Contents

100 AMERICAN INDEPENDENT FILMS

BFI SCREEN GUIDES

Jason Wood

 Publishing

First published in 2004 by the
British Film Institute
21 Stephen Street, London W1T 1LN

The British Film Institute promotes greater understanding and appreciation of, and access to, film and moving image culture in the UK.

This publication © Jason Wood 2004
Preface © Scott McGehee and David Siegel 2004

Reprinted 2005

Cover design: Paul Wright
Cover image: *Buffalo '66* (Vincent Gallo, 1998, © Cinépix Film Properties)
Series design: Ketchup/couch
Set by Fakenham Photosetting Limited, Fakenham, Norfolk
Printed in the UK by The Cromwell Press, Trowbridge, Wiltshire

British Library Cataloguing-in-Publication Data
A catalogue record for this book is available from the British Library

ISBN 1–84457–006–1 (pbk)
ISBN 1–84457–005–3 (hbk)

Acknowledgments

Numerous people have generously assisted with the completion of this book, providing advice, inspiration, encouragement and access to materials. My appreciation and thanks are therefore extended to: Marc Allenby, Geoff Andrew, Eileen Anipare, Nigel Arthur (BFI Stills), Tom Cabot, Sophia Contento (BFI Publishing), Mark Cosgrove, Andi Engel, Sara Frain, Jane Giles, Neil Hunter, Steve Jenkins, Louise Johnston (BFI National Library), Tony Jones, Asif Kapadia, Steve Lewis, Andy Leyshon, Nick Manzi, D. A. Pennebaker, B. Ruby Rich, Ben Roberts, Howard A. Rodman, Jonathan Romney, Damian Spandley, Peter Todd (BFI National Library) and Gavin Whitfield.

My special thanks are extended to both Scott McGehee and David Siegel for their generous and spirited involvement. Honourable mentions also go to Nigel Algar, Michael Leake, my wife Nicky and especially to Andrew Lockett of BFI Publishing who initiated the project and showed unerring faith in it.

In closing, I would very much like to dedicate this book to my parents.

Preface

Scott McGehee and David Siegel

For the record, we only agreed to write this preface thinking we would have some sway over the content of the book itself, and might be able to insist on the inclusion of *Billy Jack*, which was for both of us a first and formative experience with American indie film-making. But as it turns out, we've had no impact whatsoever on the author's choices, and you will find that *Billy Jack* is not, in fact, included, and as far as we know, isn't even mentioned within these pages except right here.

That being said, there are 100 other films listed, all of them somehow American and apparently 'independent' in some meaning of the word.

It's an interesting phenomenon that even the lowliest of social groups (in this case 'independent film-makers') manages to figure out a way to instil some sense of snob exclusivity to their meagre social or cultural identity. How often have we been with our fellow independent film-makers and their few remaining friends (if you can really call them that) and been party to conversations about whether or why a particular film or film-maker is not actually 'independent', as if having no money, respect or financial prospects to carry on making films were somehow a highly prized social privilege or badge of honour.

Because the American independent film movement is a more or less ad hoc affair, lacking a charismatic leader or a Vow of Independence (or any kind of vow, for that matter) to give it shape or discipline, one finds that there tend to be almost as many opinions about what qualifies a film as 'independent' as there have been entries to the Sundance Film Festival recently. Luckily, over the years, we've culled our own list of ten or so indisputable ground rules that we thought might be helpful to the reader in the context of this list of 100 films:

- Rule no. 1: No one in the entire film industry ever helped the independent film-maker make his or her film. In fact, every gainfully employed industry person the film-maker ever spoke to about the film said it was a lame, derivative, unintelligible – or at least a financially unviable – idea.
- Rule no. 2: If someone in the film industry did help somehow, the help was not substantial or financial, and/or the 'brave' film industry helper was in danger of losing his or her job by providing help. (Since everyone in the film industry seems always in danger of losing his or her job, this rule can often be brought into play.)
- Rule no. 3: The film was made for no money. The meagre goods and services involved in production were stolen or borrowed or bartered, or charged on credit cards which were already past their limit.
- Rule no. 4: If there was money involved, it wasn't nearly enough, and most importantly, it was less than lots of other films that claim to be independent that aren't as good. If the film in question had a budget larger than the budget of one's own independent film, however, the film in question is especially questionable.
- Rule no. 5: No film industry money was involved. Any real money came from investment by non-film industry dentists, or from something called a 'German Tax Fund' which (it will one day be proven) is actually a code name for non-film industry German dentists, and is wholly unreliable. If film industry money was involved, it was from an 'independent' company, such as Fine Line or Miramax or Fox Searchlight, which are by unspoken agreement somehow considered 'independent' from AOL Time Warner or Disney or the Fox News Corp despite considerable evidence to the contrary.

- Rule no. 6: The film was poorly distributed, if at all. If it found success it was against common wisdom, and by luck, fluke and happenstance, or because the film-maker personally telephoned everyone who ever attended.

- Rule no. 7: The film as an enterprise was pure financial folly. Even though it was made for no money, it miraculously stands to lose more money than it would have been made for had it been made for money. Occasionally certain distributors might profit from an American independent film due to shady accounting practices, but under no circumstances can the dentists or German dentists profit, and certainly not the film-makers.

- Rule no. 8: The film has no proper stars. If it does have stars, they have somehow fallen out of favour due to evidence of low morals, or worse, the poor box-office performance of a recent film. They worked for no money and wore no make-up except what they put on themselves.

- Rule no. 9: The film has no special effects. If it does have effects, they are not special.

- Rule no. 10: No animals were harmed in the making of the film.

We believe *Billy Jack* qualifies under this or any other reasonable set of criteria, and why it is not included here is a question to be put to the author of the book. Indeed, lots of films qualify that aren't here. (Our last film, in fact.) No doubt the author has some slap-dash criteria of his own. As *Billy Jack*'s girlfriend Jean said in explaining the founding principle of the Freedom School, 'Each man has the right to follow his own centre, follow his own conscience, do his own thing . . .'.

Which brings us to one final rule, which we call the 'Independent Spirit' rule:

- Rule no. 11: In the spirit of independence, the above rules should be ignored when it is found helpful to ignore them. If a film is good, no matter how it was produced and financed, it can be found to have an 'independent spirit' that distinguishes it from its studio-developed brethren. (And of course, if a film is bad, its relative dependence or independence will rarely be an issue.)

A writer friend of ours describes studio development as the process whereby a script that could only possibly have been written by one person is transformed into a script that could possibly have been written by anyone. We suspect that one reason we tend to like independent films is that they have usually been spared this process (for better or worse), and it shows. (They've usually been spared all sorts of other really useful things that studio films have loads of, but enough complaining.) Or perhaps the entrepreneurial spirit that is a necessary component of the independent film-maker's character does, mysteriously, have some sort of aesthetic analogue that leads to some fresh, surprising, worthwhile and entertaining movies. Or perhaps it's a simple matter of probabilities, that given enough struggling American film-makers, enough typewriters and cameras, and not quite enough film, sooner or later there will inevitably be movies made to fill a book called *100 American Independent Films.*

Strip yourself of your greed and ego trips and let the spirit enter you.
Billy Jack

Scott McGehee and David Siegel are the writers-producers-directors of *Suture*, 1994 ('Official Selection' at the Cannes Film Festival and Jury Prize at the Toronto Film Festival) and *The Deep End*, 2001 (selected for Director's Fortnight at the Cannes Film Festival). Both films won the best Cinematography Prize at the Sundance Film Festival. Together with Robert Nathan they formed an independent film production company, i5, in 1999.

Introduction

So what is an American independent film? What is meant by this elusive, contradictory and complex term, independent film-making? Jim Hillier in his introduction to *American Independent Cinema: A Sight and Sound Reader* (2001), suggests that it has always meant something different from the mainstream, be that the economic mainstream (production and distribution) or 'in aesthetic or stylistic terms' (p. ix). I have followed these basic criteria in the selection that follows . Films are selected according to this twofold understanding – economic and aesthetic. Of course, as with any selection process personal preference counts for something. For some readers this will no doubt provide the only explanation for my inclusion of Steven Soderbergh's relatively little-known *Schizopolis* (1996), which I happen to like.

That said, to my mind the film does act as an illustration of how boundaries have blurred, and indicates the current climate of American independent film-making. Aesthetically and stylistically *Schizopolis* certainly deviates from mainstream film-making practices – Richard Lester is the dominant influence, although the film pretty much exists in a world of its own – and yet it was actually funded by a major studio, Universal. Similarly, *sex, lies and videotape*, Soderbergh's debut feature and a watershed in the evolution of American independent cinema, was bankrolled by the home video division of RCA Columbia (with assistance from the UK's Virgin) and was a project on which the director did not secure the artistic privilege of final cut. Soderbergh as a director remains interesting for the position he continues to occupy. Indelibly linked with the independent sector for his formal daring and ability to imbue material with his personal signature, he often works with the benefaction of studio funding. But it is primarily as a producer with his Section Eight outfit that Soderbergh continues to display a commitment to a formally complex, rigorously intelligent cinema that may be considered outside the mainstream. Todd Haynes' *Far from Heaven* (2003) and Christopher Nolan's *Insomnia* (2002) are just two of his most recent projects.

As many of the entries and the film-makers focused upon here show, economic independence and aesthetic independence can, but need not necessarily be, mutually exclusive. As a term, 'independence' is open to multiple interpretations. In Chris Rodley and Paul Joyce's excellent television documentary *Made in the USA* (1994), Hal Hartley, who claims to take his inspiration from small businesses, declares that he has 'never understood what people mean by independent. I know what they mean by low budget.' It is worth remembering too, that Hollywood was formed by independent figures who migrated west during the 1908–13 period in response to the formation of the Motion Picture Patents Company, the first attempt at a monopoly in US cinema. Similar circumstances precipitated the forming of United Artists in 1919 by Charlie Chaplin, Mary Pickford, Douglas Fairbanks and D. W. Griffith. Independent cinema could be said to be a series of 'moments' that change according to the perspective of the beholder.

In their illuminating preface to this book, Scott McGehee and David Siegel, whose *Suture* (1993) is represented in these pages, lament the omission of T. C. Frank's [Tom Laughlin's] *Billy Jack* (1971). Other readers will no doubt raise an eyebrow when ruminating on other absences and will question why Roger Corman, Christine Vachon, Nick Wechsler, Ira Deutchman and Jeff Lipsky, to name but five, are only given passing mention. Selecting 100 films – the 'hot 100' as one colleague termed it – was an intimidating task, largely because it seems both to suggest tantalisingly the comprehensive nature of this project while actually undermining that comprehensiveness; choices had to be made at the expense of countless worthwhile films. Therefore, the selections provide an overview of the leading films and film-makers while also attempting to reflect some of the historical developments encapsulated under the umbrella of American independent film. A comprehensive analysis of American independent cinema is beyond the scope of this introduction. There is here no mention of the politically inspired Leftist film-making of the 1930s or the numerous works that evolved during the anti-communist, immediate post-war period in Hollywood. And I should add that while the intention of this selection was to suggest the broad sweep of American independent cinema, the primary aim was to be contemporary, and so most of the films here date from the mid-1980s on.

For practical reasons, it was decided that all the inclusions should be of feature length – at 56 minutes Michael Almereyda's *Another Girl, Another Planet* (1992) just sneaked under the wire. That is regrettable. Hence the unfortunate but largely unavoidable deflecting of focus from those figures working within the American avant-garde and underground cinema of the 1940s, 50s and 60s. Figures such as Maya Deren, Kenneth Anger, Jack Smith and Stan Brakhage irrefutably exerted a major influence on the American independent sector. And this influence can be viewed not only in terms of how these film-makers funded their projects (through arts organisations and public-funding bodies or out of their own pockets), but also in how they established a network of venues where such work could be enjoyed. Of equal import, the work of these directors expressed a desire to explore new approaches to the language of film, opening up the medium to new ways of communicating meaning by deviating from dominant cinema's reliance upon narrative, character and genre. The influence of these film-makers is traced in this book through the inclusion of works such as Shirley Clarke's *Portrait of Jason* (1967) and Andy Warhol's *Lonesome Cowboys* (1968), and later pictures, such as including David Lynch's *Eraserhead* (1976).

A film like Anger's *Fireworks* (1947) audaciously highlights issues of gender, expressing a sensibility and viewpoint previously denied by mainstream cinema. In doing so, it and films like it were instrumental in laying the groundwork for the subsequent New Queer Cinema cycle of films that emerged during the 90s. A similar movement occurred with the gradual emergence of films from African-American film-makers. When surveying what American independent cinema has contributed to film worldwide, the 'transformed representations of ethnic minorities – particularly African-Americans (but also Hispanics and Chinese Americans) – and of gays and lesbians' (Ibid., p. ix) registers as prominent. So by extension, therefore, the term independent has also been taken to embrace those films and film-makers whose work expresses a sensibility that contrasts with prevailing political, sexual and racial ideologies.

Take for instance Spike Lee. Few directors have done more to foreground issues of race. John Pierson, himself a major figure as a rep for American indie product from the early 80s onwards, cites Lee's *She's Gotta Have It* (1986) as a pivotal moment in both contemporary American independent and African-American cinema. Lee now cuts something of a contradictory figure in terms of his 'independence', but it is difficult to argue that he has not provided an authentic expression and celluloid representation of African-American hopes, aspirations and desires. Lee's style is fresh and inventive, showing the influence of the French New Wave, Italian neo-realism, the New German cinema of the 1970s and, in his later films, echoes of Martin Scorsese (e.g. *The 25th Hour*, 2003). Though he has retained a relative autonomy over his work through his 40 Acres and a Mule production outfit and fought to retain final cut, Lee's post-1986 output has been financed, produced and distributed by studio companies. Courted by the majors after *She's Gotta Have It* had caused a sizeable critical splash and alerted studio executives to an income sector more or less ignored since the blaxploitation heyday, Lee has made no apologies for his desire to work regularly with the major resources a studio can provide.

Other African-American directors such as Julie Dash and Charles Burnett consciously resisted assimilation into the mainstream, fearing that their methods and their message would be diluted. This refusal to assimilate is typical of numerous other directors who consciously choose to operate outside the Hollywood system. Jon Jost, for example, has continued to plough his own resolutely independent furrow, frequently expressing his criticism of the system and an independent sector he sees as increasingly susceptible to Hollywood's overtures. Jost's militancy has drawn admiration and censure in equal measure. Gregg Araki appropriated both Jost's low-budget mindset and his raw and highly individual aesthetic, but others within the industry, John Pierson among them, have dismissed Jost as a 'politically cranky, experimental film-maker' (Pierson, 1996, p. 235), turning out films on minuscule budgets that very few people actually ever see. Jost may be able to claim freedom of expression and economic autonomy, but at what cost?

Lee is one of just six directors with more than one film featured in this book. To keep a balance between variety and importance, I have imposed a maximum of two films per director. Apart from Lee and the previously discussed Soderbergh, my top-ranking directors are John Sayles, Jim Jarmusch, Hal Hartley (who remains a personal favourite and appears twice at the expense of contemporaries such as Richard Linklater and Kevin Smith) and that pioneering forefather, John Cassavetes, whose *Shadows* (1959) is very much a benchmark work. The reasons for this film's mighty reputation and importance relate both to economics (it was arduously self-funded and promoted) and aesthetics (an experimental European-influenced 'learn as we shoot' policy), both discussed later in this book. Cassavetes, who was to set up his own distribution company, had a radical effect on alternative approaches to production, exhibition and distribution in the US. Subsequently courted, seduced and then, as Pierson puts it 'screwed' (Ibid., p. 8) by the studios on *Too Late Blues* (1961) and *A Child Is Waiting* (1962), Cassavetes thereafter severed all involvement with the system, save for acting in studio projects as a means of raising finance for his own uncompromised productions. John Sayles (as a writer for hire and sometime actor), Alan Rudolph and Steve Buscemi are just three recent figures who have followed Cassavetes' lead and used studio and other acting fees as collateral for more personal ventures. Cassavetes himself retained rights to the negatives of his work and was able to exert control over subsequent exploitation, exercising a rare privilege that only Jim Jarmusch and a handful of others have also enjoyed. For Cassavetes this paradoxically sometimes hindered audience accessibility to his films in subsequent years, but his methods and spirit continue to inspire a legion of American independent film-makers.

One of the first directors to openly acknowledge the liberating power of Cassavetes' autonomy was Martin Scorsese, one of the new breed of directors accorded creative liberty in the auteur-friendly studio climate of the late 60s and early 70s initiated by Arthur Penn's *Bonnie and Clyde* (1967). The period brought to prominence other cult favourite directors, including Bob Rafelson, Robert Altman and Sam Peckinpah. Altman remains a maverick dignitary; abandoned by the studios with the advent of event movies and saturation releases, he adapted by turning to independent financing and television. In an industry founded on creativity and frequently in need of fresh ideas, Altman remains perceptive on the subject of the awkward relationship between Hollywood and independent film-making: 'The biggest assets the studios have are the independents that are fighting them' (Rodley, 1994).

The period led to the formation of classics divisions within the studios, establishing a continuing parasitical and symbiotic marriage of convenience. On an aesthetic level, this provision for innovative work within the confines of the mainstream remains very much in evidence today. One need only look at the work of Soderbergh and other figures like Wes Anderson, Paul Thomas Anderson (whose digressive, multi-character dramas owe much to Altman) and Spike Jonze, all of whom enjoy studio subsidisation allied with a degree of creative freedom.

Let me flag up three titles and dates that have become synonymous with American independent cinema as we know it today. Former Fine Line president Ira Deutchman and director Whit Stillman are just two figures who have argued that modern (post-Cassavetes) American independent cinema began with John Sayles' *Return of the Secaucus Seven* (1979). This film was one of the first independent features to announce, as part of its marketing campaign, that it was entirely self-financed and made on a very low budget. Completed for $125,000 and subsequently sold by Sayles to Specialty Films (with Libra handling sub-distribution), the $60,000 needed to cover the direct production costs came from Sayles himself. Interestingly, Sayles saw the film as an audition piece: 'I wanted to direct, and the only way you get to direct in Hollywood is to have a film to show' (Rosen with Hamilton, 1990, p. 182). Released in October 1980, the film immediately benefited from the contrast with the studio calamity that was *Heaven's Gate* (Michael Cimino, 1980). Its co-distributors were able to instil in an American press already sympathetic to the film's fine script, naturalistic performances and political insight, an acute awareness of the film's meagre budget in comparison to Cimino's $44 million monster. With Sayles personally attending screenings across the country, the film also demonstrated that a grass roots approach to promotion and outreach could work, with the film going on to achieve an impressive estimated box-office gross of $2 million.

Citing 1984 as heralding what he terms 'the first golden age', John Pierson places Jarmusch's minimalist *Stranger Than Paradise* as modern American independent cinema's point of origin. Detailing the film's bargain basement budget of $110,000 and its own organic and original aesthetic – 'identifiably European and quintessentially American at the same time' (Pierson, 1996, p. 25) – Pierson makes the case that the film represents a new departure identifiably distinct from earlier US indie fare such as Susan Seidelman's *Smithereens* (1982) in that it managed to be 'both brilliant and attainable' (Ibid., p. 27). Moreover, *Stranger Than Paradise*, with its subsequently much-imitated deadpan performances, introverted characters, sparse, ironic dialogue and static camera (which reduced the cost of filming and fascinated an impressionable Kevin Smith) grabbed attention on a truly international scale, with Jarmusch becoming the first American to win the Cannes Camera d'Or for Best First Feature. The film was then acquired by the Samuel Goldwyn Company, proving a commercial success both domestically and in key foreign markets, including France and Japan. The success of *Stranger Than Paradise* acted as a reminder to the industry that the lower the budget, the higher the potential profit margin. Other notable films released during Pierson's golden period included Sayles' *The Brother from Another Planet* (distributed by Cinecom, 1984), the Coen brothers' *Blood Simple* (Circle Releasing, 1983) and Alan Rudolph's *Choose Me* (Island/Alive, 1984).

Nineteen eighty-nine was another year when 'it all changed' (Ibid., p. 126) with the release of Soderbergh's *sex, lies and videotape*, which had a truly global impact. Soderbergh's debut – completed at the age of just twenty-six encourages parallels with Hopper's *Easy Rider* (1969), in terms of sheer impact and in the way in which it precipitated a rush among the studios to associate themselves with young, up-and-coming directors whose work, though formally audacious and apt to appeal to the counterculture, could be modestly acquired and then advantageously marketed. A $1.2-million production that offered an intelligent and adult delineation of sexual impotence, infidelity and relationship trauma in an age made weary of promiscuous coupling by the devastation of AIDS, *sex, lies and videotape* slipped relatively unnoticed into the Sundance Film Festival and thereafter indelibly altered – for better and for worse – the festival's profile forever. Sundance was founded in 1981 as a response to the Reaganite administration's hostility towards the arts, and was dedicated to the support and development of emerging screenwriters and directors of vision. Though the festival had assumed increasing importance among the independent sector and carried critical kudos, it did not figure highly on the itinerary of studio executives until a series of feverishly received screenings of Soderbergh's film. In anticipation, major film industry figures from the East and West Coasts descended upon Park City, Utah. They have returned ever since, causing many insiders – Jon Jost included – to suggest that Sundance has become a rather large and picturesque shop window for Hollywood. Though undeniably true, it would be unfair to deny the positive role Sundance has played in bringing to wider attention the work of directors such as Todd Haynes, Hal Hartley, Whit Stillman, Tom Kalin, David Gordon Green and Karyn Kusama.

sex, lies and videotape was also the film that put the fledgling, independent outfit Miramax on the map. (Miramax, a company now regarded as the corporate Goliath of American independent/arthouse production and distribution – has since been acquired by Disney, just as the once independent New Line, whose Fine Line boutique division fostered kitsch auteur John Waters, now falls under the aegis of Time Warner.) Bob and Harvey Weinstein's bold approach to positioning *sex, lies and videotape* began in Cannes with Harvey's insistence that the film should appear in the main competition. The cajoling paid off, and Soderbergh became the youngest ever winner of the Palme d'Or. On awarding a somewhat bemused Soderbergh his prize (the director commented sardonically, 'it's all downhill from here'), jury president Wim Wenders pronounced him the future of cinema.

After launching film and director internationally, Miramax adopted an equally audacious approach in the US where they eschewed the niche, limited-release pattern traditionally associated with independent titles and instead put out the film widely on multiple prints. The 'sex' aspect of the title undoubtedly helped and quickly became a part of the indie 'package'. Likewise the violent aspect of American indie pictures would be foregrounded after the success of Quentin Tarantino's *Reservoir Dogs* two years later. Miramax's gamble again brought dividends, with Soderbergh's film eventually going on to achieve a seismic worldwide gross of over $100 million. This success established over-the-top expectations for American independent films and presented many emerging film-makers with a daunting objective. The ratio of budget to box office remained a focus of attention. Both film-makers and distributors would often actively stress the meagre means for which their project was made, with both *El Mariachi* (1992) and *Clerks* (1993) making much of their completion costs (about $7,000 and $27,000 respectively).

With hindsight there is much validity in Hillier's suggestion that *sex, lies and videotape* represents the total assimilation of American independent cinema. This feeling intensifies when surveying a number of recent releases that seemingly replicate this pattern of economic assimilation and aesthetic familiarity. *Girlfight* (1999), a gritty, medium-budget picture that tackles both ethnicity and feminism through the genre of the boxing movie, was produced and distributed by Sony Classics, a division of Columbia. *Boys Don't Cry* (1999), Kimberly Peirce's compelling account of the life and murder of Brandon Teena, a young woman who for most of her adult life passed as a male, was produced and distributed by Fox Searchlight. Hal Hartley, Richard Linklater, Michael Almereyda (all directors who have embraced advances in digital production as a means of reducing budgets) and David Gordon Green are figures operating at the more esoteric, less commercial end of the independent spectrum who have had their most recent projects backed and released by the specialist divisions of studio companies. There is still a pocketful of marginal directors such as Bruce LaBruce who continue to avoid both aesthetic and economic dependency on Hollywood, but such figures in American independent cinema are now, and perhaps have for some time, clearly been the exception rather than the norm. As one moment of independence ends, another may be beginning.

Angel City
US, 1977 – 70 mins
Jon Jost

Jean-Luc Godard has claimed that Jon Jost 'is not a traitor to the movies, like almost all American directors. He makes them move' (quoted in Pym, 1977, p. 4) As Godard suggests, Jost is indeed one of the most truly independent and politicised of American film-makers. Existing at the very outer edges of radical, no-budget film-making and operating at 'the interface of the politics of form and the politics of production' (Ibid.), Jost's work offers a sustained critique of the illusionist, capitalist nature of Hollywood feature films and the economic forces they serve. That said, the polemic (like Godard's) is one of a true cineaste's and wrestles with all the traits of popular genre film-making styles and structures in the process.

Directed, written, produced, photographed and edited by Jost on a budget of $6,000, *Angel City* adopts the framework conventions of the thriller genre as it tracks down-at-heel private detective Frank Goya (Glaudini) as he attempts to solve the murder of aspiring LA actress Gloria Franklin (Golden). Goya has been hired by Franklin's husband Pierce Del Rue (Del Rue), a respected businessman and president of the powerful Rexon Corporation. Goya's investigations reveal that after Franklin's first movie, *Death on the Installment Plan*, failed, Del Rue had his wife murdered, fearing that she would prove an obstruction to his own financial interests in the industry.

Self-consciously signposting the motifs and prescribed characteristics of the genre (e.g. Goya's direct-to-audience narration which later gives way to lectures on the redistribution of wealth), Jost alerts the spectator to *Angel City*'s artificiality and by extension to that of fictional film in general. Moreover, the glamour of Hollywood is deconstructed with an aerial shot of the mythical Los Angeles, accompanied by prolonged voiceover statistics about the city. The film reveals the raw materials of cinema through various reflexive, structuralist devices – it is organised into sections '12' to '1' – and through clumsily executed camera movements and optical effects. Most notable is a sequence in which Goya reassembles the screen in the form of a jigsaw puzzle and another in which he escapes from the clutches of Del Rue while exiting the film frame. Jost's technical imperfections are themselves intrinsic parts of *Angel City*'s ideological make-up, serving to further puncture the seductive, flawless surface of the commercial feature with its seamless illusion of reality.

Jost connects crime with capitalism, a subject, along with the dominance of multinational corporations, that is especially close to his heart. Shot like a commercial, a sequence shows Del Rue strolling along a beach extolling the virtues of Rexon and the social benefits of large companies. The image is followed with an animated logo of a dinosaur embracing a globe featuring the words 'One world'.

Angel City is a visionary, highly original work that marries the Brechtian distanciation of *Alphaville* (1965) with the political commitment of *Vent D'Est* (1970). Jost himself expanded on the artist analogy of the central character by describing his film as having the subtlety of Vermeer in contrast to Hollywood films, which have the fleshy magnitude of Rubens. However, Jost's standing in the hierarchy of American independent film-makers has been diminished by the limited distribution of his films and by his own criticisms of an independent sector that he increasingly views as duplicating Hollywood's financial and economic imperatives.

Dir: Jon Jost; **Prod**: Jon Jost; **Scr**: Jon Jost; **DOP**: Jon Jost; **Editor**: Jon Jost; **Score**: Uncredited; **Main Cast**: Robert Glaudini, Winifred Golden, Pierce Del Rue, Kathleen Kramer.

Another Girl, Another Planet
US, 1992 – 56 mins
Michael Almereyda

A partly autobiographical love letter to Almereyda's native East Village, *Another Girl, Another Planet* takes its title from the seminal single by punk outfit the Only Ones. It may weigh in at just 56 minutes, but as a follow-up to the writer-director's engagingly spaced-out *Twister* (1990), this film packs a heavyweight artistic punch through its formal daring and endearingly romantic pessimism, as well as its effective, idiosyncratic use of a discontinued camera produced for children.

The simple, admittedly slight but nonetheless deftly crafted story concerns the relationship between two East Village apartment block neighbours: Nic (Nic Ratner, Almereyda's real-life neighbour playing

Another Girl, Another Planet, director Michael Almereyda's love letter to the East Village filmed on the Fisher-Price PXL 2000, a discontinued toy camera produced for children

himself), anxious and married, and bohemian Bill (Sherman), whose life appears to be a constant stream of rich encounters with strange, beguiling and capricious females. The film examines the reluctance of each man to surrender to the expectations and responsibilities of adulthood, and also observes (via male eyes) a kind of feminine pursuit of answers to the unanswerable. *Another Girl* was produced by Hartley associate Bob Gosse (an alumni of Hartley's 1984 graduation film *Kid*), and among the excellently cast ensemble lie further connections with the Long Island-born director, with *Another Girl* introducing the audience to the iconic talents of the Romanian actress Elina Löwensohn, later to be seen in *Simple Men* (1992) and *Amateur* (1994).

Influenced by the experimental, highly personal shorts of Sadie Benning, Almereyda and cinematographer Jim Denault (later to work on Hartley's similarly mesmerising and technically audacious digital exercise *The Book of Life*, 1998) imbue the monochrome material with an ethereal, otherworldly quality that manages to be extremely seductive while seemingly resembling the inside of somebody's head. The grainy, hazy, soft-focus look of the film is due to the use of the Fisher-Price PXL 2000, a high-speed instrument whose format came to be called 'Pixel vision'. Originally retailing at $45, and benefiting from the wonders of digital video production, the PXL 2000 proved to be a wholly viable economic alternative to 16mm and 35mm for a select number of low-budget/independent directors.

Almereyda was one of the relatively few independent directors at the time attempting to break new ground in terms of exploring how technology can shape an overriding visual aesthetic. He was to continue to experiment with the Pixel vision format, most notably on his subsequent picture, *Nadja* (1994) executive produced by David Lynch and Mary Sweeney.

Dir: Michael Almereyda; **Prod**: Michael Almereyda; **Scr**: Michael Almereyda; **DOP**: Jim Denault; **Editor**: David Leonard; **Score**: Uncredited; **Main Cast**: Nic Ratner, Barry Sherman, Elina Löwensohn, Mary Ward.

Badlands
US, 1973 – 94 mins
Terrence Malick

For many, Terrence Malick was the most lyrical and artistic director of the auteur-friendly US cinema of the 70s. *Badlands*, his exquisite, self-written and -produced debut, has been compared by David Thomson with *Citizen Kane* (1941) in terms of its originality and enduring influence (Thomson, 1996). Ostensibly a rural lovers-on-the-run gangster film in the tradition of Ray's *They Live by Night* (1948), the independently made *Badlands* is distinguished by the oblique approach Malick takes to his familiar material. This is perhaps most evident in the enigmatic attitude towards the psychological motivations of its characters, a pair of murderous juveniles in search of release from the banality of their existence in the American Midwest of the late 50s.

The film is loosely based on the true story of nineteen-year-old Charles Starkweather, who murdered the family of his thirteen-year-old lover, Caril Ann Fugate, before embarking with her on a killing spree through Nebraska and Wyoming. *Badlands* relocates events to Fort Dupre, South Dakota. Garbage-man and James Dean lookalike Kit (Sheen) begins courting Holly (Spacek), a fifteen-year-old immersed in trashy, celebrity-fixated magazines. Holly's father (Oates) forbids the relationship and kills his daughter's dog as punishment when she disobeys him. As Holly impassively stands by, Kit shoots her father dead. The couple rob and kill their way across the Dakota Badlands, pursued by the law, but Holly's affections for Kit wither and she turns herself in. Kit, however, is seduced by the celebrity status the media bestows upon him and is arrested only after stopping to build a monument to himself during a high-speed chase. Having played no part in the killings, Holly receives a lengthy prison term; Kit is sentenced to execution.

Presenting the narrative elements from contrasting perspectives, Malick offers an at times mysterious yet eloquent dissection of disaffection and the role the media plays in offering unsustainable alternatives to the commonplace. Self-obsessive and self-mythologising, Kit regards himself as a heroic non-conformist whose good looks and affability will mark him out as worthy of remembrance. Although this conviction blinds him to the gravity of his actions (and indeed to Holly's growing disinterest in him), it is in effect fulfilled by the esteem in which his pursuers hold him. The film is also narrated in the dispassionate, listless voice of Holly, whose description of mundane events is nonetheless littered with vocabulary from the romantic magazines in which she is constantly immersed. These disjunctions are underscored by the sensory perfection of the film and in the way Malick evocatively combines Carl Orff's ethereal music and Tak Fujimoto's painterly cinematography. Organically merging psychological and physical landscapes, *Badlands* has a mythic, iconic quality that recurred throughout Malick's hermit-like career, as does the director's interest in man's capacity for destruction and the interaction of the characters, from whom we are purposefully distanced, with the natural world around them.

Acquired by Warner Bros. following its reception at the 1973 New York Film Festival, *Badlands* marked the emergence of a skilled perfectionist with little regard for the dictates of commercial film-making. *Badlands* has been cited as an inspiration by successive generations of American directors. David Gordon Green's *George Washington* (2000) is among the most notable recent works to bear Malick's indelible mark.

Dir: Terrence Malick; **Prod**: Terrence Malick; **Scr**: Terrence Malick; **DOP**: Tak Fujimoto; **Editor**: Robert Estrin; **Score**: Carl Orff; **Main Cast**: Martin Sheen, Sissy Spacek, Warren Oates, Ramon Bieri.

Bad Lieutenant
US, 1992 – 96 mins
Abel Ferrara

Ferrara made his bona fide feature debut with the ultra low-budget 'video-nasty' *Driller Killer* (1979), following various amateur productions, excursions into Super 8 and even a pornographic movie. Ferrara has consistently dealt with themes of religion, salvation and redemption and a consideration of abject existential confusion in a morally bankrupt universe. Flawed, repellent and self-destructive characters provide the focus of this examination. Ferrara's provocative and erratic output is also marked by its unsettling visceral extremity. It comes as little surprise to also hear Ferrara pay homage to Godard, Pasolini and Fassbinder, the similarly 'serious' pre-eminent directors of post-war European art cinema. Today the prodigious director is reckoned to be, on the one hand, the most impassioned and 'driven American film-maker in American cinema' (Smith, 2001a, p. 182) and, on the other, a film-maker of 'little artistic merit' (Andrew, 1998, p. 6).

Bad Lieutenant marked a return to a more determinedly realist mode following the glossier *King of New York* (1990), and is an especially profane and sustained howl of anguish from the depths of despair. Perhaps the director's most powerfully realised work, it's certainly his bleakest. Set amid New York's violent, multicultural, urban squalor, the film features a shockingly raw and courageous performance from Keitel as the self-destructive NYPD bad Lieutenant of the title. The Lieutenant is addicted to a diet of drugs and alcohol, and his escalating gambling debts are a source of constant frustration, which he vents by sexually haranguing female members of the public. While investigating the rape and torture of a local nun, the Lieutenant is proffered redemption after seeing a vision of Christ.

Reflecting Ferrara's origins as an underground film-maker, *Bad Lieutenant* is almost entirely shorn of artifice. The credits are crude and the use of music is minimal. It offers few concessions to the conventions of mainstream cinema. At times the film resembles a particularly disturbing documentary, with Ferrara adopting a frills-free vérité approach to the self-consciously raw material; hand-held camera and jagged, abrasive editing dominate. The film is resolutely amoral in tone, to the extent that it frustratingly denies narrative closure and any restoration of moral order by allowing the rapists to go unpunished for their crimes.

Described by Martin Scorsese as being all he had hoped *The Last Temptation of Christ* (1988) would be, *Bad Lieutenant* offers Ferrara's most earnest consideration of the potentially redemptive powers of Catholicism, beneath the film's apparent blasphemy. This aspect is particularly evident in the scenes in which an increasingly wretched and contrite Lieutenant weepingly remonstrates with God for forgiveness. But on-screen depravity and moments of shuddering intensity (Keitel's masturbating while mouthing obscenities after questioning two female motorists is especially unrestrained) ensured that the film received a rocky reception upon release and radically polarised critics. It also managed to attract the scrutiny of the British Board of Film Classification, which eventually passed it uncut for theatrical exhibition. The film was penned by the director in collaboration with Zoe Lund, the star of Ferrara's rape revenge satire *Ms.45/ Angel of Vengeance* (1980).

Dir: Abel Ferrara; **Prod**: Edward R. Pressman; **Scr**: Zoe Lund, Abel Ferrara; **DOP**: Ken Kelsch; **Editor**: Anthony Redman; **Score**: Joe Delia; **Main Cast**: Harvey Keitel, Victor Argo, Anthony Ruggiero, Robin Burrows.

Being John Malkovich
US, 1999 – 113 mins
Spike Jonze

Being John Malkovich marked one of the most daring, entertaining and eccentric debuts in recent American cinema. The film was fashioned from a surreal, wildly imaginative script by Charlie Kaufman and directed with brio by pop-promo alchemist Spike Jonze. And it was produced by Michael Stipe's production company Single Cell Pictures. Though the project was enthusiastically greeted by Hollywood executives, it had been rejected as being impossible to bring to the screen.

Malkovich is about Craig Schwartz (Cusack), an out-of-work puppeteer who under duress from his animal-obsessed wife Lotte (an unrecognisably dowdy Diaz) takes a lowly filing job with LesterCorp, the occupiers of floor seven-and-a-half of a Manhattan office block. There he discovers a portal that leads directly into the head of John Malkovich. Entering the portal, Schwartz spends fifteen minutes within the star before being ejected on to the New Jersey Turnpike. In cahoots with voracious colleague Maxine (Keener playing against type as a cruel, scathing vamp), Schwartz begins charging people $200 to enjoy the experience. Unfortunately the scam opens, as he neatly describes it, 'a metaphysical can of worms' when Lotte enters and falls in love with Maxine, who has since begun dating the actor. Craig uses his puppeteering skills to permanently enter Malkovich, who it transpires is the latest in a line of conduits used by a secret society to enjoy eternal life in new bodies. So far, so simple . . .

With a nod to Warhol's famous-for-fifteen-minutes maxim, this part-screwball, part-crackpot conspiracy theory comedy is an incisive parable about the cult of celebrity and the hollowness of fame. In one of its most amusing running gags, Malkovich is forever mistakenly associated for his turn as a jewel thief, a part he has never played. The film also takes great delight in monkeying around with notions of identity (Craig peddles his scheme with the pitch: 'Have you ever wanted to be someone else?'), offering an effective meditation on crises of sexuality and gender that even allows for a positive lesbian ending.

Given Jonze's MTV background and the material's whacky premise, the director largely adopts a surprisingly sober, low-key, almost naturalistic approach. Employing subtle lighting and a downbeat orchestral score from regular Coen composer Carter Burwell, Jonze impressively navigates the various shifts in tone, incorporating the more bravado, fantastical diversionary moments with quiet confidence. Such moments include a flashback sequence from the perspective of a recently captured chimp and an immaculately conceived 'training' film as dire as only training films can be.

John Malkovich acts as the film's foundation and proves to be an extremely game target for the far-from-gentle ribbing, offering a self-obsessed and repellent caricature of his perceived, narcissistic persona. The film was variously compared to works by Borges, Buñuel and Svankmajer. Though distributed by a major studio (Universal), it is included here by virtue of its independent spirit and irreverent sensibility.

Dir: Spike Jonze; Prod: Michael Stipe, Sandy Stern, Steve Golin, Vincent Landay; Scr: Charlie Kaufman; DOP: Lance Accord; Editor: Eric Zumbrunnen; Score: Carter Burwell; Main Cast: John Cusack, Cameron Diaz, Catherine Keener, John Malkovich.

The Blair Witch Project
US, 1999 – 81 mins
Daniel Myrick, Eduardo Sanchez

The Blair Witch Project makes every effort to present itself as a factual document, opening with titles informing us that what we are about to see is the surviving footage shot by three student film-makers who mysteriously disappeared into the woods around Burkittsville, Maryland. With a nominal budget of just $25,000, Myrick and Sanchez understood that they would not be able to deliver a picture that corresponded to the contemporary approach to the horror genre – slick and expensive special effects and/or Hollywood stars – and so instead adopted an approach that has its precedent in the 70s' and early 80s' wave of mock-documentary movies of which Ruggero Deodato's *Cannibal Holocaust* (1980) is among the most notorious.

The factual feel of the film is largely achieved through the use of video and Super 8mm, formats made necessary by the low budget. Assigning their characters the names of their lead actors to further maintain the conceit, Myrick and Sanchez presented the trio with a camcorder on which they were to document the experiences of the seven-day shoot and sent them out into the woods where their only interaction with the crew would be the receipt of written instructions concerning rudimentary directions. The cast was subjected to sleep deprivation and various disorientating provocations to ensure that the resulting film, edited in its entirety from the hand-held footage recorded by the actors, had the requisite elements of authenticity, spontaneity and abject terror.

Unable to physically reveal or even suggest the fabled witch due to budget constraints, the directors employ an inventive and wholly effective approach to sound design, filling the night air with rustles, shrieks and cries that come suffocatingly closer as the characters experience social and psychological breakdown. The breakdown is in part effected by the character Heather's determination to film everything (like the 'real' crew, the characters are all assigned technical duties) and to experience 'reality' through her camera lens.

Blair Witch caused an immediate Sundance sensation and was snapped up by independent distributor Artisan. It mirrored the deliberately 'artless' approach exhibited in pictures such as *Night of the Living Dead* (1968), offering a fresh alternative to the attractively packaged but ultimately tiresome teens-in-peril cycle. *Blair Witch* was also undoubtedly the first film to truly harness the phenomenal power of the Internet as a marketing tool – the directors created a

The Blair Witch Project: An unsettling, documentary style horror that rapidly became a modern day marketing phenomenon

website to perpetuate the impression that the film was a documentary. Even though costly prints and advertising spend pushed the completion budget way over the originally quoted $25,000, in terms of profit against production costs, the film has gone on to be one of the most commercially successful films ever, grossing over $100 million worldwide and triggering a host of inferior sequels and reproductions.

Dir: Daniel Myrick, Eduardo Sanchez; **Prod**: Gregg Hale, Robin Cowie; **Scr**: Daniel Myrick, Eduardo Sanchez; **DOP**: Neal Fredericks; **Editor**: Daniel Myrick, Eduardo Sanchez; **Score**: Tony Cora; **Main Cast**: Heather Donahue, Michael Williams, Joshua Leonard.

Blood Simple
US, 1983 – 99 mins
Joel Coen

A contemporary film noir with an acute awareness of the origins of the genre, *Blood Simple* owes a debt to James M. Cain's tales of duplicitous females and two-time male losers trapped in a net of betrayal, murder and double crossing. The film opens with a suitably cynical voiceover monologue which observes that 'the world is full of complainers. But the fact is, nothing comes with a guarantee', setting the tone for the stagnant moral universe which this stylish and confident debut sucks us into. Direction is credited solely to Joel, though brother Ethan shared key roles. *Blood Simple* concerns Marty (Hedaya), a cuckolded bar owner who hires Visser (convincingly portrayed by rangy character actor Walsh, who also provides the opening narration), a sleazy private detective, to kill his wife Abby (McDormand) and Ray (Getz), the bar employee she is having an affair with. A million miles from the customarily cool big screen gumshoes, the constantly sweating, reptilian Visser encapsulates the Coen brothers' desire to put a mischievous but undoubtedly auteurist and entertaining spin on familiar genres. It's a trick they've continued to use with success, establishing themselves as among the most consistent, idiosyncratic and entertaining artists currently at work in contemporary cinema.

Blood Simple originated from a three-minute teaser trailer assembled to secure funding and makes virtuous use of its low-budget status, relatively obscure cast, and stark and unfamiliar rural Texas locations where, as the opening narration ominously informs us, 'you're on your own'. The film was beautifully shot by Barry Sonnenfeld, the first of his three cinematographic outings for the Coens before establishing his own directorial career. It deploys an inventive use of *mise en scène* and an especially audacious attention to texture and high-contrast lighting effects. And in the grand tradition of noir, *Blood Simple* is almost endlessly dark. Reflective of the murky goings-on, surprisingly sexless furtive couplings and the pervading unhappiness and nihilism of its characters, colour in the film is used to sparing but startling effect. Hence the vulgar neon signs, the garish pool of blood accumulating under what appears to be Marty's corpse, and the catch of silver-blue fish, slowly spoiling on his desk.

Leavening the brew and confounding expectations are blackly comic interludes and gruesome yet strangely silent visual set-pieces. Moments such as when a knife skewers Visser's tarantula-like hand borrow freely from the modern American horror movie, an unsurprising debt given Joel's association with Sam Raimi, for whom he edited *The Evil Dead* (1982). Similarly, the film delights in repeating aural motifs (the Four Tops' 'Same Old Song' recurs to resonant and disarming effect) and exaggerated and disquieting sound effects, including the perpetual hum of a fan and the wince-inducing sound of Marty's index finger being broken.

Cold-blooded and claustrophobic, the film was instantly acclaimed, not least by J. Hoberman, who cited it as the most influential film noir since *Chinatown* (1974) (Hoberman, 2000). With a clutch of festival accolades, including Best Dramatic Feature at 1985's Sundance and Best Director and Best Actor (Walsh) at the 1986 Independent Spirit Awards, *Blood Simple* went on to become a modest commercial success. It was later re-released in a fifteenth anniversary 'director's cut', which, with characteristic Coenesque perversity, runs slightly shorter than the original.

Dir: Joel Coen; **Prod**: Ethan Coen; **Scr**: Ethan Coen, Joel Coen; **DOP**: Barry Sonnenfeld; **Editor**: Roderick Jaynes, Don Wiegmann; **Score**: Carter Burwell; **Main Cast**: John Getz, Frances McDormand, Dan Hedaya, M. Emmet Walsh.

(Next page) Something wicked this way comes . . . the cuckolded Marty (Dan Hedaya) hires Visser (M. Emmet Walsh) to kill his wife in neo-noir *Blood Simple*

Boogie Nights
US, 1997 – 156 mins
Paul Thomas Anderson

One of the most striking recent features of American independent cinema is the return to the formal risk-taking and elaborate, multi- or parallel narrative structures adopted by the leading post-studio-system maverick directors of the 70s and early 80s. *Boogie Nights* made explicit Anderson's debts to the work of three of the key directors of this earlier period: Altman, Demme and Scorsese. The film was made a year after Anderson's low-key debut feature, *Hard Eight* (1996), with backing and sizeable funding from mini-major New Line.

Boogie Nights begins with the title displayed in neon lights on a San Fernando Valley movie marquee circa 1977, and asserts its formal daring and stylistic exuberance in an opening four-minute sequence that, through a variety of impressively mounted cranes and Steadicam shots, moves into a bustling nightclub to introduce several leading characters. There, with a little help from a roller-blade-wearing porn starlet (Graham), lowly busboy Eddie Adams' (Wahlberg) trouser talent is spotted by porn impresario Jack Horner (Reynolds), who exclaims, 'I've got a feeling in those jeans there's something wonderful waiting to get out'. Horner, with the help of kooky 'actress' Amber Waves (Moore) transforms Eddie, alias Dirk Diggler and on-screen persona Brock Landers, into the biggest porn superstar of his generation.

The film evolved from *The Dirk Diggler Story*, a short completed by Anderson when he was just seventeen, and is informed by the director's own private viewing habits and authoritative knowledge of pornography as both industry (the film deals with the seismic repercussions of the emergence of the home video market) and art form. It is, in part, a loose, unofficial re-telling of the life of porn star John 'Johnny Wadd' Holmes. The film's almost uncanny reproduction of an authentic porno aesthetic (extended long takes, desperate storylines and cheesy formal flourishes) owes much to the on-set consultancy of porn legend Ron Jeremy.

Anderson's intelligently and exhilaratingly deployed visual flair and distinctive eye for period detail (nostalgic fun is poked at garishly opulent interiors and ill-fated technological advances such as the 8-track) are more than matched by his ability to negotiate the tricky tonal shift between comedy/parody and drama. Anderson cites F. W. Murnau's *Sunrise* (1927) and Demme's *Something Wild* (1985) as inspiration in terms of 'gearshift movies' (Smith, 2001b, p. 172). When the tight-knit, fun-loving surrogate family implodes amid Oedipal tensions and cocaine-fuelled arrogance and paranoia, Anderson makes impeccable use of soundtrack to steer the film into darker but still morally neutral waters. The feel-good soul and disco tracks slowly give way to a contemplative, melancholy score by Michael Penn that compounds the profound loneliness and longing underlying the hedonism and excess.

The cherry on top of an ambitious, sprawling, exhibitionist epic are the performances of a well-marshalled ensemble cast. Anderson regulars John C. Reilly and Philip Baker Hall particularly excel, as do William H. Macy and Philip Seymour Hoffman as respectively, a cuckolded cameraman and a repressed gay crewmember. The latter two characters movingly express the director's interest in the often fraying and tenuous threads that bind and connect people, a pervading theme to which he has subsequently returned.

Dir: Paul Thomas Anderson; **Prod**: Lloyd Levin, John Lyons, Paul Thomas Anderson, Joanne Sellar; **Scr**: Paul Thomas Anderson; **DOP**: Robert Elswit; **Editor**: Dylan Tichenor; **Score**: Michael Penn; **Main Cast**: Mark Wahlberg, Burt Reynolds, Julianne Moore, Heather Graham.

Born in Flames
US, 1983 – 80 mins
Lizzie Borden

Before taking up directing, Borden was a self-taught editor, who had
worked on projects such as Murray Lerner's *From Mao to Mozart* (1980)
and sculptor Richard Serra's *Stahlwerk*. *Born in Flames* was a largely
self-financed $40,000 project that began in 1977, but this skilful and
provocative blending of art and activism took six years to reach fruition.
It quickly achieved recognition as a seminal chapter in both
independent and feminist film-making. Borden's working conditions
and lack of finance resigned her to a single shoot per month. Working
without a script and with scant regard for continuity, the resulting
footage was painstakingly self-assembled on a Steenbeck installed in
Borden's home.

    Born in Flames was inspired by former Detroit resident Borden's
arrival in New York and her surprise at the degree to which the
contemporary feminist movement suffered from divisions along race
and class lines. The film is intended as a political discovery process
and an attempt to show how a microcosm of black, white and
Hispanic women could all come together to address issues of
inequality. Highlighting the emerging feminist sensibility at the
beginning of the Reagan administration, the film is an allegorical tale
that inventively and resourcefully draws upon elements of the science-
fiction genre.

    It is set ten years after a peaceful social revolution has created all
men as equal. The streets of New York City are murmuring with the
discontent of the seemingly forgotten female populace. Most prominent
among the dissenters are Adele (Satterfield), a member of the militant
women's army; Honey (Honey), a black presenter on the all-black, pirate
Radio Phoenix; and Isabel (Bertei), who performs on the anarchistic Radio
Regazza. The women are closely monitored by the FBI for signs of revolt.
The prison death of a fellow feminist campaigner finally unites the

Revolutionary radio in *Born in Flames*

disparate factions, precipitating the sabotage of the party-controlled media and a unified battle for liberation and equality.

A project that is very much improvisational in terms of performances (director Kathryn Bigelow, incidentally, also features) and execution, the perennially topical *Born in Flames* employs its restricted resources with style and imagination. The vibrancy and danger of New York's streets and the dynamism of the pirate radio stations and simmering countercultures are impressively rendered through a combination of well-paced editing, authentic news reportage and quasi-surveillance techniques. A suitably revolutionary and disparate soundtrack, which fuses elements of rap, reggae and punk, further complements the film's revolutionary air and agitprop spirit. Moreover, Borden's stimulating approach makes generous concessions towards both amusement and entertainment, allowing her to sustain an intelligently posited feminist discourse in what Susan Barrowclough describes as a 'rare example of political film-making that doesn't rule out pleasure in order to preserve its integrity' (Barrowclough, 1984, p. 42).

Dir: Lizzie Borden; **Prod**: Lizzie Borden; **Scr**: Lizzie Borden; **DOP**: Ed Bowes, Al Santana; **Editor**: Lizzie Borden; **Score**: The Bloods, The Red Crayolas, Ibis; **Main Cast**: Honey, Adele Bertei, Jeanne Satterfield, Flo Kennedy.

Bottle Rocket
US, 1996 – 91 mins
Wes Anderson

Originating as a thirteen-minute short, the irreverent and imaginative *Bottle Rocket* pricked the interest of Texas-based writer L. M. Kit Carson, who helped smooth the film's passage from enthusiastic local screenings to the giddy heights of Sundance. First-time independent directors have frequently benefited from the fortuitous benefaction of a more experienced guiding hand (Keitel's involvement with *Reservoir Dogs*, 1991; Soderbergh's nurturing of McGehee and Siegel and Gregg Mottola), and it was at Sundance that *Bottle Rocket* found further patronage from producer James L. Brooks, who succeeded in convincing Columbia to finance a reputed $5 million transformation from promising short to fully fledged feature. Thus, Anderson found himself faced with a potentially fairy-tale scenario dreamily envisioned by countless aspirant independent directors.

The film was shot in and around Austin, Texas (thus prompting comparisons with Linklater's similarly coincidental and offbeat *Slacker,* 1991), and begins with an escape from a minimum-security mental facility by the directionless but amiable Anthony (Luke Wilson), who has been recovering from a recent breakdown. Anthony's escape is orchestrated by his wild-card friend Dignan (Owen Wilson), who sets about installing Anthony as his partner-in-crime in a house burglary. Dignan is later joined by Bob Mapplethorpe (Musgrave), another easily susceptible, long-time cohort, who is desperate to escape the clutches of his overbearing brother. Dignan attempts to bring to fruition his dreams of a career as a master criminal; his lack of appropriate skills receives no comment. After pulling a heist on a bookstore, the fugitives take to the road where love unexpectedly blooms between Anthony and Inez, a Paraguayan motel maid (Lumi Cavazos). However, the trio realise that they are in over their heads when Dignan's hair-brained scheme introduces menacing crime lord Mr Henry (Caan) into the equation.

The heart of the film lies in its engaging, irrepressible and charming chronicle of larger-than-life characters bound together by unconventional morals and relationships. Such a quizzical and indomitably off-kilter sense of characterisation served as the foundation for two later, fruitful Anderson/Wilson collaborations, *Rushmore* (1998) and *The Royal Tenenbaums* (2001). Beautifully written and performed with a potent combination of abandon and tenderness (especially by Owen Wilson), *Bottle Rocket* takes place in an immaculately constructed alternative universe, in which the foolishness of adults is consistently marked by the intelligent observations of children. Most evident here is the moment where Anthony's young sister exasperatingly asks what will become of him.

Though executed with flair and consummate style by Anderson and his team of talented technical collaborators (Yeoman, Moritz and designer David Wasco have all retained their associations with him), the film was considered too esoteric and arcane for Columbia, which ultimately baulked at backing a costly theatrical release campaign. The film nevertheless acted as a useful advertisement for Anderson's idiosyncratic talent, although it went unreleased until a belated appearance on DVD. By this time, however, Anderson had already served notice of his abilities with *Rushmore*, on which he secured some creative autonomy with not inconsiderable studio backing. If *Bottle Rocket*'s troubled circulation is to be viewed as testimony to the dangers independent directors face when working within the studio system, Anderson's ensuing experiences would equally suggest that in the right corporate hands maverick talents can be successfully nurtured.

Dir: Wes Anderson; **Prod**: Polly Platt, Cynthia Hargrave; **Scr**: Owen Wilson, Wes Anderson; **DOP**: Robert Yeoman; **Editor**: David Moritz; **Score**: Mark Mothersbaugh; **Main Cast**: Owen Wilson, Luke Wilson, Robert Musgrave, James Caan.

Boys Don't Cry
US, 1999 – 118 mins
Kimberly Peirce

Four and a half years in the making, and nearly abandoned when a leading actor appeared impossible to find, Peirce's compelling debut is an original and irrefutably haunting study of gender and sexual transgression. It started life as as a Columbia Film School thesis project before evolving into a feature through the involvement of superlative producer Christine Vachon.

Boys Don't Cry tells the remarkable true story of Brandon Teena (Swank), a twenty-one-year-old petty criminal found raped and murdered in an abandoned farmhouse near Falls City, Nebraska. The perpetrators, ex-con John Lotter (Sarsgaard) and self-mutilator and arsonist Thomas Nissen (Sexton), were revealed as friends of Teena's girlfriend, Lana Tisdel (Sevigny). What elevated the crime above the usual grim, Midwestern fare, catapulting it onto the front pages of America's tabloids, was the revelation that Teena was actually Teena Brandon, a young woman from Lincoln, who had for her adult life passed herself off as male.

The film is in part an attempt to reclaim the story from the tabloids that treated it with salacious glee. Peirce, whose exhaustive research included interviewing pre-op transsexuals and butch lesbians, was keen to gain an understanding of both the motivations for Brandon's desire and a wider insight into why a girl would want to pass/dress as a boy. Explained Peirce: 'I've always been interested in women dressed as men, because that's how I grew up, as a tomboy swinging from trees' (Leigh, 2001, p. 110). Brandon was the subject of *The Brandon Teena Story*, a 1994 Susan Muska and Gréta Ólafsdóttir documentary that revealed her self-perception as a transgendered person and not a lesbian or a woman. In sharp contrast, Peirce consciously avoids a factual, biopic approach and reveals nothing of Teena's life pre-Brandon. And though in part inspired by the novelistic journalism of Norman Mailer's *The Executioner's Song* and the unsentimental approach to rural American nihilism and violence evidenced by Brooks' *In Cold Blood* (1967), Peirce also intercuts the semi-fictionalised and at times harrowing narrative (the rape sequence induced nausea in the actors) with a transcendent expressiveness reminiscent of Malick's *Badlands* (1973). Peirce was herself quick to cite the inspiration of neo-realist works such as Hunter's *River's Edge* (1986) and Van Sant's *My Own Private Idaho* (1991), and her cinematographer Jim Denault certainly imbues the otherwise unremarkable landscapes with a tender, lyrical sense that conveys Brandon's romantic yearning.

Former *Beverley Hills 90210* star Hilary Swank is faultless and utterly convincing, giving an Academy-Award winning performance of luminous intensity and poise. The supporting cast, particularly Sevigny, is similarly impeccable. The film's progress was initially dampened by a surprising and unsuccessful defamation of character lawsuit bought by the real-life Tisdel. But *Boys Don't Cry* then went on to enjoy both critical and commercial success, bagging Peirce the FIPRESCI (International Federation of Film Critics) award at the London Film Festival and numerous nominations at the Independent Spirit Awards. Gender confusion continued beyond the film frame, most publicly at the Toronto Film Festival premiere, where Lindsay Law, then head of Fox Searchlight, the film's North American distributor, commended Brandon for 'her bravery', only for Peirce to then thank Brandon for letting her tell 'his story'.

Dir: Kimberly Peirce; **Prod**: Jeffrey Sharp, John Hart, Eva Kolodner, Christine Vachon; **Scr**: Kimberly Peirce, Andy Bienen; **DOP**: Jim Denault; **Editor**: Lee Percy, Tracy Granger; **Score**: Nathan Larson; **Main Cast**: Hilary Swank, Chloë Sevigny, Peter Sarsgaard, Brendan Sexton III.

Boyz N the Hood
US, 1991 – 107 mins
John Singleton

After the success of Lee's *Do the Right Thing* (1989) and in a climate of increasing cultural heterogeneity in which black artists had assumed diverse profiles in which the gap was bridged between black and white consumers, Hollywood opened the door wider to a new wave of young black directors. These directors were eager to produce polished, marketable films with mass appeal. Singleton, a twenty-three-year-old USC graduate, was one of the first to emerge with this high-profile debut, which was financed and distributed by Columbia.

The film opens with a *Stand By Me* (1986) reference: the quest to see a dead body conducted by three ten-year-old friends, who are already inoculated against the consequences of bloodshed by their brutal South Central LA surroundings. *Boyz* then jumps forward seven years to the now teenaged boys, Tre (Gooding Jr), step-brothers Doughboy (Cube) and Ricky Baker (Chestnut), in an even more violent present. Ricky is a gifted athlete and young father, whose life offers promise, while Doughboy, the family scapegoat, is already falling victim to the pervading culture of drugs and killing. Tre is kept on the straight and narrow by his disciplinarian father Furious Styles (Fishburne), a neighbourhood survivor who instils in Tre a sense of self-pride and respect. Circumstances conspire to break the trio's bond, but they remain on good terms until a tragic incident tears them apart.

Boyz was fashioned from a Singleton script based on his experiences growing up in the South Central area. Dubbed an 'American film of enormous importance' by Roger Ebert of the *Chicago Sun-Times* (Ebert, 1991), *Boyz* is a sobering rites-of-passage drama that delivers a powerful polemic about male black-on-black violence. Making its message abundantly clear, *Boyz* opens with the statistic that one in every twenty-one black males will be murdered at the hands of another, and ends with a title card imploring an increase in peace. Singleton spreads his targets wide but rarely uses a scattershot approach, offering intelligent, coherent and balanced observations on the Eurocentric nature of the college education system and the hard-won rewards of community. Perhaps most remarkable is the film's willingness to tackle the issue of paternal responsibility through its criticism of Ricky's irresponsibility and its praising of Furious' tough-love approach. The implication that the absence of a father is likely to result in anti-social behaviour or death and the general affirmation of the paternal over the maternal (a flashback sequence reveals Tre's mother, played by Angela Bassett, abdicating her parental duties) do, however, provoke questions concerning representations of gender.

Singleton's thematic confidence is matched by assured visual aesthetics. Though citing Spike Lee as an influence, Singleton's approach is subtler and more restrained than Lee's, ensuring that the unfolding drama and performances remain centre stage. The director is rewarded by the excellence of his principals; Gooding Jr is especially outstanding in an early role. Ice Cube, former NWA member and one of rap's highest profile stars, lends Doughboy a tragic nobility in a role that prefigured what would become a familiar transition to acting for black musicians (and a key component of the marketing and success of any film boasting a hip hop element).

The film was a commercial box-office success, grossing over $57 million in the US. *Boyz'* popularity among young, black, American males helped sustain the continued visibility of young, black directors in Hollywood and precipitated a crop of ethnic ghetto violence movies, tagged 'New Jack Cinema'.

Dir: John Singleton; **Prod**: Steve Nicolaides; **Scr**: John Singleton; **DOP**: Chuck Mills; **Editor**: Bruce Cannon; **Score**: Stanley Clarke; **Main Cast**: Larry Fishburne, Cuba Gooding Jr, Ice Cube, Morris Chestnut.

Buffalo '66
Canada/US, 1997 – 110 mins
Vincent Gallo

Prior to *Buffalo '66*, Gallo was best known for the demonic intensity of his acting, and had previously enjoyed success as a model, painter and then a musician in the experimental and influential New York band Gray. His acting credits included a number of independent pictures, including Alan Taylor's *Palookaville* (1995) and Abel Ferrara's *The Funeral* (1996). Gallo has a restless, idiosyncratic talent, and *Buffalo '66* marked his vaguely autobiographical, definitely personal, even maverick debut.

Buffalo '66 is ostensibly a poignant yet provocative love story. It opens with Billy Brown (Gallo) being expelled from prison onto the wintry, suburban streets. Heading back to his hometown of Buffalo, Billy kidnaps Layla, a blonde tap-dancer (Ricci), and forces her to pose as his adoring wife on a visit to the home of his indifferent, abusive but football-crazy parents (Gazzara and Huston). During a fraught, hostile dinner, Billy's insecurities and his parents' simmering resentments rise to the surface.

Gallo follows the trend of many previous actors-turned-directors – and especially Cassavetes – favouring performance over narrative. The film is constructed as a loosely connected series of intricately stylised set-pieces linked by surreal, esoteric and often musical vignettes. Each of the cast is allowed at least one show-boating and invariably show-stopping moment, most memorably, perhaps, Gazzara's Frank Sinatra mime. Similarly, Mickey Rourke (an actor enjoying something of a renaissance in independent productions, witness Buscemi's *The Animal Factory*, 2001) delivers an impressive, direct-to-camera monologue that reveals how Billy came to owe him money. In a role that appears to have been constructed to satisfy male viewers seeking an element of wish fulfilment, Ricci still just about shades the acting honours, cementing her burgeoning indie icon status in the process.

As a comment on parental abuse and the horrors of blue-collar suburbia, the film is surprisingly lucid and moving, with Gallo's adoption of a washed-out naturalism (the film was shot on vintage reverse stock, a result of the director's obsession with detail), proving highly effective. At times painfully funny (Billy's desperate search for somewhere to take a piss during the opening brings tears to the eyes), the film however, will undoubtedly be best remembered for its stylised visual aesthetic, meticulous production design and formal daring. *Buffalo '66* employs inventive, unconventional editing techniques, perhaps most impressively in the form of the flashbacks to Billy's unhappy childhood that begin as small frames within frames before multiplying and enlarging to fill the screen. Gallo has a fondness for off-kilter tableaux, and his sense of framing is equally audacious, denoting both distance (the reverse angle shots around the dinner table in Billy's home) and tentative intimacy (the shot from above of Billy and Layla on the motel bed).

Gallo's publicising of the film was exuberant. The director responded to questions about how he got his stars to appear in a micro-budget production with an incredulous, 'How do you think? I fucking paid them.' Backed by a stack of impressive nominations (including the Grand Jury prize at Sundance and a Best First Feature Independent Spirit Award), *Buffalo '66* wasted little time in achieving cult status.

Dir: Vincent Gallo; **Prod**: Chris Hanley; **Scr**: Vincent Gallo, Alison Bagnall; **DOP**: Lance Accord; **Editor**: Curtiss Clayton; **Score**: Vincent Gallo; **Main Cast**: Vincent Gallo, Christina Ricci, Ben Gazzara, Anjelica Huston.

Candy Mountain
France/Switzerland/Canada, 1987 – 92 mins
Robert Frank, Rudy Wurlitzer

Candy Mountain is a co-production that begins in New York before
meandering cross country and concluding in Canada, but it is
nonetheless described as a resolutely American film by its two well-
matched collaborators. Robert Frank is an acclaimed photographer (his
1958 book *The Americans* depicted American iconography and the
mythic allure of the road in a downbeat light), who segued into film-
making, establishing his reputation with the unscripted Beat classic *Pull
My Daisy* (1959). With a passion for the road movie genre (as evidenced
by his work on Monte Hellman's *Two-Lane Blacktop*, 1971), scriptwriter
Rudy Wurlitzer similarly mined the tarnished mythology of America,
notably in Peckinpah's *Pat Garrett and Billy the Kid* (1973).

Informed by Wenders' *Kings of the Road* (1976), *Candy Mountain*
tracks the dispiriting personal odyssey of ambitious but untalented New
York musician Julius (O'Connor), whose quest for glory leads him to
feign an association with Elmore Silk (Yulin), the J. D. Salinger of guitar
making. Charged with luring the legendary craftsman from hiding and
retirement, Julius initially contacts Elmore's brother Al (Waits). Financially
lighter (he is repeatedly sold cars which he either trades or crashes),
Julius heads for the Canadian border and the remote home of Silk's
former French lover (Ogier), who re-directs him to a barren seaboard
town. There, Julius finally tracks Silk down, only to discover that in return
for a lifetime of security and freedom Silk has signed an exclusive deal
with a Japanese businesswoman (Kazuko Oshima). A helpless bystander
as Silk destroys his remaining guitars, a tired and broke Julius attempts to
hitch a ride home.

Wurlitzer draws upon Frank's background, specifically his struggles
with the eternal art/commerce dichotomy; the pressures of fame; his
journeys towards selfhood; and the defining importance of music (Frank
had directed the seminal Rolling Stones' documentary, *Cocksucker Blues*,

1972, the third celluloid collaboration between the pair). Having to satisfy the demands of the various international financiers, Frank/Wurlitzer also tapped into Frank's desire to make a film about a journey from the centre of one culture to the margins of another. The pair also debunk the romantic notion of the open road as a symbol of freedom. *Candy Mountain* certainly strikes a sobering note and can perhaps be seen as providing a natural conclusion to the American road movie.

Pio Corradi's photography – redolent of Frank's own – imbues the shifting landscapes and their weird, cranky and frequently lonely populace with a timelessness and distinctly iconic quality. In a key moment, a toothless van driver warns the initially optimistic Julius that 'life ain't no candy mountain' before, like so many others, smartly ripping him off. The music, co-ordinated by Hal Wilner and provided by luminaries such as Arto Lindsay and Marc Ribot, is essential, intelligently foregrounding both character and action. Endorsing the film's endearing, countercultural sensibility, the film-makers cast from an esoteric pool of musicians and were repaid with accomplished and entertaining turns from the likes of Tom Waits, Dr John, David Johansen and Joe Strummer. The 'regular' actors aren't bad either, especially O'Connor as the bowed but not quite beaten Kerouac-lite hero.

Dir: Robert Frank, Rudy Wurlitzer; **Prod**: Ruth Waldburger; **Scr**: Robert Frank, Rudy Wurlitzer; **DOP**: Pio Corradi; **Editor**: Jennifer Auge; **Score Coordinator**: Hal Wilner; **Main Cast**: Kevin J. O'Connor, Harris Yulin, Tom Waits, Bulle Ogier.

Chan Is Missing
US, 1981 – 80 mins
Wayne Wang

Chan Is Missing was shot vérité style on raw, grainy black and white 16mm for $23,000, with a combination of grants from the American Film Institute and completion funding from the National Endowment for the Arts. It offers a witty, off-beat and quizzical take on the Chinese-American experience and the collision between Eastern and Western cultures. Such subjects were close to the heart of Hong Kong-born writer-director Wayne Wang (named in homage to his father's favourite American actor) who, following the success of 1985's *Dim Sum*, was credited with patenting the Chinese-American movie. Moreover, the on-screen discussion and representation of issues relating to ethnicity and diaspora were to act as a profound influence on more politicised emerging directors such as Spike Lee.

A sprawling, meandering travelogue, the film is set amid San Francisco's Chinatown, with its contrasting communities of American-born Chinese who have largely embraced US culture, and the freshly arriving Taiwanese and Hong Kong immigrants striving to remain true to their roots. *Chan* tracks the search of two taxi drivers, Jo (Moy) and his nephew Steve (Hayashi) for Taiwanese immigrant Chan Hung. It transpires that Hung has mysteriously disappeared with the $4,000 Jo and Steve had given him to establish them as independent cab operators. Their enquiries turn up a miasma of conflicting theories concerning Chan's whereabouts, including his implication in the murder of a supporter of the People's Republic. Told by a scholar that they must 'think Chinese' to solve the mystery, Jo and Steve recognise that the more they analyse Chan's character the more unknowable and contradictory he becomes. Acknowledging that some things happen without reason, they call off their search.

Wang's ensuing career both in and out of the mainstream has revealed an uncompromising and chameleon-like approach to form and structure. Indeed *Chan*, described by the director in an interview with Tony Rayns as 'almost totally abstract' (Rayns, 1985), is no exception. Displaying a playful propensity for allusion and a disregard for orthodoxy, Wang kicks things off with an entertaining Cantonese version of 'Rock around the Clock' by Hong Kong pop star Sam Hui before mixing seemingly disparate generic conventions. Beginning as a detective mystery with film noir overtones (suspenseful editing, off-kilter camera angles, Marlowesque voiceover), the film changes tack to adopt a more naturalistic, observational aesthetic for its philosophical and at times melancholic exploration of contradictory attitudes to identity and values. With filming often taking place on tight schedules with friends and acquaintances, this aesthetic also in part derives from the original film conception as a thirty-minute, non-fiction piece about cabbies.

Edited over nine months, the film was eventually completed by Wang himself following a disagreement over the film's structure with original editor Geraldine Kataka. Part of the problem with the editing process was that Wang had originally set up shots to suggest that the point of view throughout was possibly from the perspective of an omniscient Chan. When it became clear that this technique was not sustainable, Wang was forced to make drastic editing reconstructions. Premiered on 16mm at the Pacific Film Archive and subsequently screened to great interest at the New Directors and Films Festival in New York, *Chan Is Missing* was subsequently acquired by New Yorker films and blown up to 35mm for US theatrical distribution.

Dir: Wayne Wang; **Prod**: Wayne Wang; **Scr**: Wayne Wang, Isaac Cronin, Terrel Seltzer; **DOP**: Michael Chin; **Editor**: Wayne Wang; **Score**: Robert Kikuchi-Yngojo; **Main Cast**: Wood Moy, Marc Hayashi, Laureen Chew, Judi Nihei.

Chuck and Buck
US, 2000 – 96 mins
Miguel Arteta

Arteta's low-budget *Chuck and Buck* gained wider attention than his previous feature, *Star Maps* (1997), causing intense interest at Sundance and major independent festivals worldwide. At the Independent Spirit Awards the film received numerous acting nominations and triumphed in the Best Feature under $500,000 category.

Intelligently scripted by actor Mike White, it's a well-performed and initially unassuming if off-beat buddy movie concerning Buck (White), a twenty-seven-year-old who has never fully navigated the transition to adulthood, and his childhood friend Chuck (Weitz), now a successful Los Angeles music executive on the brink of marriage. The two are reunited for the funeral of Buck's mother, rekindling Buck's memories of their childhood games. Buck decides to effect a more permanent continuation of their relationship, trailing Chuck and his fiancée Carlyn (Colt) back to their home. From this point the film segues into darker, distinctly uncomfortable psycho-sexual territory, with Buck's pursuit of Chuck becoming an obsessive stalking exercise.

The film was shot on digital video by Mexican cinematographer Chuy Chávez, and its bright, candy-coloured look, with cartoonish reds and vivid colour combinations, perfectly reflects the lolly-loving Buck's mental state and childish sensibility. Surrounding him with the books, toys and general accoutrements of his childhood, Arteta also cannily incorporates a bubblegum soundtrack, including the endearingly chirpy 'Freedom of the Heart' by Sanford, Hormel and Joey Waronker. By contrast, Chuck is located in more subtle, adult contexts: the efficient office environment and, perhaps most pertinently, his designer home. The two worlds are destined to collide, with Buck observing, 'I like your house, it's kind of old personey'. Also of formal interest are Buck's recollections of his childhood, which are given a convincingly grainy, home-movie look that imbues them with an intense emotional currency.

Buck's ignorance of the adult world's machinations and its reliance on small talk, particularly evident at an industry bash Chuck invites him to attend, evokes Mike Leigh's perceptive take on the horrors of social etiquette and those terrible moments involving people who have no awareness of it. Similarly, Buck's inability to accept Chuck's attempts to brush him off leads to another comical but excruciating event, Buck's hiring of a local theatre troupe of out-of-work, untalented actors (all subsequently unanimous in their decision to leave the play off their CVs) to perform an embarrassingly autobiographical play offering a frank account of his affections. On reading the play the theatre manager/director tellingly exclaims, 'It's like a homoerotic misogynistic love story'.

And indeed it is, as it emerges that the film's title is also a euphemism for the 'sucking and fucking' in which the pair indulged as kids and which Chuck has suppressed way down in his subconscious. On steering the film into even darker, more uncomfortable waters, Arteta and White gained credit for rejecting traditional, mainstream depictions of the sanitised nature of childhood, but invited criticism for the way in which they equate homosexuality with emotional immaturity (Buck also becomes infatuated with his macho leading man) and unsocial, obsessive behaviour.

Dir: Miguel Arteta; **Prod**: Matthew Greenfield; **Scr**: Mike White; **DOP**: Chuy Chávez; **Editor**: Jeff Betancourt; **Score**: Joey Waronker; **Main Cast**: Mike White, Chris Weitz, Beth Colt, Lupe Ontiveros.

Clean, Shaven
US, 1993 – 80 mins
Lodge Kerrigan

Filmed over a two-year period because of its low budget, Kerrigan's debut feature is representative of the more radical end of the independent spectrum. As a director, Kerrigan's adoption of an independent sensibility is not purely a result of enforced economics, but more a reflection of his aesthetics and his desire to attack mainstream cinematic conventions.

As such, *Clean, Shaven* implements a determinedly non-linear approach, instead painting an impressionistic, fractured and ambiguous portrait of Peter Winter (Greene), a schizophrenic and self-mutilator who undertakes a cross-country search for the daughter from whom he is denied access by her adoptive parents. Winter's release from an institution coincides with the discovery of the mutilated body of a young girl, a crime for which Winter is suspected and trailed by a homicide detective. Kerrigan withholds and denies information concerning Winter's complicity, forcing the viewer to share his protagonist's mental fragility and twisted perception of the world. At the beginning of the film Winter grows annoyed with a child for bouncing a ball against his windscreen. He gets out of the car and while the camera lingers on the vehicle, out of shot there is a terrible scream. The aftermath is never revealed, denying the spectator the comfort afforded by the usual generic conventions surrounding the roles of hunter and the hunted.

Set in a bleak, drab landscape, from which director of photography Teodoro Maniaci's camera picks out abstract, ugly structures of metal and concrete, the film also takes an extremely expressionistic and inventive approach to sound design. There is virtually no dialogue but instead a cacophony of discordant screeching, squawking sounds, much of which emanates from Winter's car radio and from the noises that emerge as a result of his belief that he has been fitted with a radio receiver allowing the authorities to monitor his whereabouts. In a nearly unwatchable moment, Winter, whose self-mutilation is a result of his intense self-loathing (hence his inability to use mirrors, which he smashes or tapes over), gouges out his nails with a knife in an attempt to find the device.

Kerrigan presents a non-sanitised picture of mental illness that exists in stark contrast to traditional Hollywood flicks such as *Forrest Gump* (1994) which depict 'the mentally damaged as founts of simple wisdom' (Kemp, 1995, p. 43). In this regard the writer-director is greatly assisted by Greene who gives an intense, courageous and intelligent performance to render Winter's troubled psyche. *Clean, Shaven* is an uncompromising and provocative work by a film-maker with an astute understanding of the medium and a desire to use it to question standard modes of representation.

Dir: Lodge Kerrigan; **Prod**: Lodge Kerrigan; **Scr**: Lodge Kerrigan; **DOP**: Teodoro Maniaci; **Editor**: Jay Rabinowitz; **Score**: Hahn Rowe; **Main Cast**: Peter Greene, Molly Castelloe, Megan Owen, Robert Albert.

Clerks
US, 1993 – 90 mins
Kevin Smith

Tagged as 'a hilarious look at over-the-counter culture' and pitched squarely at the slacker generation, *Clerks* takes an eventful day in the life of young convenience store clerk Dante (O'Halloran) and his friend and fellow wage slave at the neighbouring video store, Randal (Anderson). Rudely awoken at 6am to be told that he has to work on his day off, Dante, the film reveals, has an incident-packed shift, which takes in the explicit sexual confessions of his girlfriend, the impending nuptials of a high school ex and an impromptu hockey match staged on the store's roof. A fight with Randal and a constant stream of eccentric and offensive customers further ensures a day Dante, who in a moment of pathos exclaims, 'The real tragedy is that I'm not even supposed to be here today', is unlikely to forget.

Smith, a multiplex 'movie-brat' with a particular penchant for Spielberg and Lucas, had his sensibilities challenged by a double-bill of Linklater's *Slacker* (1991) and Hartley's *Trust* (1990) as a twenty-one-year-old during his single semester in film school. Citing *Slacker* as the formative influence on his decision to become a film-maker, Smith similarly drew inspiration from Hartley's ability to adapt to economic constraints by simply placing the emphasis on dialogue. Enthralled by Jarmusch's visual minimalism and Spike Lee's reduction of narrative to a single location and concentrated time frame, Smith went so far as to thank the aforementioned directors for 'leading the way' in his closing credits.

Financed on credit cards by twenty-three-year-old Smith and shot on black and white 16mm stock (an economic consideration, not an artistic one), *Clerks* was completed with impressive ingenuity on a micro-budget of $27,000. Filming took place at night in the Leonardo Quickstop convenience store where Smith worked on a minimum wage. The fact that the shutters remain permanently closed throughout is neatly incorporated into the film as a recurring joke.

Over-the-counter culture as depicted in *Clerks*

In terms of editing, cinematography and composition, *Clerks* is crudely executed, though it does employ an endearing and inventive structuring into mini-episodes. It is, however, on the 'talk is cheap to film' aesthetic that the film thrives, propelled by Smith's sharp, scabrous and profusely profane dialogue and scattershot observational riffs on issues relating to friendship, hygiene, job prospects and the fragile fabric of life. Captured in long, static takes, the characters display an adolescent if often hilarious fascination with sex, but thankfully Smith's writing and the impeccable performances of the young cast (who reveal a natural aptitude for delivery and timing) ensure that the effect is rarely boorish or immature. As was the vogue following the success and influence of Tarantino's first two features, *Clerks* also offers numerous witty asides and observations on popular culture, most memorably the ramifications concerning the conclusion of *Return of the Jedi* (1983).

Warmly received at Sundance and a highly visible Miramax triumph (the $3 million domestic gross ensured that it became an oft-quoted paradigm of low-budget success), *Clerks* also brought Smith generational spokesman status and a loyal, vaguely obsessive coterie of diehard fans.

Dir: Kevin Smith; **Prod**: Kevin Smith, Scott Mosier; **Scr**: Kevin Smith; **DOP**: David Klein; **Editor**: Kevin Smith, Scott Mosier; **Score**: Scott Angley; **Main Cast**: Brian O'Halloran, Jeff Anderson, Marilyn Ghiglotti, Lisa Spoonauer.

Crumb
US, 1995 – 120 mins
Terry Zwigoff

An eclectic documentary-maker firmly rooted in underground comic book culture, Zwigoff formed a lasting friendship with the artist Robert Crumb in the mid-60s. Bonded through a love of esoteric music, particularly ragtime blues and traditional jazz, the pair played together in Crumb's band, The Cheap Suit Serenaders. More pertinently, however, the relationship spawned this film, an affectionate, intimate and often complex document of Crumb's life and work, which deservedly won the Grand Jury Prize at the 1995 Sundance Film Festival.

The film was executive produced by David Lynch and filmed without restriction over a six-year period. *Crumb* begins by tracing the origins of Crumb's talent as a sensitive child, hailing from relatively humble beginnings, who was encouraged to draw by an older brother in order to escape the bullying of high-school jocks. The film reveals some of the formative experiences that would exert an influence on his art and personality (the seventeen-year-old Crumb developed a sexual attraction to Bugs Bunny) and then details how with *Fritz the Cat*, *Mr Natural* and *Keep on Truckin'* Crumb became the archetypal underground artist of 60s' counterculture. Accorded celebrity status, Crumb began to indulge both in print and in reality his myriad sexual peccadilloes, in particular his fetishistic fixation with domineering, big-bottomed women. He was increasingly inspired to graphically depict his darker side, and accusations of pornography and misogyny soon followed.

In this often unflattering but frequently humorous portrait of an undeniably fascinating artist, Zwigoff largely retains an impressive objectivity, soliciting the animated participation of supporters and detractors of Crumb's work, examples of which are beautifully represented on screen with lingering camera pans of comic strips and larger scale drawings. Art historian Robert Hughes passionately argues that Crumb's work is in the subversive, misanthropic Rabelaisian

Gun crazy. Artist Robert Crumb in *Crumb*

tradition, while female commentators such as fellow cartoonist Trina
Robbins describe his output as self-indulgent, racist, pornographic and
deeply misogynistic. The jocular Crumb himself refuses to be drawn on
the debate, preferring instead to shrug off the issue with a laidback
affability that at times causes frustration in others, most notably Kathy
Goodell (one of several ex-girlfriends), who is moved to deliver a blow to
the head of the now happily married Crumb.

Crumb also examines Robert's relationship with his two brothers,
Charles and Maxon, who both appear in the film. Tellingly, the end
credits reveal that sisters Sandra and Carol declined to be interviewed,
indicating the warped maleness of the Crumb household. We also learn
that the chronically depressed, housebound Charles committed suicide
shortly after the film's completion. It is in the relentlessly voyeuristic
presentation of Crumb's hugely dysfunctional family that the film
perhaps falters, presenting Charles and Maxon as freakish curiosities, as

well as examples of the fate that Robert's talent and ability to function within society allowed him to avoid. That said, *Crumb* remains a compelling, exhaustive work and is required viewing for admirers of documentaries or those whose interest was pricked by *Ghost World* (2001), Zwigoff's inspired fiction debut.

Dir: Terry Zwigoff; **Prod**: Lynn O'Donnell, Terry Zwigoff; **DOP**: Maryse Alberti; **Editor**: Victor Livingston; **Music Arrangements**: David Boeddinghaus; **Main Cast**: Robert Crumb, Aline Kominsky, Charles Crumb, Maxon Crumb.

Dark Days
US, 2000 – 82 mins
Marc Singer

An astonishing debut from novice documentarist Singer, *Dark Days* is all the more impressive as Singer had no formal training as a film-maker and was inspired by the compelling subject matter alone. The result is a work of genuine social and sociological import.

The film focuses on the homeless denizens of the labyrinthine subway tunnels in and around Manhattan's Penn Station. Risking life and limb, the desperate, disparate men and women on whom Singer turns his unflinching camera-eye build temporary shelters which they equip as best they can despite abject poverty and surrounding squalor. Overrun by vermin and forced to exist with little running water and scant sanitation, the subterranean dwellers are at least accorded the blessing of being off the streets, even if only under them. For many featured in the film this has been home for as long as twenty-five years, but their habitation is threatened when Amtrak, the subway owners, announce plans for eviction.

The film's pervading candour and integrity was in part generated by the bond Singer forged with his subjects over the course of filming, which took place intermittently throughout the 90s. Working in arduous and adverse film-making conditions, Singer invited many of those featured to participate in technical duties, and for the majority of the filming shared their living conditions, periodically emerging, mole-like, only to replenish film stock. As a result, the sensitive interviews Singer conducts are perceptive and illuminating, contributing to a moving patchwork of torn and tattered lives. As the film progresses, Singer's objectivity understandably wavers and after having grown so close to his subjects he becomes personally involved in the fight to avoid eviction and the seeking of resettlement.

Dark Days makes a tangible virtue of the various impositions of the production, and is strikingly shot on grainy, monochrome black and white 16mm to lend the film the texture and sensibility of vintage photojournalism. By contrast, Singer displays a canny awareness of the power of other cinematic devices, often setting his charged images to an atmospheric score by contemporary breaks maestro DJ Shadow. Editor Melissa Neidich works wonders condensing the years of material to a cogent and coherent length.

Though eschewing the no-thrills simplicity espoused by Frederick Wiseman, *Dark Days* recalls the abundant ironies, hardships, conflicts and passions found in Wiseman's work and also shares a questioning attitude to the institutions and corporations that shape our lives. It comes as little surprise to learn that Singer received advice regarding structure and objectivity from two Goliaths of the documentary world, D. A. Pennebaker and Chris Hegedus, during the editing of the film. *Dark Days* went on to win three major awards at Sundance (including the Audience Award) and the 2000 Indie Spirit Best Documentary Award.

Dir: Marc Singer; **Prod**: Marc Singer; **DOP**: Marc Singer; **Editor**: Melissa Neidich; **Score**: DJ Shadow; **Main Cast**: Rick Rubell, Mike Harris, Tommy Tito, Ralph Greg.

Daughters of the Dust
US, 1991 – 112 mins
Julie Dash

The first film directed by an African-American female to gain national
distribution, *Daughters of the Dust* established Dash as an original and
independent voice and a seminal figure for black feminist critics. The film
was originally intended as part of a planned series of films dealing with
the experiences and forgotten histories of black women during the last
century (Dash's 1982 American Film Institute graduation film *Illusions*
being the first part). The fraught passage of *Daughters* through
financing, production and distribution can in part be attributed to Dash's
insistence on total artistic control. Other factors which gave the film
difficulties were its uncompromising Afrocentric, female perspective and
highly sophisticated aesthetic, qualities to which a largely white industry
and critical cognoscenti were unaccustomed.

Meticulous in even the smallest detail, and informed by Dash's
attention to historical fact (as reflected in the exquisite costume design
and eye for playful subversion), *Daughters* is a visually ravishing and
hugely sophisticated costume drama set in the islands off the South
Carolina coast at the turn of the century. A far cry from the urban terrain
explored by emerging male African-American film-makers of the time,
the film tells the impressionistic tale of a Gullah family who meet for a
last supper before the migration of its members to a new life on the
mainland. Central to the film is the tension between matriarch Nana
Peazant (Lee Day), who wants the family to remain together, and Haagar
(Kaycee Moore), who leads the journey away from roots and ancestral
African heritage towards a new future.

Dash is an avowed disciple of influential black writers such as Toni
Cade Bambara, Toni Morrison and Alice Walker (fans of whom provided
a ready audience for *Daughters* when it received its limited theatrical
release), and she also followed their preference for non-linear structure,
enabling the incorporation of voices past, present and future. Though

originally conceived as a silent, the film uses dual narration, contrasting Nana's commentary with that of an as yet unborn child. It's an audacious device that demonstrates an awareness of the importance of oral storytelling in West African culture and which helps provide a clear link between the experiences of multiple generations of African-American peoples.

Beautifully rendered (it won a cinematography award at Sundance), with an arresting depiction of landscapes, *Daughters of the Dust* visually emphasises the spiritual and organic relationship between a people and their land and culture. Often mythic in tone, the film also abounds in images that denote an intense symbolism, intelligently signifying both the scars of slavery (a flashback to an indigo-processing plant establishes that the Gullah people depicted in the film are the descendants of slaves) and the customs, practices and superstitions, largely religious, waiting in the new world.

Unfortunately, Dash subsequently suffered similar funding problems to those that beset her when making *Daughters*. At the time of writing she has been forced to use television as the canvas on which to further extend her oeuvre.

Dir: Julie Dash; **Prod**: Julie Dash; **Scr**: Julie Dash; **DOP**: A. Jaffa Fielder; **Editor**: Amy Carey, Joseph Burton; **Score**: John Barnes; **Main Cast**: Cora Lee Day, Alva Rogers, Barbara-O, Trula Hoosier.

The Daytrippers
US, 1995 – 88 mins
Greg Mottola

The Daytrippers, Columbia Film School graduate Mottola's debut feature, owes much to the fortuitous attentions of Steven Soderbergh. After being impressed by the writer-director's short, *Swinging in the Printer's Room*, Soderbergh offered to assume the producer's role to guide Mottola through the tricky process of bringing his sardonic, social satire to the screen. Others obviously had faith in Mottola's smart, bittersweet script: Campbell Scott (who also takes a small cameo as an unassuming author) acted as executive producer, and relatively well-known actors such as Stanley Tucci and Marcia Gay Harden agreed to appear for greatly reduced fees.

The film was shot in a whirlwind sixteen days on a $700,000 budget. Allegedly based on a true incident, *The Daytrippers* is a delightfully droll, decidedly idiosyncratic road movie of sorts, in which supposedly happily married Long Island teacher Eliza (Davis) discovers a note that suggests her husband Louis (Tucci), a successful Manhattan-based publisher, is having an affair. Seeking the sanctuary and advice of her family, Eliza is persuaded by her domineering, manipulative mother (Anne Meara) to travel to the city to confront him. The henpecked patriarch (Pat McNamara) is assigned the role of driver, and it becomes a full family outing when Eliza's kooky sister Jo (indie heavyweight Posey) and her pretentious boyfriend Carl (a wonderfully odious Schreiber) are invited along for the ride. In a tightly packed car with no heater (and cinematographer John Inwood certainly gives the film an authentic, wintry feel), it doesn't take long for family tensions to reach breaking point.

The director, acutely aware of the financial constraints of the production, wisely adopts an unfussy minimalist style (in one scene Mottola sets up a car chase only for it to peter out immediately, at which point Jo exclaims 'well that was the shortest car chase in history'). This approach manages to be deceptively and economically revealing about the fractured spaces the characters inhabit and the suffocating claustrophobia of the family unit. Mottola's shot selection suggests that all is not as it should be, for example Eliza and Louis never appear in the same frame during their nocturnal ride home from an evening on the town. Intrusive hand-held camera shots continually capture the extent to which these individuals are gnawing at each other's fraying nerves.

Mottola's perceptive, painfully funny script, a delicate balancing of pathos and bathos, allows the director to intelligently explore the lower-middle-class milieu he creates for his characters – all vividly realised by an on-form cast – and the culture/class dichotomy presented by Carl's wonderfully inane artistic endeavours, excruciatingly explained to Eliza's uncomprehending mother. The hapless but harmless Carl's comeuppance at a literary bash is a cruel but nonetheless wickedly enjoyable moment in a film liberally sprinkled with beautifully observed situations that are the embodiment of social awkwardness, the last of which offers a neat subversion of gender stereotypes.

A genuinely charming low(ish)-budget triumph, *The Daytrippers* suffered rejection by Sundance before going on to triumph at Slamdance and Toronto.

Dir: Gregg Mottola; **Prod**: Nancy Tenenbaum, Steven Soderbergh; **Scr**: Gregg Mottola; **DOP**: John Inwood; **Editor**: Anne McCabe; **Score**: Richard Martinez; **Main Cast**: Hope Davis, Parker Posey, Liev Schreiber, Stanley Tucci.

Donnie Darko
US, 2001 – 122 mins
Richard Kelly

Donnie Darko was a startlingly original debut from a then twenty-six-year-old fresh out of film school. It is as consistently intelligent, esoteric, dreamlike and downright perplexing as anything in contemporary American cinema. A disparate generic cocktail that comprises elements common to science fiction, high-school satire, horror and tales of suburban dissatisfaction, the film is also liberally sprinkled with a multiplicity of filmic allusions. Most prominent examples include *Harvey* (1950), *It's a Wonderful Life* (1946), *Carrie* (1976) and *Back to the Future* (1985); *Ordinary People* (1980) and, inevitably, *American Beauty* (1999) also come to mind. *Donnie Darko* is also imbued with the general other-worldliness of David Lynch. That the finished product should still be so confident and tonally assured is remarkable.

The 80s-set film concerns troubled teen Donnie Darko (Gyllenhaal in a magnetic performance that augurs well for his future), whose recent psychiatric treatment for what appears to be a form of paranoid schizophrenia has caused escalating conflict among his uptight parents. While sleepwalking, Donnie meets Frank, a menacing six-foot figure sporting a fake-fur suit and disturbing rabbit mask who informs him that the world will end in precisely twenty-eight days, six hours, forty-two minutes and twelve seconds. Donnie returns home from his reverie to see a jet engine being lifted from his bedroom; had he been there it would have killed him. Any hopes of normality following the forming of a relationship with Gretchen (Jena Malone), a new arrival at Donnie's conservative school, are crushed by further visitations from Frank, who compels Donnie to commit a series of rebellious crimes.

This blackly comic film is initially, for the most part, concerned with making incisive comments about personal and familial dysfunction, teenage introspection, the moral Right and the charlatanism of new-age self-help gurus (in the insightful US DVD commentary, Kelly describes

Donnie as 'a spiritual superhero'). The film then moves into darker, phantasmagoric territory as the central character's hallucinatory episodes increase and eventually take over. The previously dry and acutely observed if off-kilter depiction of suburban life gradually recedes to be replaced with a frequent and dizzying use of slow- and fast-motion photography and the disjunctive use of sound and image to depict the wormholes in time and parallel realities with which Donnie becomes increasingly and portentously fascinated. It is during these latter stages that *Donnie Darko*, with its overtones of universal interconnectedness, arguably teeters on the brink of collapse, compelled by its astringent sense of ambition, twisted logic and desire to uncork myriad inexplicable enigmas and mysteries.

Donnie Darko was executive produced by Drew Barrymore, who lends acting support. A surprisingly credibly creepy Patrick Swayze also features, sacrificing Hollywood fees for independent kudos. The film's limited US release was hampered by the events of September 11 and a curmudgeonly critical response to a rapturous Sundance reception. Subsequently, however, the film has acquired a sizeable reputation (the *Village Voice*'s J. Hoberman described it as 'a most original and venturesome American indie': Hoberman, 2001) and achieved rapid and probably enduring cult status.

Dir: Richard Kelly; **Prod**: Chris Ball, Adam Fields, Nancy Juvonen, Sean McKittrick; **Scr**: Richard Kelly; **DOP**: Steven Poster; **Editor**: Sam Bauer, Eric Strand; **Score**: Michael Andrews; **Main Cast**: Jake Gyllenhaal, Maggie Gyllenhaal, Patrick Swayze, Mary McDonnell.

Don't Look Back
US, 1967 – 96 mins
D. A. Pennebaker

A landmark documentary, *Don't Look Back* evolved from what William Rothman calls 'the first generation of cinéma vérité film-makers' (Rothman, 1997, p. xi), who expressed a passionate commitment to 'truth'. Jean Rouch and his contemporaries influenced an emerging group of American directors of the late 50s and 60s who sought in their own ways to reveal the reality of specific subjects and social conditions. Pennebaker and his peers of the Direct Cinema group (Richard Leacock, Robert Drew, and Albert and David Mayles) refuted the notion that the presence of the camera had any significance, believing that they were offering a purely objective depiction of reality.

Pennebaker's film accompanies a young Bob Dylan on his 1965 tour of Britain. It was filmed using a hand-held camera, and is distinguished by an absence of voiceover narration and the replacement of montage with extended long takes to offer an approximation of real time. It begins with Dylan's iconic performance of 'Subterranean Homesick Blues', with the aid of outsized cue cards, and culminates in a tumultuous concert at London's Royal Albert Hall. *Don't Look Back* here captures Dylan, accompanied by an entourage spearheaded by manager Albert Grossman, as he undergoes the uneasy transition from folk singer to rock star. Dylan is by turns bored, arrogant, affected and disaffected. The film examines the dichotomies in the singer's increasingly fractured persona (such as his awarenesss of the artificiality of his image and paradoxical obsession with it) and his often fraught and uneasy interactions with fans, journalists and British music contemporaries.

When considering the signficance of the film, it is necessary to recall that following the expulsion of Direct Cinema films from prime-time American TV networks, *Don't Look Back* (shot in 1965 but not released until 1967) was from the very outset intended to be shown in theatres. This intention was made easier to realise by the ascension of Dylan as a 'star'. The film therefore represents the moment that the commitment to 'truth' became a cinematic concern as opposed to a purely televisual one. Rothman cites the independently made *Don't Look Back* as marking the true birth of cinéma vérité in America.

Don't Look Back also marked a moment when advances in 60s' film technology began to make an impact on screens. The film was shot on a twelve-volt, battery-operated, home-made, 16mm camera with an Auricon movement and a feedback loop DC motor drive. And it had improved, crystal-determining, sound-recording equipment with increased playing time per roll. *Don't Look Back* thus became a hugely influential cultural and indeed countercultural document that shaped future documentary techniques (the 'fly-on-the-wall' method is credited to the film), pop videos (the opening sequence is interminably replicated) and music concert features. Evidence of the influence of *Don't Look Back* is discernible in works as diverse as the Mayles' *Gimme Shelter* (1970) and Wim Wenders' *The Buena Vista Social Club* (1999). The film had its detractors, though. Reviewing the film upon its release, Andrew Sarris in the *Village Voice* pointed out that Pennebaker's film was only as good as its subject (Thompson and Gutman, 1991, p. 88) while the *Monthly Film Bulletin* described the film as 'shapeless', 'embodying all the deficiencies of cinéma vérité', and detailed the extent to which the work was 'staged', (*Don't Look Back* review, 1969, p. 201). The claims to objective observation must be viewed sceptically, given that the urgent 'whip-pan and shifts in focus often meant that the viewer was more aware of the camera's presence than before' (Andrew, 1999, p. 170). Formal semantics aside, however, the film and its maker more than deserve their rightful place in cinema history.

Dir: D. A. Pennebaker; **Prod**: Albert Grossman, John Court; **Scr**: D. A. Pennebaker; **DOP**: Jones Alk, Howard Alk; **Editor**: D. A. Pennebaker; **Score**: Bob Dylan; **Main Cast**: Bob Dylan, Joan Baez, Donovan, Alan Price.

Do the Right Thing
US, 1989 – 120 mins
Spike Lee

Do the Right Thing offers a cohesive and successful fusion of independent sensibilities with studio funding and resources. The film was produced by Lee's Forty Acres and a Mule company, like Lee's subsequent output, and was financed and distributed by a major studio (Universal), a situation that has clouded Lee's status as a truly independent film-maker.

The film is set over a single, scorching summer's day and features multiple characters and digressions. In this, *Do the Right Thing* partly retains the formal and structural audacity of Lee's *She's Gotta Have It* (1986). But here, as elsewhere, Lee has strenuously resisted the marginalisation that has blunted the works of many other black directors, and fought to ensure that his committed foregrounding of issues relating to race reaches the widest audience possible.

The film is largely framed from the perspective of pizza delivery boy Mookie (Lee), who has a fractious relationship with his employer Sal (Aiello), and is set on a single block in Brooklyn's Bed-Stuy, with its multicultural characters, including blacks, Hispanics, Italian-American pizza vendors and Korean storeowners. Presenting a polemical microcosm of the simmering racial tensions in American society, *Do the Right Thing* effortlessly and confidently negotiates tonal and formal shifts from incisive, well-written comedy and vivid hip-hop musical (the Public Enemy anthem 'Fight the Power' is deployed to powerful effect) through to the full-scale race riots and the burning down of Sal's pizzeria precipitated by the police choking of Radio Raheem (Bill Nunn). The film was inspired by racial violence and incidents of police brutality in the Queens neighbourhood of Howard Beach (particularly the murder of graffiti artist Michael Stewart), and is imbued with a keen awareness of the power of moral and political activism. Even so, Lee – who claimed that he intended the film to provoke thought – was criticised in the

American media and by conservative black intellectuals for advocating violent action as a means of redressing injustice. Still, Mookie's uneasy, mournful reconciliation with the paternalistic Sal, the final call for common sense from the voice of radio DJ Señor Love Daddy (Samuel L. Jackson), and opposing quotes from Martin Luther King and Malcolm X suggest a more ambiguous and pensive note.

Do the Right Thing is skilfully edited (the various denizens of the block are introduced in a series of vignettes) and choreographed (Lee baits his feminist critics by opening with Perez's wildly sexual boxing-cum-dancing). The film's overall exuberance and technical panache are most memorably demonstrated in a series of hilarious, direct-to-camera monologues in which members of the various ethnic groups trade insults. Though controversially denied the Palme d'Or at Cannes because jury head Wim Wenders believed that Mookie lacked heroic status (Soderbergh's *sex, lies and videotape* with its video-fixated masturbator took the prize), *Do the Right Thing* was an immediate cultural sensation. Cited as 'one of the most important American films produced in the last fifteen years' (Allon, Cullen and Patterson, 2000, p. 276), it confirmed Lee's spokesman status and proved instrumental in establishing a commercially viable black cinema.

Dir: Spike Lee; **Prod**: Spike Lee; **Scr**: Spike Lee; **DOP**: Ernest Dickerson; **Editor**: Barry Alexander Brown; **Score**: Bill Lee; **Main Cast**: Danny Aiello, Ossie Davis, Spike Lee, Rosie Perez.

Down by Law
US, 1986 – 107 mins
Jim Jarmusch

Jarmusch's third feature fine-tunes the director's disregard for genre and convention, beginning as a tale defined by urban naturalism before taking a scenic detour to include elements of the prison movie, the noir thriller and the fairy-tale romance. Jarmusch also brings his own esoteric sensibility to bear on the buddy movie, crafting a comic and characteristically off-beat variant in which miscommunication, a common Jarmusch theme, is key.

The film charts the exploits of two New Orleans deadbeats: pimp Jack (Lurie) and radio DJ Zack (Waits), both of whom are framed by the corrupt local police for crimes they unwittingly commit. Thrown together in jail, their hothead similarities breed a simmering antagonism until the pair find a fresh butt for their sniping in new cellmate Roberto (Benigni), a diminutive Italian tourist and alleged murderer with a passion for Robert Frost and Walt Whitman. Ridiculed for his rudimentary grasp of English, Roberto ultimately acts as a solidifying force, leading his inmates to freedom across a Southern bayou.

Down by Law shares with *Stranger Than Paradise* (1984) and subsequent Jarmusch pictures an arresting tripartite structure (before prison, in prison, after prison) that allows for a wry exploration of the theme of American culture colliding with a foreign element – and ultimately interacting despite cultural differences. Again, Jarmusch favours tone and atmosphere over narrative and action, omitting, as is his wont, vital visual details of the trio's perilous jailbreak. The defining style is often absurdly pared down and minimalist, a term the director rejects, preferring to think of his work as simply 'reduced'.

The visuals are evocatively rendered in high-contrast black and white, with Wenders' lensman Robby Müller capturing both the seediness of late-night New Orleans and the silvery, eerie beauty of the swamps in which the men seek freedom. The jazz-tinged score, courtesy of frequent

Jarmusch collaborator Lurie (with songs also largely from Waits'
impressive *Rain Dogs* album), similarly contributes to *Down by Law*'s
tonal assurance. The contrasting performance styles of the leading
players are utilised to fine effect (Lurie is, as ever, the embodiment of
cool) with Benigni's gloriously over-the-top gesticulating and energetic
fizz lending the film a broad accessibility that led many critics, who also
felt that it offered little in the way of narrative progression, to define the
film's humour as determinedly lowbrow. Indeed, many of Roberto's
idiosyncratic interpretations of the English language such as 'I ham a
good egg' raise an easily won smile, but there's also depth and surprising
poignancy too, as in his mantra 'it's a sad and beautiful world'.

Down by Law remains the director's favourite of his own movies,
largely for the celebratory atmosphere in which it was shot. Recalls
Jarmusch: 'We had a really wild time. In retrospect I don't know how we
got through it' (quoted in Keogh, 2001, p. 129). Selected for Official
Competition at Cannes, the film also maintained Jarmusch's close ties
with the New York Film Festival, where it was platformed prior to its US
release.

Dir: Jim Jarmusch; **Prod**: Alan Kleinberg; **Scr**: Jim Jarmusch; **DOP**: Robby Müller; **Editor**:
Melody London; **Score**: John Lurie; **Main Cast**: Tom Waits, John Lurie, Roberto Benigni,
Nicoletta Braschi.

Drugstore Cowboy
US, 1989 – 101 mins
Gus Van Sant

Having won the LA Film Critics' award for best independent feature and attracted intense festival attention, *Mala Noche* (1985) enabled Van Sant to upgrade from a $25,000 budget to a $6 million one for this subsequent Hollywood indie. Though similarly set in the director's hometown of Portland, Oregon, *Drugstore Cowboy* transposes the gay milieu of his improvisatory black and white micro-budget debut for a more linear, conventional and less associative tale involving a quartet of junkies.

Led by the charismatic and paranoiacally superstitious Bob Hughes (Dillon), the young, makeshift surrogate family (a defining theme that recurs throughout Van Sant's work, as does an interest in alienation and outsiderism) is completed by Bob's long-term girlfriend Dianne (Lynch)

Matt Dillon as junkie outlaw Bob Hughes receives some sobering advice from William Burroughs' ex-priest in *Drugstore Cowboy*

and fellow couple Rich (LeGros) and Nadine (Graham). They support their habit by knocking off drugs and money from local pharmacies in a series of increasingly perilous raids. Events take a more sombre turn when Nadine overdoses, causing Bob to re-evaluate his life and check into a rehabilitation programme in an attempt to straighten out. Set during the early 70s (the authentic outfits and attentive production design are superb), the film is narrated in flashback by a fatally wounded Hughes, who we learn is the victim of a vicious attack by an amoral junkie.

The film was adapted by Van Sant and Daniel Yost from an unpublished autobiographical novel by convicted felon James Fogle. It offers further evidence of the director's ability to respond with empathy to both environment and the failings and foibles of his characters. Refreshingly, Van Sant resists adopting a judgmental and sanctimonious tone towards chemical addiction, and presents the activities of his protagonists as partly a reaction to the numbing boredom of lower-middle-class suburbia and the oppression of everyday existence. In such circumstances drugs present a genuine allure, which Van Sant never shies away from depicting. Counterculture icon William Burroughs contributes a cameo as a junkie ex-priest (his *The Discipline of D. E.* formed the basis for one of Van Sant's earliest shorts).

Robert Yeoman's understated cinematography lends the film a gritty realism, but as in the more determinedly surreal *My Own Private Idaho* (1991) Van Sant also punctuates proceedings with a series of stylishly exuberant interludes to replicate Bob's superstitious paranoia (he harbours a fear of dogs and red hats) and descent into a chemical haze. Another of Van Sant's strengths as a director lies in his ability to coax intelligent performances of depth and subtlety from his cast. Van Sant here draws an articulate and surprisingly nuanced performance from former teen idol Dillon, resurrecting his faltering career in the process.

Dir: Gus Van Sant; **Prod**: Nick Wechsler, Karen Murphy; **Scr**: Gus Van Sant, Daniel Yost; **DOP**: Robert Yeoman; **Editor**: Curtiss Clayton, Mary Bauer; **Score**: Elliot Goldenthal; **Main Cast**: Matt Dillon, Kelly Lynch, James LeGros, Heather Graham.

Easy Rider
US, 1969 – 95 mins
Dennis Hopper

Easy Rider originated as an idea by Peter Fonda and was expanded into a loose story outline by Fonda and Dennis Hopper. With Fonda producing and the livewire Hopper slated to direct, financing for the project, known as *The Loners*, was in a state of flux until a chance meeting with Bob Rafelson and Bert Schneider's independent Raybert company provided the required $360,000 to make a picture Fonda promised would challenge the rules of film-making and the given representations of contemporary American society.

Easy Rider tells the story of anti-authoritarian bikers Wyatt 'Captain America' Earp (Fonda) and Billy (Hopper) who, buoyed by the proceeds of a cocaine deal, and with alcoholic, part-time lawyer George Hanson (a star-making turn from Nicholson) in tow, 'went looking for America and couldn't find it anywhere'. Dealing with male camaraderie, the quest for freedom and America's pioneering spirit, the film offers a rebellious riposte to Establishment platitudes. Laszlo Kovacs's sweeping cinematography of iconic national landmarks such as Monument Valley lends the film a mythic symbolism, but this is undercut by both the indolence and drug dependency of the protagonists and the depiction of the country as populated by narrow-minded bigots. The film closes with Earp and Billy admitting that they 'blew it', being slain by a group of vicious rednecks.

Though in places technically raw and riddled with imperfections (Hopper cited underground film-making and French new wave as inspirations), the film saw Hopper crowned Best New Director at the 1969 Cannes Film Festival. The subsequent critical and commercial reaction to both the film and its huge-selling, rock-orientated soundtrack

(Next page) Billy (Dennis Hopper), Wyatt Earp (Peter Fonda), and George Hanson (Jack Nicholson) on the road in search of America in *Easy Rider*

was phenomenal. *Easy Rider* grossed over $50 million during its initial release (according to Hopper, the film made all its money back in one week and in one theatre [Biskind, 1998, p. 74]), putting it and its makers at the forefront of the industry and contemporary counterculture. The film is also retrospectively viewed as establishing the road movie as a key post-60s genre.

Perhaps most importantly the film precipitated in Hollywood a move towards pictures dealing with the counterculture, revealing among studios and major companies (*Easy Rider* was distributed by an initially wary Columbia) a willingness to grant independent producers and artists a new autonomy. The studios' changed attitude ushered in a period of relative artistic freedom and experimentation, epitomised by the 'New Hollywood' directors, figures such as Peckinpah, Altman and Bogdanovich, who found themselves comfortably accommodated within the mainstream.

Easy Rider's loose, less consequential narrative structure and preference for character over plot is at the beginning of one road that leads straight to the American indie boom of the 80s and 90s.

Dir: Dennis Hopper; **Prod**: Peter Fonda; **Scr**: Peter Fonda, Dennis Hopper, Terry Southern; **DOP**: Laszlo Kovacs; **Editor**: Donn Cambern; **Score**: Hoyt Axton, Mars Bonfire, Roger McGuinn; **Main Cast**: Peter Fonda, Dennis Hopper, Jack Nicholson, Antonio Mendoza.

Eating Raoul
US, 1982 – 83 mins
Paul Bartel

Bartel was working as an animator when spotted by Gene Corman, and was taken under the wing of Gene's mogul brother Roger with his first film project *The Secret Cinema* (1969). Like Corman's numerous other protégés, Bartel came to occupy the niche between independent films and cheaply made, subversive variants on traditional genre pictures. Invited to direct *Private Parts* (1972), quickie, low-budget *Rollerball* (1975) and remake *Death Race 2000* (1975), Bartel's work revealed a preoccupation with sex and violence, the main staples of the exploitation genre. Also prone to sating his bad taste sensibilities and displaying a penchant for what was commonly considered outrageous, risqué humour, Bartel earned a reputation as a purveyor of the strange and unusual, inspiring comparisons with John Waters.

Eating Raoul is arguably the film for which Bartel is most fondly remembered and which most clearly encapsulates his maverick provocateur ethos. The film endured a traumatic genesis. Financed piecemeal by Bartel's parents over a five-year period and supported by a plethora of actors working on the cheap, the picture was predominantly shot on weekends when cast, cheap equipment and materials were available. The finished film attracted negligible distributor reaction, but it immediately acquired a mighty must-see reputation on the late-night, cult circuit following a series of sell-out shows.

Bartel and regular B-movie cohort, the formidable Mary Woronov, star as Paul and Mary Bland, an intellectual, highly cultured and moralistic married couple disgusted by the hedonism and perversity of their LA neighbours. Harbouring dreams of a rural restaurant retreat complete with a well-stocked wine cellar, but lacking the cash to achieve it, the pair fortuitously hit upon an ingenious scheme that involves Mary masquerading as a prostitute. Luring unsuspecting prospective johns to their doom, Paul and Mary make a killing selling the men's bodies to a local dog food plant. Things, however, hit a snag when Hispanic delivery boy Raoul (Beltran) threatens to blow the whistle on their ghoulish activities, and so the Blands are forced to concoct an elaborate plan to kill, cook and eat him.

Bartel serves up an ordinary tale of everyday cannibalism, a blackly comic, deliciously deadpan satire on covert racism and intolerance, moral conservatism and cultural snobbery. Avoiding the kitsch and often self-consciously unrestrained style of Waters, the more literary and often surprisingly refined *Eating Raoul* is informed by Bartel's previous experience as a playwright and jobbing writer. The film's mordant wit and observational prowess are accentuated by deft performances, with Bartel and company wisely, and somewhat against the grain, playing their roles relatively straight.

Up until his untimely death in 1999 Bartel continued to offer incisive if 'trashy' and knowingly absurd critiques of the more repellent aspects of bourgeois society. Like Corman before him, Bartel also became a useful resource for emerging independent directors. Jim Jarmusch was just one beneficiary of Bartel's support, in the form of completion funding for *Stranger Than Paradise* (1984).

Dir: Paul Bartel; **Prod**: Anne Kimmel; **Scr**: Richard Blackburn, Paul Bartel; **DOP**: Gary Thieltges; **Editor**: Alan Toomayan; **Score**: Arlon Ober; **Main Cast**: Paul Bartel, Mary Woronov, Robert Beltran, Susan Saiger.

El Mariachi
US, 1992 – 80 mins
Robert Rodriguez

Hispanic director Robert Rodriguez burst onto the scene with this Mexican-set feature that was to become as exalted for its low budget as for its routine if stylishly executed content. With the dexterous Rodriguez handling the majority of key technical duties and casting through a combination of family, friends and non-actors, the $7,000 cost of shooting and editing soon made *El Mariachi* a touchstone for aspirant film-makers. The immediate effect on the industry was an increase in the number of films being independently shot on non-film stock (*El Mariachi* was originally shot on video as a straight-to-video production for the Spanish-speaking market). The film's success was also responsible for a mistaken understanding of the costs involved in getting a film into distribution. As it turned out, the film was acquired by Columbia after motoring to the Audience Award at 1993's Sundance. The studio spent significantly on post-production, including a 35mm blow-up and a sizeable marketing campaign, to bring the completion and releasing costs up to the $1 million mark. With that backing behind it, the $7,000 budget of the film was subsequently called into question. John Pierson is unequivocal: 'I don't call the Rodriguez budget "alleged"; he sold a $7000 movie cut on video and didn't personally spend another cent on it'. (Pierson, 1996, p. 235).

Whatever its financial status, there can be no doubting the constrictive economic origins of the film and the adversities a determined, self-sufficient Rodriguez was forced to overcome to make it. Having completed numerous prize-winning home movies in Austin, Texas, Rodriguez raised the money for *El Mariachi* by accruing various loans, working as a guinea pig for cholesterol medication while penning the screenplay, and finally by selling his body to medical science. The narrative and structure are conventional enough: a young, black-clad mariachi (Gallardo, boyhood friend of Rodriguez and star of his home movies) drifts into a small Mexican border town, and through a combination of mistaken identity (a similarly attired gun-toting killer has arrived the same day) and a simmering attraction to local barmaid Domino (Gomez), soon finds himself embroiled in a vengeful warlord's blood feud.

Well aware of the formal and generic sources from which the film freely draws (the Leone Western, the stunt-fixated Hollywood action flick, Hong Kong martial arts pictures, and the melodramatic and romantic conventions of silent cinema), Rodriguez gleefully adopts an exuberant visual style to parodic but undeniably thrilling and polished effect. Rodriguez whips the whole shebang along at an enjoyably breakneck and breathless pace, employing an at times dizzying array of zooms, wide-angle lenses, intricately edited set-piece shoot-outs and an inventive understanding of the possibilities of sound design. His ironic, often deliciously droll dialogue is another plus, and the casting of non-actors and the 'found' locations and props lend the film an atmospheric authenticity that belies both its modest design and its more excessive if thoroughly unpretentious cinematic trickery.

Unlike some other directors working in the independent sector (though few mined the action genre), Rodriguez made little secret of his aspirations to work within the Hollywood mainstream. *El Mariachi* provided instant gratification, becoming a respectable commercial success and the launch-pad for a successful studio career for Rodriguez that began with *Desperado* (1995), a big-budget makeover of his debut.

Dir: Robert Rodriguez; **Prod**: Robert Rodriguez, Carlos Gallardo; **Scr**: Robert Rodriguez, Carlos Gallardo; **DOP**: Robert Rodriguez; **Editor**: Robert Rodriguez; **Score**: Marc Trujillo; **Main Cast**: Carlos Gallardo, Consuelo Gomez, Peter Marquardt, Jaime De Hoyos.

Eraserhead
US, 1976 – 89 mins
David Lynch

Indebted to *The Alphabet* (1968) and *The Grandmother* (1970), the director's early shorts that similarly explored themes of repression, fear and psychological paranoia, Lynch's experimental and provocative debut feature remains one of the most distinctive, blackly comic and disturbing of modern pictures. *Eraserhead* was shot at the American Film Institute over a five-year period on a micro budget (the cast and crew mostly comprised friends and associates). The film's abstract, other-worldly visual style evokes vintage Americana (an abiding obsession with Lynch), European expressionist film, surrealism, the horror genre and the American avant-garde movement of the 1940s.

Set in a nightmarish urban landscape ravaged by decay, *Eraserhead* largely steers clear of traditional narrative or structure to operate on a more purely sensory and subconscious level, the faintly familiar and very funny family dinner scene which verges on social satire aside. Henry Spencer (Nance) is a hapless and hopeless shock-haired innocent struggling to comprehend the world he lives in. Mostly confined to his dingy, under-lit apartment, Henry draws comfort from his increasingly bizarre sexual dreams and from the soothing song sung by a hamster-faced girl who he imagines to be living inside his radiator. His reveries are, however, punctured by the news that his girlfriend Mary (Stewart) is pregnant. The 'child' is born premature and, unable to stand its constant crying and wretched appearance, Mary is driven back to the bosom of her outlandish family. Henry is left alone with the pestilent creature, and his dreams soon take on a more disturbing complexion, including, in a gruesome sequence that gives the film its title, his own decapitation.

Riddled with images relating to intercourse and castration that connote a morbid interest in sex, physicality and the cycle of birth and death, *Eraserhead* also clearly offers a personal take on the claustrophobic pressures and anxieties of responsibility. It was made while Lynch was a struggling artist-turned-film-maker coping with the birth of his daughter and recent marriage. The director's representation of women as predatory and demanding, and infants as purely monstrous must have made arresting viewing for his family (the mechanics involved in realising the reptilian 'baby' remain a source of wonder, as does the creation of the tiny chickens which spring to life, oozing blood as Henry carves them). Lynch himself has described *Eraserhead* as 'a dream of dark and troubling things', undoubtedly the best way to view it when searching for a meaning.

Shot in black and white (with emphasis on the black), *Eraserhead* is imaginatively and expertly executed. The film contains surreal, often grotesque set-pieces and employs a generally disorientating design, exemplified by Henry's decapitated head plummeting through the film frame, the milky pool into which Henry and his neighbour sink after

Jack Nance as Henry in the nightmarish and surreal *Eraserhead*

coupling, and the inventive use of architecture. These aspects are complemented by a hugely effective and disarming aural backdrop, which constructively employs a cacophony of industrial hissings, thuds and clanks. Upon release the film immediately found favour on the late-night cult repertory circuit. It also enraptured Mel Brooks, who hired Lynch to direct his production of *The Elephant Man* (1980).

Dir: David Lynch; **Prod**: David Lynch; **Scr**: David Lynch; **DOP**: Frederick Elmes; **Editor**: David Lynch; **Score**: Peter Ivers, David Lynch; **Main Cast**: Jack Nance, Charlotte Stewart, Allen Joseph, Jeanne Bates.

The Evil Dead
US, 1982 – 86 mins
Sam Raimi

One of the most remarkable and infamous horror films of the modern era, *The Evil Dead* originated as a thirty-minute preview titled *Within the Woods* that was used as bait by Raimi to snare contributions from potential investors. Expanding upon the short's infectious blending of horror, gory live-action animation, graphic violence and humour, Raimi completed the film for the relatively low cost of $400,000, which in part explains its grainy visual aesthetic (the result of a subsequent transfer from 16 to 35mm), gleeful irreverence and experimental bent.

Filming on the project, then titled *Book of the Dead*, took place in 1980 in Tennessee and Michigan locations. The film's premise and structure are attentive to the conventions of the horror genre. A group of twenty-something male and females take a sojourn to a remote woodland cabin where they discover a strange book titled the 'Book of the Dead'. An accompanying tape made by an archaeologist reveals that the book was found among the Khandarian ruins of a Sumerian civilisation. Unfortunately, in playing the tape, which also includes ancient incantations, the group unwittingly summon the hitherto dormant demons of the forest that in turn possess the party one by one. Only Ash (Campbell, future Raimi regular and the film's executive producer) survives the demonic onslaught to single-handedly engage in the battle of good versus evil.

Raimi's film recalls such notable examples of the genre as *The Exorcist* (1973) (from which *The Evil Dead* takes many of its make-up ideas) and *The Texas Chainsaw Massacre* (1974), and also has a knowing reflexivity and black, tongue-in-cheek humour that has informed the recent strain of post-modern contributions to the horror cycle, such as *Scream* (1996). At times exceedingly violent – albeit in a comic-book fashion – the film revels in its shock tactics and low-budget gore, in which Bart Pierce's impressively executed stop-motion special effects form the centrepiece. However, alongside the film's outrageous mayhem there's also palpable suspense and a genuinely unsettling, claustrophobic and nightmarish air. The film is expertly cut (Joel Coen worked on the editing) and atmospherically lit in ominous clouds of fog. The frequent deployment of first-person camera in the film's initial stages successfully evokes the encroaching presence of the marauding demons. Moreover, the use of crane and Panaglide shots lends *The Evil Dead* a momentum and technical flair that masks its meagre economic means and somewhat muted characterisation.

The film caused a sensation at the 1982 Cannes Film Festival, where horror scribe Stephen King described it as 'the most ferociously original horror film of the year', (quoted in King, 1982). *The Evil Dead* was subsequently acquired by risk-taking British distribution outfit Palace Pictures. Only marginally trimmed after a viewing by the British censors, the film was simultaneously launched theatrically and on video. However, some local councils intervened, objecting largely to a distasteful scene in which a tree apparently rapes a woman; videos of the film were banned and seized. One of the first so-called 'video-nasties', *The Evil Dead* nonetheless became the best renting title of 1983 and an instant cult success.

Dir: Sam Raimi; **Prod**: Robert Tapert; **Scr**: Sam Raimi; **DOP**: Tim Philo; **Editor**: Edna Ruth Paul; **Score**: Joseph Loduca; **Main Cast**: Bruce Campbell, Ellen Sandweiss, Betsy Baker, Hal Delrich.

Faster, Pussycat! Kill! Kill!
US, 1965 – 83 mins
Russ Meyer

An independent director-producer-writer-editor-cameraman and distributor, Russ Meyer is popularly credited with inventing the skin flick with the series of unashamedly adult films he produced between 1959 and 1963. These pictures were considerable commercial successes, and films such as *The Immoral Mr Teas* (1959) were harbingers of Meyer's vehicles for buxom Amazonian women. Meyer's films from this period are also marked by a technical excellence lacking in those of his contemporaries, and from the mid-60s onwards the director began to explore more ambitious territories, producing a number of stylishly executed, low-budget outlaw action pictures that marry high nudity content with outrageously trashy narratives, tongue-in-cheek dialogue and domineering female characters. *Faster, Pussycat! Kill! Kill!* galvanised Meyer's burgeoning cult standing and arguably remains the most popular and typical of his pre-studio pictures firmly aimed, as it was, at the undemanding drive-in market.

Set in rugged desert terrain, *Pussycat* features Meyer starlets Satana, Haji (as Satana's female lover) and Williams as a trio of homicidal, Porsche-racing go-go dancers blazing their way across California. Kidnapping a young girl (Bernard) after the black-clad dominatrix Satana breaks her boyfriend's back with a single karate chop, the scantily dressed women head for a secluded farmhouse after a talkative gas attendant informs them that the head of the bizarre household (Stuart Lancaster) has a considerable fortune hidden beneath his floorboards. To get it, they must first contend with the father's lustful advances and the equally physical attentions of his slow-witted but strapping son, Vegetable (Dennis Busch).

Shot effectively in black and white, *Pussycat* is an arresting combination of the distastefully lurid, the camp and the highly comic. All three elements frequently combine in the ripe, over-the-top dialogue: his eyes transfixed on Satana's ample cleavage, the gas attendant extols the virtues of seeing America, eliciting Satana's feisty response, 'You won't find it down there, Columbus!' Proving that Meyer's interests extended beyond bust size, *Pussycat* has a compositional assuredness that combines an eye for the surreal and visually absurd with expertly choreographed fight sequences and suspenseful cross-cutting. An effective and exuberant action picture, the film displays many of the attributes found in the early Don Siegel pictures.

Roundly criticised for objectifying women and pandering to vulgar wish fulfilment fantasies, Meyer, who was not adverse to using such responses in his marketing campaigns, defended his work, highlighting that not only are women always the heroines but that they have a sexual appetite and physical strength equal to their male counterparts. Women are rarely victims but are frequently powerful victors, and as such offer a sense of empowerment. John Waters, who displays an obvious debt to Meyer, declared *Pussycat* not only the best movie ever made but also the best ever likely to be made. In 1983 and then 1995 the critical reassessment of Meyer's work was bolstered by a major retrospective at the National Film Theatre, where the film was 'revered by riot girls, feminists and dykes alike for its un-PC portrayal of tough, sexy, ironic women in control (Giles, 1995, p. 11). The circle was completed when *Pussycat* was successfully revived in the US in the mid-90s, playing at prestigious art-house venues such as New York's Film Forum. On originally seeing the film in the mid-70s, feminist critic B. Ruby Rich was 'appalled', but she overturned her initial dismissal on seeing it again, labelling the film 'an unexpected celebration of bad-girl empowerment' (Rich, 1995, p. 65).

Dir: Russ Meyer; **Prod**: Russ Meyer, Eve Meyer; **Scr**: Jack Moran; **DOP**: Walter Schenk; **Editor**: Russ Meyer; **Score**: Paul Sawtell; **Main Cast**: Turu Satana, Haji, Lori Williams, Susan Bernard.

F for Fake (Vérités et mensonges)
France/Iran/W. Germany, 1973 – 85 mins
Orson Welles

F for Fake is perhaps the quintessential American independent film in both spirit and practice. (As Geoff Andrew comments, 'It is probably fair to say that the godfather and father of American independent cinema were, respectively, Orson Welles and John Cassavetes', Andrew, 1998, p. 97.) Welles was forced to work under tighter constraints after *Citizen Kane* (1941) and *The Magnificent Ambersons* (1942). Turning to minor Hollywood companies and European investors in order to pursue his ambitions, Welles also used appearance fees from lucrative acting jobs, talk-show slots and advertising roles for the funding of highly personal projects that were unpolluted by Hollywood finance or input. *F for fake*, his penultimate completed work, is such an entity.

In 1972, partly to reduce a sizeable tax bill, Welles began work on a television film about Elmyr de Hory, a famous art forger and, as *F for Fake* later suggests, the subject of a book titled *Fake* by Clifford Irving. Having negotiated the rights to the interviews and out-takes that François Reichenbach had conducted with Hory for a BBC documentary, Welles began editing the film from Paris when news arrived that Irving's recent Howard Hughes biography, purportedly based on extensive interviews, was an utter fabrication. The idea of a self-reflexive feature about the art of illusion, creativity and fakery was born.

Welles was no stranger to embellishment and charlatanism, having lied about his childhood and sweet talked his way into his first acting role by falsifying his experience. And his talent for convincing fakes was illustrated through the infamous panic-inducing *The War of the Worlds* radio broadcast and *Citizen Kane*'s deftly executed sequences of faux newsreel footage.

Undertaken in collaboration with Welles' partner Oja Kodar, *F for Fake* was, then, a joyous, irreverent experience that acted as an exorcism of many of Welles' personal demons, most notably his inability to finish a film. A knowing meditation on notions of authorship and the act of attribution, the film was also in part a response to a particularly hurtful article by Pauline Kael titled 'Raising Kane', which questioned Welles' contribution to *Citizen Kane*. Welles was further seduced by Hory's disdain for art experts and the Establishment, and he identified with the precarious financial situations and need to creatively avert impending disaster that led to Hory's and Irving's respective acts of deceit.

The film's playful nature is laid bare at its beginning with the promise by Welles, who foregrounds the film's thematic preoccupations and illusory sleight of hand by appearing as a magician, that for an hour he will tell the truth. Re-appearing to reveal that the hour elapsed seventeen minutes ago, Welles confesses that he has since been lying his head off. Deploying a dizzying array of media and formal devices such as reportage, fiction, found footage and interview materials, a cohesive and entertaining fabric is created by Welles' skilful if protracted manipulation in the editing suite.

Finally premiered at festivals in New York, London and San Sebastian, Welles was left distraught by the film's abject commercial failure.

Dir: Orson Welles; **Prod**: Dominique Antoine, François Reichenbach; **Scr**: Orson Welles, Oja Kodar; **DOP**: Christian Odasso, Gary Graver; **Editor**: Marie-Sophie Dubus, Dominique Engerer; **Score**: Michel Legrand; **Main Cast**: Orson Welles, Oja Kodar, Elmyr de Hory, Clifford Irving.

Gas Food Lodging
US, 1991 – 101 mins
Allison Anders

Anders is a UCLA film school graduate who got her break as a
production assistant on Wenders' *Paris, Texas* (1984) after bombarding
the director with letters. She used her own upbringing and subsequent
first-hand experiences of single parenthood for her breakthrough feature.
A deeply felt, unflinching familial drama about two sisters living in a
desolate, backwater desert town with their divorced mother, *Gas Food
Lodging* avoids offering a sanctimonious homily about the bonds
between mothers and daughters (a staple of mainstream fare covering
similar terrain), and instead presents a gritty and authentic representation
of blue-collar lives edging ever closer to the poverty line.

Nora (Adams) scrapes a living waiting tables at the local truck stop
while single-handedly raising her daughters in a cramped, decrepit trailer.
Elder daughter Trudi (Skye) has just turned seventeen and, bored with life
in Laramie, has taken to skipping school, drinking until late and making
out with high-school Lotharios. As Trudi's reputation for raising hell grows,
the tension between her and her mother escalates. Younger daughter
Shade (Balk) is also undergoing a sexual awakening, but after suffering
rejection at the hands of dreamy Darius (Donovan Leitch) she seeks solace
at the local Spanish cinema, where she loses herself in the romantic
adventures of Mexican matinee siren Elvia Rivero. There's no such escape
for the equally romance-starved Nora, though a flirtation with a local
satellite engineer may offer temporary respite from her arduous existence.

The film is rigorously unsentimental in tone. Anders' perceptive
writing and sense of character capture the frustrations of the two
generations of women, offering a powerful if understated depiction of
the resilience required for survival. Eschewing dreams for realism, Anders
offers no easy conclusion but does intermittently leaven the tone with a
series of brief interludes in which glimpses of happiness are revealed,
most notably in a scene where Shade and her new Mexican-American

boyfriend dance with impromptu abandon. Perhaps most impressive, however, are the violent, no-holds-barred confrontations between Trudi and her mother in which Nora's determination that her eldest daughter escape her own fate is palpable.

Contributing to the film's plausibility are the principal performances. Adams impressively conveys a semi-lifetime of drudgery and disappointment, while Skye (of whom much was expected after the film) lends Trudi a sullen petulance born of frustration and ennui. Lower down the acting credits is former Dinosaur Jr. songsmith J. Mascis who also contributes an evocative, suitably frills-free score. (The relationship between lo-fi musicians and American indie pics remains harmonious – witness Lou Barlow's work on *Kids* (1995) and the collaborative work on *Heavy* (1995) by Sonic Youth's Thurston Moore.) In formal terms, *Gas* adopts a predominantly simple, low-key approach with cinematographer Dean Lent (another UCLA graduate) effectively rendering the arid, weather-beaten landscapes that serve as the film's setting and metaphorical parameter.

Generational female angst in *Gas Food Lodging*

Gas is another notable example of the relatively few female-directed American independent movies. What is perhaps a more telling statistic is that Anders is one of the few female directors who has gone on to regularly produce subsequent features, including *Mi vida loca* (1993), *Grace of My Heart* (1996) and *Sugar Town* (1999).

Dir: Allison Anders; **Prod**: Bill Ewart, Dan Hassid, Seth Willenson; **Scr**: Allison Anders; **DOP**: Dean Lent; **Editor**: Tracy S. Granger; **Score**: J. Mascis; **Main Cast**: Brooke Adams, Ione Skye, Fairuza Balk, James Brolin, Robert Knepper.

George Washington
US, 2000 – 89 mins
David Gordon Green

The debut feature of then twenty-five-year-old Green, *George Washington* is a beguiling, elegiac coming-of-age drama and a lyrical meditation on the fragility of human existence. Impressively naturalistic, the film also displays an astute appreciation for the ethereal strangeness of human interaction and the minutiae of rural small-town life.

The film follows the lives of a group of black teenagers hanging out in derelict buildings and at the local train depot over a long, hot summer in a poor North Carolina town, and examines the fickle ties of friendship and the tentative steps towards adulthood and responsibility. The group's journey to adulthood is hastened by a brutal accident that leaves one member dead and the others struggling to come to terms with their culpability. Most affected is a super-hero fixated youth, who through one of the film's many humorous, poignant ironies is forced to wear an ungainly helmet for medical reasons. He yearns to become the nation's first black American president, and to emulate his hero from whom the film takes its somewhat elliptical title.

As with many notable US independent debut pictures, finance for the film was obtained through a mixture of guile, determination and tenacity on the part of the director, who toiled at a variety of blue-collar jobs in order to raise funds. Green credits this period as providing the inspiration for his perceptive, delicately subtle dialogue (and no doubt the fondness for washed-out, industrial locations), which is alive with the nuances of everyday conversation. Perhaps most impressively, Green never falls foul of patronising his ensemble of youthful characters, played mostly by non-professional actors, some of whom were residents of the town in which the film was shot. The uniformly excellent performances suggest a mutual respect, cultivated through the communal spirit Green instilled by

George (Donald Holden), the superhero fixated youth in *George Washington*, David Gordon Green's tender and lyrical coming of age drama

having the cast and crew live side-by-side throughout the production. Many of the on-screen friendships accurately mirror those that were developing off-screen. The film is a covert work in terms of politics, but the mainly black cast were chosen simply because the majority of people where Green wanted to shoot just happened to be black.

Green eschewed working with the now 'norm' of digital video technology and its utilisation of grainy, hand-held vérité style camera work, instead choosing to shoot with anamorphic lenses. Tim Orr's luminous, sun-dappled photography lends the film an enthralling textural beauty that in conjunction with the long, lingering edits does much to evoke the seminal 70s' works of Malick, a director whose brand of visual lyricism is much admired by Green. The film's steadfast refusal to employ the clichés of the genre (*Sleazenation* declared it the benchmark by which coming-of-age dramas will come to be judged) and its attempts to intelligently reflect the troubled path towards adulthood and moral responsibility place *George Washington* in such exalted recent company as *River's Edge* (1986) and *Gummo* (1997), albeit with added tenderness and beauty.

Dir: David Gordon Green; **Prod**: David Gordon Green, Sacha Mueller, Lisa Muskat; **Scr**: David Gordon Green; **DOP**: Tim Orr; **Editor**: Steven Gonzales, Zene Baker; **Score**: Michael Linnen, David Wingo; **Main Cast**: Candace Evanoiski, Donald Holden, Damian Jewan Lee, Curtis Cotton III.

Girlfight
US, 1999 – 110 mins
Karyn Kusama

Girlfight marked the bristling, tenacious and intelligent debut of Karyn Kusama, a former assistant to John Sayles. Though it undoubtedly deals a disservice to Kusama (who trained as a fighter during her youth) to overstress the Sayles connection, the film is produced by Sayles' long-time collaborator Maggie Renzi, edited by Sayles' assistant editor Plummy Tucker and is executive produced by and features the man himself in a minor acting role. This is a film outwardly about the precision and control required of pugilists, but there are shades of Sayles in the film's lean and disciplined aesthetic and in the way it focuses upon a socially disadvantaged protagonist who to succeed must do so against considerable odds.

Diana Guzman (newcomer Rodriguez) is a Brooklyn high-school senior with a track record of getting into corridor fights. Her home life is equally fractious and often punctuated by rows with her widowed, bullying father Sandro (Calderon). While accompanying her bookish younger brother Tiny (Ray Santiago) to the gym for the boxing lessons he loathes but which his father insists he takes, Diana discovers a thirst for the sport. Without her father's knowledge, she coaxes an ex-pro, Hector (Tirelli), to train her using the lesson money intended for Tiny. As her natural talent and dedication shine through, Diana develops a new sense of self-worth, quickly rising through the ranks of local male and female fighters. Meanwhile, a mutual attraction develops between Diana and Adrian (Douglas), the gym's most promising male prospect, but is instantly put under pressure when the pair are drawn to face each other in a high-profile bout.

The boxing world is traditionally a male domain. Kusama puts the largely tired, formulaic conventions of the boxing picture through their paces by investing the material with a feminist perspective. Diana's male counterpart is wryly named after Sylvester Stallone's wife in the *Rocky* series). By doing so, she creates a dramatic, intelligent and affecting tale about not only female but also racial and economic empowerment. Moreover, Kusama largely avoids the pitfall of overwrought sentimentality (the scenes in which Diana confronts her father with the physical abuse that drove her mother to suicide are especially hard hitting and well handled), thanks to her own accomplished script and a towering turn by Rodriguez in the central role. As Diana, Rodriguez exudes a raw, almost feral brooding energy and, with her permanently furrowed brow, gives the sense that she carries the weight of the world. It is a performance of compelling conviction and, given the arduous training patently required, no little dedication. Kusama's boxing background serves her well, lending the gym sequences and pre-bout banter an appropriately downbeat realism that evokes Huston's *Fat City* (1972). It's a sensibility mirrored in the bruising fight sequences, authentically shot with a minimum of sensationalism or excess using stolid medium shots.

Garlanded at Sundance with Best Director and Grand Jury prizes, *Girlfight* is a notable entry to the crowded ranks of sport-as-metaphor films, and hopefully signals the emergence of a distinctive new film-making talent.

Dir: Karyn Kusama; **Prod**: Sarah Green, Martha Griffin, Maggie Renzi; **Scr**: Karyn Kusama; **DOP**: Patrick Cady; **Editor**: Plummy Tucker; **Score**: Theodore Shapiro; **Main Cast**: Michelle Rodriguez, Jaime Tirelli, Paul Calderon, Santiago Douglas.

Go Fish
US, 1994 – 83 mins
Rose Troche

Go Fish is an overtly lesbian debut described by writer-director Troche and actress/co-writer and former partner Turner as being by and for lesbians. The project began life as *Ely and Max*, fifteen minutes of footage screened at the 1993 Sundance Film Festival. Initially directed in Troche's free time, the film was intended to address the lack of films for lesbian audiences (Donna Deitch's *Desert Hearts*, 1985, excepted) and as an antidote to the stereotypical, titillating predominantly male depiction of lesbianism popularised in mainstream pictures such as *The Hunger* (1983).

The project ran into trouble once the meagre funds raised by Troche evaporated, but following a letter from the director, financial support was pledged by Kalin Vachon Productions Inc (formerly Apparatus), the independent film-maker-friendly outfit founded by lesbian producer Christine Vachon and Chicago-born director Tom Kalin. John Pierson's influential Islet (a valuable resource and source of support for American independent film-makers since the mid-80s) provided completion funding.

Named after a children's card game much beloved in the States, the stylishly shot, grainy black and white film is a fresh, Chicago-set romantic serio-comedy that frankly portrays the day-to-day lives of five women friends – Max (Turner), Kia (McMillan), Ely (Brodie), Daria (Anastasia Sharp) and Evy (Melendez) – and the search for romance by the perennially single Max. The film's technically mesmerising associative editing style (Troche does her own edits) evidences the director's affiliation with the Chicago avant-garde tradition. It's little surprise to learn that Troche cites the influence of the experimental video work (a key subculture for the lesbian community) of artists such as Cheryl Dunne and Sadie Benning.

Immediately eclipsing its antecedents, *Go Fish* became a 1994 Sundance sensation and the first film to be actually sold during the festival. Islet had whipped potential buyers into a frenzy, pitching the film as threatening to do for lesbian audiences what Lee's *She's Gotta Have It* (1986) did for black audiences; unsurprisingly Goldwyn hungrily took Pierson's bait. With the sexual identity of the characters a given, the film feels refreshingly free of both stereotypes and didacticism. It became a perhaps unlikely box-office success, in part as a result of a canny marketing campaign intended to neither downplay the lesbian content nor exclude male or heterosexual female viewers. *Go Fish* was nevertheless released in Gay Pride month during the auspicious twenty-fifth anniversary of Stonewall.

Go Fish also established a new visibility for lesbian films and lesbian film-makers in the predominantly male domain of the New Queer Cinema movement, as well as finding universal critical favour. Influential gay critic B. Ruby Rich campaigned for the film, citing it as the daughter of Jan Oxenberg's technically raw but politically sophisticated lesbian comedy, *A Comedy in Six Unnatural Acts* (1975), (Hillier, p. 94).

Dir: Rose Troche; **Prod**: Rose Troche, Guinevere Turner; **Scr**: Rose Troche, Guinevere Turner; **DOP**: Ann T. Rossetti; **Editor**: Rose Troche; **Score**: Brendan Dolan, Jennifer Sharpe, Scott Aldrich; **Main Cast**: V. S. Brodie, Guinevere Turner, T. Wendy McMillan, Migdalia Melendez.

Gummo
US, 1997 – 89 mins
Harmony Korine

Written for Larry Clark, *Kids* (1995) marked the beginning of an
auspicious and controversial career for the cine-literate Korine. The son
of a documentary film-maker, Korine partly retained the format's vérité
style and use of non-actors for his own directorial debut, mischievously
named after the least well-known Marx brother. Made with the rare
privilege of final cut, Korine's wildly original *Gummo* polarised critics like
few other films in recent American cinema history. Many praised it as the
most authentic, inspiring and original work in decades, while others were
repelled by its squalid tone and free-form, experimental appearance;
Janet Maslin of the *New York Times* dubbed it the worst film of the year
(Hillier, p. 200).

Set among the urban poor of Xenia, an Ohio backwater community,
the film eschews linearity and plot (terms Korine despises) to instead
offer an expressionistic and fragmented series of snapshots (Korine
imagined the film as a collage of still photographs), stories and memories
to deal frankly with the ennui of small-town American adolescence.
Gummo's protagonists are Solomon (Reynolds) and Tumbler (Sutton),
two impoverished and malnourished teenage malcontents from broken
homes who evade boredom by shooting stray cats and selling their
carcasses. The money they make enables them to buy the glue and
aerosol cans that provide respite from their harsh existence.

The subject of adolescent suffering may be a common staple of
independent and mainstream American cinema (Solomon and Tumbler
also resemble literary figures such as Tom Sawyer and Huckleberry Finn),
but Korine's 'teen' movie has a closer kinship to works such as Buñuel's
Los Olvidados (1950); the director himself cites Alan Clarke as his primary
influence. Having spent many months among the community in which he
filmed, Korine was keen to avoid a patronising, 'trash-chic' depiction of
the people's lives, treating his cast with integrity and affection. There's

also a refreshing moral ambivalence and refusal to condemn, achieved in part through an understanding of the social and economic factors that have afflicted an underclass which the director felt had been marginalised or simply ignored by the American media.

At times *Gummo* resembles a home movie (albeit an extremely stylised one) in terms of the spontaneous, private moments it captures, including two skinhead brothers fighting and Solomon's mother (Linda Manz) giving him a bath. Contrastingly, its authentic blue-collar neo-realism is suffused with an intense, lyrical beauty courtesy of Jean-Yves Escoffier's luminous photography, perhaps best evidenced in a transcendent scene in which teenagers frolic in a swimming pool during a summer storm. Dave Doernberg's off-kilter production design heightens the sensory surrealism, most memorably during the opening sequence in which a waif-like boy (Sewell, credited simply as 'Bunny Boy') wanders the grey highways sporting outsized pink rabbit ears.

Misspent youth: Solomon (Jacob Reynolds) and Tumbler (Nick Sutton) quell the boredom of small-town life by shooting stray cats and selling their carcasses to buy glue to get high in Harmony Korine's opinion-dividing *Gummo*

Gummo fell foul of the censors, who objected to the association of children with drugs and a scene in which the camera reveals the bug bites on the legs of a four-year-old child forced to share his home with a legion of cockroaches. During the hiatus over cuts the ever-precocious Korine considered junking the project. This now seems unthinkable.

Dir: Harmony Korine; **Prod**: Cary Woods; **Scr**: Harmony Korine; **DOP**: Jean-Yves Escoffier; **Editor**: Chris Tellefsen; **Score**: Randy Poster; **Main Cast**: Jacob Sewell, Nick Sutton, Lara Tosh, Jacob Reynolds.

Heavy
US, 1995 – 103 mins
James Mangold

Mangold was an Alexander Mackendrick pupil at the California Institute of the Arts. His career got off to an uncertain start after notching up a single writing credit on Disney's *Oliver and Company* (1998). Returning to Columbia University, Mangold studied under Milos Forman, whose considered approach to characterisation and ability to observe potentially turbulent situations with a quiet intensity, was to act as a formative influence on *Heavy*, Mangold's evocative, melancholic and atmospheric self-penned debut.

The film is set in an upstate New York pizza joint owned by the widowed Dolly (Winters) and run with the aid of her doting, overweight son Victor (Taylor Vince). In an attempt to enliven the atmosphere and in anticipation of a possible romance for Victor, Dolly hires fresh-faced college dropout Callie (Tyler), much to the chagrin of Dolly's other waitress, Delores (Harry). The normally withdrawn, inarticulate Victor does indeed take an instant shine to Callie and, despite the attentions of Callie's self-obsessed muso boyfriend Jeff (Evan Dando), a tentative bond develops between the pair. When Victor's crush turns to infatuation he stumbles to consciousness, determining to diet in an attempt to win Callie's heart. But events slowly unravel, forcing Victor into a world of change, of which he has no experience and little hope of maintaining control.

With a poignant, brooding score by Sonic Youth's Thurston Moore, *Heavy* is a quietly authoritative work in which unhappiness, regret and emotional stagnation are eloquently observed. The film is marked by a deft use of *mise en scène*, which makes notable use of bright primary colours to suggest Victor's cosseted, childlike worldview (his room is that of a teenager, decorated with comics and baseball pendants) and his inability and reluctance to extricate himself from his past. It is Victor's reticence, fleetingly punctured by the exuberant Callie's attentions, that suffocates his dreams of becoming a professional chef and of revealing to the community the fact that his mother has died. Confronted by an angry Callie when Dolly's passing is finally revealed, Victor replies, 'I didn't want things to change'.

Mangold extends and accentuates this metaphor of wearying inertia, styling Dolly's restaurant and her ramshackle house to resemble environments from a bygone era. Inextricably linked to this era is Delores, whose aversion to Callie (a character well served by Tyler's gamine beauty) is founded on being tortuously reminded of her own youth and rapidly fading looks. Mangold's casting of former Blondie pin-up Deborah Harry in the role is a gently ironic touch – and also continues the tradition of casting musicians, such as Tom Waits and Joe Strummer, in American independent projects. In terms of performances, the film belongs to the truly remarkable Taylor Vince who signals a deep well of emotional repression through his nervous, wandering eyes alone.

A worthwhile addition to the suburban ennui sub-genre of American independent film (*Trust*, 1990, and *Spanking the Monkey*, 1994, are further examples), *Heavy* brought Mangold a Sundance Special Jury prize and the approbation of leading American critics. Writing in the *Los Angeles Times*, Kevin Thomas described the film as 'a small, quiet miracle of a movie in which tenderness, compassion and insight combine to create a tension that yields a quality of perception painful to experience' (Thomas, 1996, p. 159).

Dir: James Mangold; **Prod**: Richard Miller; **Scr**: James Mangold; **DOP**: Michael Barrow; **Editor**: Meg Reticker; **Score**: Thurston Moore; **Main Cast**: Pruitt Taylor Vince, Shelley Winters, Liv Tyler, Deborah Harry.

Henry: Portrait of a Serial Killer
US, 1986 – 83 mins
John McNaughton

Inspired by a television documentary on convicted mass-murderer Henry Lee Lucas, McNaughton set about creating a film loosely based on the killer's life. Lucas claimed to have killed more than 300 people but has, a caption at the start of *Henry* informs us, recanted many of his confessions.

Released from prison following the murder of his prostitute mother, Henry (Rooker) supplements his job as a bug exterminator with the murders of countless strangers, most of them female. He shacks up in a Chicago apartment with fellow ex-con and sometime drug dealer Otis (Towles), who Henry finds to be a willing accomplice in his murderous pursuits. Seeking sanctuary from her abusive husband, Otis's abused sister Becky (Arnold) moves in, and a tentative bond develops between her and Henry. Becky is raped by an increasingly depraved Otis, who is then murdered by Henry. Henry seems to be on the brink of forming a relationship with Becky, but the film chillingly concludes with Henry, alone, depositing a blood-stained suitcase by the roadside before silently disappearing into the night.

Working in low-budget mode, McNaughton aims for dispassionate objectivity, adopting a low-key documentary style that the film impressively sustains throughout. Conversation and carnage are rendered in the same detached matter-of-fact manner, an approach that marks out the film's intelligence and the film-maker's resolute refusal to offer the kind of exploitative, cheapo titillation that are the hallmarks of other films of this nature. *Henry* also deploys excellent sound design throughout, perhaps most impressively in the opening panning montage of Henry's victims, a sequence that substitutes visceral gore for a discordant soundtrack of screams and cries.

A later DIY video sequence, revealing Henry and Otis invading the home of a young family, is the film's most chillingly realised and excruciating set-piece and McNaughton's formal *coup de grâce*. The camera is clumsily dropped on its side while Henry slopes off to execute a young interloper; he returns to find Otis attempting to rape the dead mother. Off-screen we hear Otis exclaim, 'I want to watch it again', and as the camera pulls back we realise that Henry and Otis are reviewing the tape for their own pleasure. As the tape rewinds on Otis's television screen, McNaughton lingers on the image before thankfully cutting away. A thorn in the side of the censor (and later an inspiration for *Funny Games*, 1997), the moment has provoked myriad debates about voyeuristic pleasure and the role of the spectator in connection with on-screen violence.

Henry avoids the presentation of the serial killer as larger-than-life entertainment – a route taken by *The Silence of the Lambs* (1991) – and similarly offers no cathartic, psychological or sociological explanation for Henry's actions. Likewise, there's no sense of moral rectitude concerning the killings, with Henry for the most part presented as the most well-balanced character. A chilling, uncompromising and intelligent vision, the film was dealt a dreaded X certificate in the US and remained unreleased for four years after its original completion.

Dir: John McNaughton; **Prod**: John McNaughton, Lisa Dedmond, Steven A. Jones; **Scr**: Richard Fire, John McNaughton; **DOP**: Charlie Lieberman; **Editor**: Elena Maganini; **Score**: Robert McNaughton; **Main Cast**: Michael Rooker, Tracy Arnold, Tom Towles.

High Art
US, 1998 – 101 mins
Lisa Cholodenko

An assistant editor on *Boyz N the Hood* (1991) and *To Die For* (1994), Cholodenko was inspired by the emergence of several New Queer directors such as Tom Kalin, Todd Haynes and Gregg Araki to put her Hollywood career on the backburner and relocate to New York to enrol in the film-making programme at Columbia University. It was there, following two well-received shorts, *Souvenir* and *Dinner Party*, that she developed *High Art*, a frank portrayal of the darker side of contemporary lesbian society and a notable entry in the New Queer canon.

High Art contrasts the higher echelons of the New York art scene, with its attendant cliques and cannibalistic cut-throat ambitions, with the equally self-obsessed mores of bohemian (read heroin-addicted) loft-living types. The film begins with Syd (Mitchell), an assistant editor at trendy Manhattan photo magazine *Frame*, suffering a leak in her apartment. The trail is followed to upstairs neighbour Lucy Berliner (Sheedy), a recluse who sardonically drawls, 'Nobody's taken a bath here recently'. After meeting Lucy's live-in German lover Greta (Clarkson), a former actress and Fassbinder darling, and the rest of the heroin-loving crowd, Syd is introduced to a book of Lucy's photographs and immediately becomes stricken. Informed by colleagues that she has uncovered the whereabouts of New York's most acclaimed photographer, Syd is urged to coax Lucy out of seclusion. Lucy consents to deliver an assignment for *Frame* on the proviso that Syd acts as editor. On a trip upstate to search for inspiration, a passionate affair begins.

In the film, Cholodenko deals with issues such as infidelity and heroin addiction (perhaps most importantly the burned-out, wasted lives addiction trails in its wake), and drew praise from many leading gay cultural commentators, including B. Ruby Rich, for refusing to present a sanitised version of some of the realities of queer relationships (Rich, 2001, pp. 114–18). The cogency of the film's argument against addiction in all its guises is in large part thanks to Clarkson's riveting performance and that of an understated Sheedy, whose waning career was temporarily resurrected by an Independent Spirit Best Actress Award. Cholodenko also examines the borders between private and public representations of the body, offering an intelligent dissection of the cult of personality by presenting Syd's 'star-fucking' as an almost vampiric act of self-opportunism. The film is, however, also leavened with a deadpan humour, including a receptionist who attempts to convey her highbrow sensibilities by reading Dostoevsky on the job, despite confessing that she's 'not sure she's getting it'.

The film features the photographic work of Jack Pierson, JoJo Whilden and Nan Goldin, the latter obviously informing Lucy's character (*Sight & Sound*'s Leslie Felperin defended the film against accusations of having plagiarised Goldin's life and work [Felperin, 1999]). *High Art* boasts a suitably confident sense of composition with Tami Reiker's richly lit, wonderfully fluid, languorous cinematography perfectly augmenting the film's by turns sultry and illicit tones.

Dir: Lisa Cholodenko; **Prod**: Dolly Hall, Jeff Levyhinte, Susan A. Stover; **Scr**: Lisa Cholodenko; **DOP**: Tami Reiker; **Editor**: Amy E. Duddleston; **Score**: Shudder to Think; **Main Cast**: Ally Sheedy, Radha Mitchell, Tammy Grimes, Patricia Clarkson.

Hoop Dreams
US, 1994 – 171 mins
Steve James

Among the most celebrated of documentary features, *Hoop Dreams*
follows four years in the lives of William Gates and Arthur Agee, two
black teenage basketball prodigies from the Chicago housing projects
who, aged fourteen, are offered semi-scholarship places at the
prestigious, largely white St Joseph's College. At almost three hours long
(the film-makers vehemently fought to avoid editing to a more
conventional length), the film looks at how the fortunes of the two
teenagers intersect and diverge as they fight to impress talent scouts,
retain the financial and moral support of their respective families and
overcome institutionalised racism in a bid to achieve their sporting goals.
Once professional status is attained, untold wealth and international
recognition tantalisingly await.

Existing within the tradition of the anthropological/ethnographic
documentary, *Hoop Dreams* presents a telling, tarnished representation
of the American dream and a damning chronicle of the black experience
in contemporary America. For young black men such as William and
Arthur, excellence in sport seems the only viable means through which to
escape their economic and social plight. But being good at sport is not
merely enough; academic exams also have to be passed, and the
scholarship at St Joseph's brings with it private fees and expenses which
ultimately Arthur's family are unable to meet. In perhaps the film's most
consciously political moment, Spike Lee gives a talk at William's summer
school to reveal how young black men will be exploited by talent scouts
and coaches in the name of money and reputation. Another scene in
which prospective talents are paraded reinforces Lee's words and evokes
the days of slavery and the trading of black men as physical
commodities.

Edited from 250 hours of footage, the expansive time frame and
narrative trajectory charting the progress of William and Arthur are leant

added poignancy and emotional engagement through the intimate interviews with members of the Agee and Gates families. The film offers a positive depiction of black motherhood as it looks at how Arthur's mother Sheila keeps her family together in the face of extreme poverty and her husband Arthur's crack habit. Critics such as bell hooks charged the film with offering a stereotypical view of black families, pointing to the unreliable, largely absent black fathers in the film (hooks, 1995, p. 23). Interestingly, and in contrast to hooks' argument, the film concludes with William, who speaks out against the ethic of competition encouraged by society, becoming a committed, doting parent.

A combination of direct-to-camera interviews and fly-on-the wall footage, *Hoop Dreams* is simply but effectively executed. Filmed largely on Betacam format, which contributes to the film's raw and grainy aesthetic, its main virtue is perhaps its lack of sentimentality and its non-didactic handling of issues of race and class. A critical and commercial success upon release, it enjoyed rave notices following Sundance and New York festival screenings. There was a swelling of support for the film to receive a Best Picture Academy Award nomination, but controversially, the film failed even to secure a nomination in the Best Documentary category. Roger Ebert in the *Chicago Sun-Times* described it as among the greatest viewing experiences of his lifetime (Ebert, 1994).

Dir: Steve James; **Prod**: Fred Marx, Steve James, Peter Gilbert; **Scr**: Fred Marx, Steve James, Peter Gilbert; **DOP**: Peter Gilbert; **Editor**: Fred Marx, Steve James, Bill Haugse; **Score**: Tom Yore; **Main Cast**: William Gates, Arthur Agee, Emma Gates, Ken Curtis.

Impostors
W. Germany/US, 1979 – 110 mins
Mark Rappaport

Impostors was the multi-tasking Rappaport's fifth feature as director, writer, producer and editor, following earlier well-received if under-exposed films such as *Casual Relations* (1973) and *Local Colour* (1977). It is a characteristically baroque and theatrical endeavour that again draws heavily on the over-blown style and rejection of realism associated with operatic traditions.

Rappaport's stock was higher in Europe than in the US, and it was thanks in part to European finance that *Impostors* saw the independent, New York-based director working on a marginally increased budget, compared to his previous films. Although still tethered by the need for economic restraint (including shooting on a limited number of locations), Rappaport could now use more elaborate sets, hire professional actors, and make an advance on the attention to lighting, bold colour design and cinematography (courtesy of Fred Murphy) that had characterised his previous work, *The Scenic Route* (1978).

Described by the director as containing enough plot to 'choke a horse' (quoted in *Journal of the University Film and Video Association*, 1983), *Impostors* makes few concessions to fully rounded characters, causality or believability. Instead it unfolds as a series of emotionally driven and often narratively distinct tableaux in which Rappaport boldly flaunts the film's artifice and theatricality by frequently framing his interchangeable characters against rear-projected sets and boldly designed backdrops. Punctuated with a Rappaportian flavouring of literary references, red herrings and comical non sequiturs, the ever-shifting story, as far as it can be distilled, concerns twin brothers Chucky (the Ridiculous Theatre Company's Ludlam) and Mikey (Burg), who thrill audiences with their magic act. Neither illusionists nor related, they are in fact a pair of camp murderers on the trail of hidden Egyptian artefacts. Theirs is a pseudo-sexual relationship founded on jealousy, and things threaten to come to a head when Mikey – whose heterosexual dalliances inspire Chucky's most violent murderous desires – begins an affair with their alluring new assistant, Tina (McElduff). The object of the affections of an aristocratic young admirer (Evans), Tina may just have valuable information concerning the near-mythic riches the 'twins' seek.

Both parodic and self-reflexive, *Impostors* is a film well versed in mainstream/Hollywood cinematic conventions and romantic clichés (at one point a character declares that 'everything we know about love we've learned from the movies') that to original and esoteric effect combines elements of the thrillers of the 1940s with the spirit of vaudeville. Not for nothing did Rappaport suggest that his cast attempt to achieve an 'amalgam of the Marx Brothers and Peter Lorre, the Three Stooges mixed with Dostoevsky' (quoted in Field, 1982). Yet beneath the play-acting, highly sexualised double entendres, murderous mayhem and droll, ironic dialogue (when Mikey exclaims that 'this trail of bloodletting has to stop', Chucky proffers, 'It will, it will . . . but not yet'), there lurks a sardonic handling of issues relating to contemporary romance, sexual difference and identity, and the malaise between and among the sexes.

Dir: Mark Rappaport; **Prod**: Mark Rappaport; **Scr**: Mark Rappaport; **DOP**: Fred Murphy; **Editor**: Mark Rappaport; **Score**: Various; **Main Cast**: Peter Evans, Ellen McElduff, Charles Ludlam, Michael Burg.

In the Company of Men
US, 1997 – 93 mins
Neil LaBute

Partly funded by an insurance settlement following a car accident, *In the Company of Men* marked playwright LaBute's transition from stage to screen. LaBute is a practising Mormon and the author of provocative plays such as *Filthy Talk for Troubled Times*, and his unflinching feature debut continued his fascination with the more loathsome, odious aspects of contemporary society and its voracious appetite for cruelty and humiliation.

With a minimalist, pared down visual style of largely static camera, medium long-shots, unfussy, well-lit interior locations and its favouring of acerbic dialogue over action, *Men* immediately drew comparisons with David Mamet's early features, *House of Games* (1987) and *Things Change* (1988). Talk, of course, is cheap to film and the simple formal requirements of these directors' plays ensured that both men were well suited to adapt to the potentially rocky terrain of independent/low-budget film production.

LaBute's film focuses on two white-collar executives, Chad (Eckhart) and Howard (Malloy), chosen by their company to help establish a new out-of-town division. Licking their emotional wounds following the fall-out from recently terminated relationships, the pair conspire to strike a blow for their sex by seducing and abandoning a female target. Office typist Christine (Edwards) fits the bill perfectly. She is beautiful and susceptible to romance, but the fact that she is also deaf makes her the perfect victim and the instrument by which Chad and Howard will exact their revenge. 'Let's do it, let's hurt someone', they cheerfully decide.

Featuring lines such as, 'I don't trust anything that bleeds for a week and doesn't die', the film is a knowingly provocative but astringently intelligent observation of misogyny and male insecurity. By locating the majority of the film in a bland, sterile and patriarchal corporate environment (we rarely see beyond the office walls to the world outside, also of course an economic consideration) LaBute makes an important point about the institutional nature of misogyny. Similarly, a scene in which Chad (one of the most monstrous and irredeemable cinematic creations in quite some time) demands to see the balls of a black underling as proof of his commitment, reveals a simmering undercurrent of racism. The film takes a microscopic look at the contemporary workplace and its gender divisions, and has a distinctly anthropological feel. It is instructive that the only work we see being done is by women, while all the bitching and back-biting is done by men.

The film suffered accusations of misogyny, with its director accused of literally denying women a voice. At the eye of this stormy debate was the film's denouement, in which LaBute perhaps deliberately employs shock tactics to court controversy. Chad, who is revealed as contemptuous of all things as opposed to just a hater of women, is allowed to go unpunished, returning to his life of cosy domesticity. Howard (realised with a weasely intensity by Hal Hartley regular Malloy) is meanwhile revealed as the film's most nauseating, irredeemable character, ultimately reduced to impotently begging an uncomprehending Christine for forgiveness.

Dir: Neil LaBute; **Prod**: Mark Archer, Stephen Pevner; **Scr**: Neil LaBute; **DOP**: Tom Hettinger; **Editor**: Joel Plotch; **Score**: Ken Williams, Karel Roessingn; **Main Cast:** Aaron Eckhart, Matt Malloy, Stacy Edwards, Emily Cline.

In the Soup
US, 1992 – 95 mins
Alexandre Rockwell

In his mind, New Yorker Adolpho Rollo (Buscemi) is a highbrow auteur, an internationally acclaimed director in the European mould whose capacity to depict the angst, alienation and general suffering of mankind has elevated him to that higher critical plane reserved for true artists. In reality, Rollo is an out-of-work writer with a lengthy, unsold script – 'Unconditional Surrender' – whose dependency upon hand-outs from his mother to pay the rent on his crummy apartment is a source of intense embarrassment. Deciding to put his cherished masterpiece on the market, Rollo attracts the attentions of Joe (Cassel), a warm-hearted gangland philistine whose efforts to raise finance for the filming of the project go beyond the conventional. However, Joe's ability to impress Angelica (Beals), Rollo's beautiful but hitherto unapproachable neighbour, convinces the would-be Fellini to turn a blind eye to his new benefactor's unfamiliarity with the law.

Pitting artistic suffering against generosity of spirit, the cultured against the uncultivated, Rockwell's delightful, hugely enjoyable feature subverts expectation by sympathising with the latter on each occasion. Beginning as if a paean to the hardships associated with artistic endeavour, the film actually pokes fun both at Rockwell's own background as a 'serious' artist with a tendency towards pretension (prior to *In the Soup* the director had two largely unremarkable features to his name: *Hero*, 1983 and *Sons*, 1989) and at the general notion of the tortured independent film-maker. In this regard, the film acted as a precursor to DiCillo's more sympathetic *Living in Oblivion* (1995). Rockwell's satirical swipes at artistic affectation (in Adolpho's script Nietzsche and Dostoevsky play ping-pong) are matched by the surreal touches he brings to an understanding of a life of crime and the visual set-pieces that result following the introduction of Joe's haemophiliac brother, Skippy (Patton).

Former Cassavetes associate Cassel is in charismatic form as the minor criminal with a passion for life and a belief that whatever one's intellect it's 'not artistic to look down on people'. Matching him is indie stalwart Buscemi (later to pay a variation on the role in *Oblivion*), who brings a characteristic wounded intensity and wide-eyed innocence to Adolpho. Indeed, the film is well cast throughout, with *Flashdance* (1983) favourite Beals (Rockwell's wife) also giving a committed performance. Affirming the film's indie sensibility are cameos from Rockets Redglare and as sleazy producers of a gratuitous cable chat show *The Naked Truth*, Carol Kane and Jim Jarmusch.

Jarmusch is also evident in terms of the film's defining formal aesthetic. The film is beautifully photographed in sumptuous black and white by Phil Parmet, using a combination of studied aimlessness and Ozu-inspired tonal assurance (Adolpho would no doubt have approved of this aesthetic concession to high art). But as if to act as a counterpoint and to underline the film's hugely affecting emotional core, for one brief, glorious moment *In the Soup* bursts into colour, evoking Joe's transparent *joie de vivre* and infectiously extemporary approach to life. The film won two prizes at the 1992 Sundance, the Grand Jury Prize and a Special Jury Prize in honour of Cassel's performance.

Dir: Alexandre Rockwell; **Prod**: Jim Stark, Hank Blumenthal; **Scr**: Alexandre Rockwell, Tim Kissel; **DOP**: Phil Parmet; **Editor**: Dana Congdon; **Score**: Mader; **Main Cast**: Steve Buscemi, Seymour Cassel, Jennifer Beals, Will Patton.

Juice
US, 1992 – 91 mins
Ernest Dickerson

Boasting an impressive curriculum vitae, including John Sayles' *Brother from Another Planet* (1984) and collaborations with Spike Lee, cinematographer Dickerson made his debut feature amid an explosion of films directed by African Americans that dealt with urban violence. Alongside Matty Rich, John Singleton and Mario Van Peebles, Dickerson also offered further evidence of a new breed of socially aware African-American directors. With a blistering score assembled by Hank Shocklee and numerous rap figureheads in cameo roles, *Juice*, independently produced by Island World but subsequently acquired by Paramount, also continued the growing trend of embracing the hip-hop idiom within mainstream film-making practices. This approach enabled the directors to reach wider audiences and offered an escape from the artistic ghetto that Ed Guerrero describes as having curtailed the careers of predecessors including Charles Burnett, Haile Gerima and Julie Dash (Guerrero, 2001, pp. 69–73).

Juice is an impassioned thriller set in Harlem that examines the implosive relationships between four young school-shy friends whose days are spent hanging out, trading insults with rival gangs and visiting record stores. Of the group, Q (Epps) is a young, would-be DJ with a vinyl obsession, Raheem (Kain) an estranged baby father and Bishop (Shakur) a loaded gun waiting to go off. The youngest of the group, the corpulent Steel (Hopkins), acts as the good-natured butt of the others' jokes. A local DJ talent competition offers Q a means of escape from his bleak surroundings, but Bishop's increasing thirst for money, violence and power leads the group into a store robbery that goes disastrously wrong when Raheem is killed.

Juice offers a convincing and despairingly authentic depiction of the hopelessness of inner-city existence, and has at its heart gritty performances by a young and relatively unknown cast. Displaying a fearsome escalating psychosis, the iconic Shakur excels in the first of several big screen roles from rap musicians adding streetwise gravitas and marketing potential to film projects. *Juice* is stylishly shot, though not excessively so, in dark, muted tones and steely blues by Larry Banks (Dickerson interestingly chose not to shoot). The film reveals the fatal consequences of violence – gang-related or otherwise – on the African-American community, while also making highly visible the challenges faced by black, working-class ghetto families trying to keep their children on the straight and narrow.

The anti-violence rhetoric and moral worldview is underlined by the climactic shot of a distraught Q being praised for having the 'juice' to kill Bishop, a moment that also emphasises Dickerson's concern over the respect that murder accords young black males among their peers. Dickerson perceptively highlights the role the media plays in this regard by equating Bishop's bloodlust with an intelligently juxtaposed viewing of Cagney's demise in *White Heat* (1949) and a news bulletin detailing the bloody death of an acquaintance of the protagonists. Critically and commercially overshadowed by the previous year's *Boyz N the Hood*, *Juice* nonetheless displays an assuredness and a distinguished polemical power.

Dir: Ernest Dickerson; **Prod**: David Heyman, Neal H. Moritz, Peter Frankfurt; **Scr**: Gerard Brown, Ernest Dickerson; **DOP**: Larry Banks; **Editor**: Sam Pollard, Brunilda Torres; **Score**: Hank Shocklee, Keith Shocklee, Carl Ryder, Gary G. Wiz; **Main Cast**: Omar Epps, Khalil Kain, Jermaine Hopkins, Tupac Shakur.

Just Another Girl on the I.R.T.
US, 1992 – 97 mins
Leslie Harris

Vying with Julie Dash's *Daughters of the Dust* (1991) as the first film directed by an African-American female to be commercially released (Dash secured the alarming statistic by mere months), *Just Another Girl on the I.R.T.* nonetheless stands as a pivotal point in African-American cinema. Made for $250,000, *Girl* was financed over an arduous three-year period during which Harris flooded organisations with grant proposals. Some paid off, precipitating assistance from the American Film

'The film Hollywood dared not make': Ariyan Johnson as Chantel in *Just Another Girl on the I.R.T.*

Institute, the National Endowment for the Arts, the New York State Council on the Arts and the Jerome Foundation. Investment was also obtained from authors Terry McMillan, Michael Moore and Nelson George. On the basis of a black and white short Harris had made to act as bait to potential investors, Spike Lee declined to assist.

Shot over seventeen days on colour Super 16mm in Manhattan and Brooklyn, the film aims to capture the vitality and coming of age of Chantel (Johnson), a smart, sassy, black teenage home girl, who every Saturday rides the IRT subway from her home in the Brooklyn projects to a job on Manhattan's West Side. Chantel's gaggle of vivacious girlfriends offer zingy comment on the accoutrements of hip-hop culture (a well-chosen soundtrack of mostly female performers provides fitting aural accompaniment). But their knowledge of more pressing issues such as AIDS and contraception is less informed, and Chantel finds herself pregnant after a night of passion with new squeeze Tyrone (Thigpen), who soon neglects her. Refusing to acknowledge reality, Chantel abandons her premature child in a rubbish bin. The film, concludes however, by revealing a well-heeled Chantel making her way through community college with her healthy young child in tow.

Girl is filmed in an urgent, intermittently effective vérité style with first-person narration and direct camera address, and informed by real-life tales of young New York mothers abandoning their children, prompting a telling and cautionary insight into teenage sexuality. To ensure educational value and authenticity in this regard, Harris worked with advisors from Planned Parenthood and Brooklyn Teen Pregnancy Network. The writer-director consciously sidesteps the violent guns and drugs terrain being mined in films, such as *Straight Out of Brooklyn* (1991) and *Juice* (1992) by male African-Americans, providing something all too rarely seen on screen: a multidimensional African-American female character drawn from a female perspective. However, and despite its ground-breaking content, *Girl* is undermined by its unpersuasive and hollow upbeat conclusion and a general tendency to err towards didacticism, an entirely conscious erring, argues Amy Taubin (Taubin,

2001b, pp. 36–9). Despite a strong central performance from newcomer Johnson and some energetic editing, the film struggles to marry polemic to execution.

Stressing its independence with the closing title 'the film Hollywood dared not make', *Girl* nonetheless proved to be something of a false dawn in terms of expanding the opportunities afforded to African-American female film-makers in what is a historically white and patriarchal industry.

Dir: Leslie Harris; **Prod**: Erwin Wilson, Leslie Harris; **Scr**: Leslie Harris; **DOP**: Richard Connors; **Editor**: Jack Haigis; **Score Supervisor**: Eric 'Vietnam' Sadler; **Main Cast**: Ariyan Johnson, Kevin Thigpen, Ebony Jerido, Chequita Jackson.

Kids
US, 1995 – 91 mins
Larry Clark

Written by an eighteen-year-old Harmony Korine, *Kids* shares a clear
lineage with Clark's controversial collections of photographs (the most
notorious of which is perhaps 1971's *Tulsa*) of bored, disaffected,
adolescent speed-freaks. Informed by a similarly uncompromising
sensibility, *Kids* also adopts a pseudo-documentary realist aesthetic,
namely the use of hand-held camera, grainy film stock and a naturalistic,
unforced approach to editing. *Kids* is the tale of a group of promiscuous,
misogynistic New York teenage boys. Led by Telly (Fitzpatrick), whose
particular peccadillo is seducing virgins, the group enjoys the occasional
spot of skateboarding but mostly passes the time by taking whatever
drugs are available, stealing beer, indulging in mindless violence and
sleeping around. However, AIDS casts its menacing shadow when Jenny
(Sevigny), one of Telly's conquests, is diagnosed as HIV-positive.

The film polarised critics and audiences alike, with many finding
Clark's clarion call to the parents of America a sleazy, sensationalist and
exploitative exercise that allowed the director, repeatedly labelled an
aging reprobate by the right-wing press, to indulge on screen a
predilection for adolescent flesh. Moreover, the AIDS subplot was viewed
as a spurious attempt to lend the material a morality it otherwise lacked.
Kids was heavily scrutinised by the censors, and created a media furore in
America, with parents (oblivious to the fact that Clark is a parent himself)
objecting to the unwholesome picture the film paints of American youth
and their absent, uncaring parents. Cannily citing objective detachment,
Clark claimed to have merely held a mirror up to American society; it
didn't like the view one bit. Various 'Do you know where your *Kids* are'
articles appeared to fan the flames of controversy, all of which were used
in the marketing of a film that went on to achieve considerable
commercial success. In Britain, an outraged *Daily Mail* led the calls for the
film to be banned.

The film's supporters, in part seduced by its somewhat forced realist credentials (*Kids* exhibits an almost inconsequential approach to sound quality), found the film to be a gritty, essential meditation on the horrors of youth in a society marked by casual attitudes to and the easy availability of sex and drugs. *Kids'* characters may be ruled by their lusts but they are still too naive to understand the consequences of their actions. Clark certainly doesn't pull his punches; the sex scenes, in which the female is normally non-compliant, are as frank, messy and determinedly un-erotic as the frequent outbursts of gang-related beatings are sickeningly violent. Moreover, the relentlessly grim and sordid tone is a persuasive argument against accusations that the film glamorises the activities on display. The fittingly lo-fi score comes courtesy of Folk Implosion's Lou Barlow.

Kids is provocative, troubling, taboo-tackling and undeniably powerful. Its main legacies are a committed reworking of documentary techniques in the name of fiction and a gloves-off approach in a series of increasingly explicit films dealing with the corruptibility and malaise of America's youth. Clark would himself return to similar territory with *Bully* (2002).

Dir: Larry Clark; **Prod**: Cary Woods; **Scr**: Harmony Korine; **DOP**: Eric Edwards; **Editor**: Christopher Tellefsen; **Score**: Lou Barlow, John Davis; **Main Cast**: Leo Fitzpatrick, Justin Pierce, Chloë Sevigny.

Killer of Sheep
US, 1977 – 84 mins
Charles Burnett

Burnett emerged from the 70s' movement of university-based Los Angeles film-makers who, through the establishment of independent black productions, sought to oppose Hollywood's discriminatory structure and the blaxploitation films it sanctioned. Focusing on the authentic depiction of the common working-class black experience and the realism of suburban and inner-city life, Burnett and his contemporaries had little interest in existing within a commercial framework, but instead strove to establish a black-consciousness audience.

Photographed in frills-free black and white with a largely non-professional cast on the slenderest of budgets, *Killer of Sheep* has a compelling immediacy and a determinedly gritty aesthetic that owe much to the Italian neo-realist cinema of the 40s. Its disjunctive approach to character and structure and its raw, uncompromising tone also recalls Cassavetes. Set in an impoverished black neighbourhood in South Central LA, Burnett's feature debut 'focuses' (it largely eschews a traditional trajectory) on Stan (Sanders), a black slaughterhouse worker whose monotonous, miserable existence engenders increasingly intense feelings of alienation and disconnectedness. Stan is an insomniac increasingly removed from wife (Moore) and troublesome son (Drummond), whose life assumes the characteristics of a tiresome dream from which he is powerless to stir.

The project bears Burnett's signature in every department as he wrote, produced, edited and shot it. *Killer of Sheep*'s dreamy, often transcendental and, to some, problematically unfocused tone frequently pauses for brief vignettes and seemingly minor interludes and reminiscences (for Richard Combs, Cassavetes' 'rambling encounter sessions are models of cohesion' by comparison, [Combs, 1977]). In this regard Burnett's approach can be viewed as audaciously replicating his protagonist's partly somnambulant state as he drifts from one encounter

Henry Gayle Sanders as Stan, a disaffected slaughterhouse worker in *Killer of Sheep*

to the next. An essentially decent man 'working myself into my own hell' in a hostile and emotionally barren climate, Stan at one point in conversation with a colleague holds a warm coffee cup to his cheek, wistfully explaining that its heat reminds him of making love to a woman. The moment offers a reminder of the small pleasures that in hardship often serve to sustain the human spirit.

Killer of Sheep is rich in metaphor, for example the relationship between sheep and sleeplessness and Stan's performing of a job in which he is mired in hopelessness and hideousness. The inventive editing technique further enhances the film's allegorical power. This is perhaps most tellingly achieved in a juxtaposition of shots of a victimised child with a 'Judas' sheep leading the other animals to slaughter. Detailing with insight, eloquence and without resort to stereotype the plight and loss of self suffered by members of the black community, Burnett also makes explicit reference to that community's rootedness and cultural heritage in the assemblage of a phenomenal soundtrack featuring jazz and blues artists such as Paul Robeson and Little Walter. This is a film that continues to influence American independent cinema. David Gordon Green cited it as a major influence on his similarly mesmeric *George Washington* (2000).

Dir: Charles Burnett; **Prod**: Charles Burnett; **Scr**: Charles Burnett; **DOP**: Charles Burnett; **Editor**: Charles Burnett; **Score**: Various; **Main Cast**: Henry Gayle Sanders, Kaycee Moore, Charles Bracy, Angela Burnett.

The Killing of a Chinese Bookie
US, 1975 – 109 mins
John Cassavetes

Originating from a discussion between Cassavetes, Sam Shaw and Martin Scorsese, *The Killing of a Chinese Bookie* was a calculated attempt at something with commercial appeal following the revitalisation of the gangster genre by *The Godfather* (1974). However, Cassavetes was dismissive of the portrayal of gangsters in Hollywood 'entertainments' and wanted to reveal the redundancy of their values in both a material and spiritual sense. Cassavetes also saw gangsters as symbolic of film industry corruption, frequently referring to studio executives (many of whom accepted background roles in a restaurant scene only to be pointedly excluded from the final edit) as 'gangsters' for their cut-throat business manner.

Written quickly by Cassavetes and drawing on his own experiences of the New York strip-club scene and Paris's legendary Le Crazy Horse, *Bookie* concerns Cosmo Vitelli (Gazzara), showman and proud owner of the chichi Crazy Horse West, an LA strip joint where choreographed routines are staged under the supervision of Mr Sophistication (Meade Roberts). Keen to ensure the club's survival, Cosmo finds himself in hock to the Mob and bound to commit a contract killing on their behalf.

Cassavetes admitted to having been influenced by Penn's *Mickey One* (1964) and the television drama *The Family Rico* (also featuring Gazzara). *Bookie* dispenses with the traditional tropes of the genre and reflects Cassavetes' vehement distrust of movie clichés: 'I loathe the simplicity of Hollywood. I hate it. I've seen all the philosophy I want to see, all the structured talk, all the mannered methods . . . I like to make films that are difficult' (quoted in Carney, 2001a, p. 403). Shooting sequentially, Cassavetes sought to explore the extent to which ordinary people define themselves through their work and their successes and failures. The film avoids action (the director deliberated over whether to show Cosmo carrying out the killing) and cheap thrills (Gazzara's improvised line, 'What kind of strip-club is this? Nobody takes their clothes off', was prompted by the director's dislike of nudity), and becomes a fractured and deliberately oblique examination of male insecurity. *Bookie* also represents a desire to capture the complexity of human behaviour, exemplified by the pivotal moment where Cosmo, having lost everything to the hoods, deliberately thanks them. Illustrative of a basic integrity, the scene, lasting barely five minutes, was filmed on two cameras over a whole evening with Cassavetes amassing over fourteen hours of material in his obsession with detail, spontaneity and nuance.

With AFI student Frederick Elmes replacing Al Ruban, who clashed with Cassavetes over the use of gels (Michael Ferris operated a second camera and Cassavetes a hand-held third), it was an ill-tempered eleven-week shoot during which the actors, particularly Timothy Carey and Seymour Cassel, consistently fought. Determined, however, to duplicate the success of *A Woman Under the Influence* (1974), Cassavetes went for broke, hiring fifty staff in New York and Los Angeles and committing to self-distributing on over a hundred prints. Expensive publicity materials added half a million to the $1 million budget. Disastrous previews took place on 15 February 1976. Reviled by critics (most virulently by Judith Crist and Vincent Canby, who likened the film to someone using words they barely understood) *Bookie* opened a few days later in the wake of Scorsese's *Taxi Driver*. With many advanced bookings cancelled, Cassavetes had little choice but to pull the film from distribution. Widely re-appraised, the film is today regarded as being among Cassavetes' best work and is considered to be a profound influence on modern film-making.

Dir: John Cassavetes; **Prod**: Al Ruban; **Scr**: John Cassavetes; **DOP**: Frederick Elmes, Michael Ferris, Mitchell Breit; **Editor**: Tom Cornwell; **Score**: Bo Harwood; **Main Cast**: Ben Gazzara, Timothy Carey, Seymour Cassel, Azizi Johari.

The Kill-Off
US, 1989 – 97 mins
Maggie Greenwald

The Kill-Off concerns the inhabitants of a grim, wintry East Coast resort who are at the mercy of the malicious and salacious town gossip, Luane Devore (Gross). It was adapted by Greenwald from pulp novelist Jim Thompson's characteristically hard-boiled, misanthropic look at the seedy underbelly of American life. Communicating her venomous missives via telephone, the bed-ridden Devore merrily spreads news of the latest scandals involving her neighbours, making public incestuous relationships, drug dependencies, teenage pregnancies and the like. It's only a matter of time before one of the paranoid victims of her idle tittle-tattle decides to silence her vicious tongue once and for all.

The film was Greenwald's second feature outing following *Home Remedy* (1988), a popular festival screener that acted as a calling card for *The Kill-Off*, which was acclaimed at Sundance. Earning comparisons with the Coens' *Blood Simple* (1983), the film suggested the emergence of a confident, forthright female voice. Pamela Woodbridge's intensely claustrophobic and oppressive production design contributes to the film's suitably hard-bitten tone, while Declan Quinn's atmospheric camera work evokes an authentically downbeat, Thompsonesque tone of seediness, pernicious moral decay and general despair. Evan Lurie's discordant, jazz-infused score is similarly effective in suggesting a small-town world deviant and twisted to its very core. *The Kill-Off* also makes a compelling virtue of its sound design (efficiently edited by James Kwei), aurally forewarning through dial tones and sound waves (accompanied by panning shots of overhead telephone wires) the moments when Devore is about to make her poisonous calls. Gross is convincingly repugnant and sadistic as Luane and is well supported by a cast of relative unknowns.

Perceived as a lower budget Kathryn Bigelow due to her tendency to work within genres more popularly mined by male film-makers,

Greenwald was perhaps inevitably feted as a feminist director upon the release of the film. Such views were largely predicated on both the relative dearth of female directors working in the medium, indie or otherwise, and the writer-director's talent for creating strong female characters able to compete on an equal footing with their male counterparts. In terms of assessing the extent of feminist sensibility in Greenwald's work, her follow-up films, the idiosyncratic Western *The Ballad of Little Jo* (1993) and *Songcatcher* (1999), are perhaps more instructive. Gender polemics and the merits of her later work aside, *The Kill-Off* is certainly a highly distinguished, brooding and intelligent contribution to the modern noir genre to compare with Stephen Frears' highly praised *The Grifters* (1990) as one of the finest, most faithful and evocative big-screen Thompson adaptations.

Dir: Maggie Greenwald; **Prod**: Lydia Dean Pilcher; **Scr**: Maggie Greenwald; **DOP**: Declan Quinn; **Editor**: James Kwei; **Score**: Evan Lurie; **Main Cast**: Loretta Gross, Andrew Lee Barrett, Jackson Sims, Steve Monroe.

The Last Seduction
US, 1993 – 110 mins
John Dahl

Dahl had made two impressive if derivative additions to the neo-noir genre, *Kill Me Again* (1989) and *Red Rock West* (1992). His modestly budgeted *The Last Seduction* combined the malevolent, avaricious femme fatale of the 40s with a more explicit and unrestrained eroticism to become one of the most notable modern thrillers since the similarly dark-hearted *Blood Simple* (1983). *Red Rock West* failed to secure a theatrical release in the States (partly because of short-sighted financing), premiering on cable and video; *The Last Seduction* looked set to suffer the same ignominious fate. However, European critics were beguiled by the film's world-weary cynicism and steadfast amorality and, following a rapturous reception at the London Film Festival, *The Last Seduction* was rapidly restored to American theatres, becoming a sleeper hit.

Fleeing from New York after double-crossing her husband Clay (Pullman) on a lucrative cocaine deal, ruthless career criminal Bridget Gregory (Fiorentino) goes to ground in the small town of Beston. Advised by her lawyer to keep a low profile, Bridget takes a job with an insurance company and begins a casual affair with Mike Swale (Berg), an attractive but none too bright white-collar local. Bridget crushes Mike's overtures towards a deeper relationship, but the arrival of a private investigator (Bill Nunn) sanctioned by Clay causes Bridget to realign her affections towards her 'designated fuck'. Having disposed of the investigator in a cleverly staged accident, Bridget then manipulates Mike into a scheme involving the murder of the unfaithful spouses of wealthy clients. Coerced into a contract killing as a means of securing Bridget's devotion, Mike is unwittingly dispatched to New York to kill her husband.

The first of Dahl's films that he did not write, *The Last Seduction* boasts a wickedly dark and blackly comic script courtesy of Steve Barancik that creates one of the most compelling, hard-faced and sexually frank on-screen female characters in recent memory. Described by her own lawyer as 'a self-serving bitch', Bridget is entirely unafraid of using men as a means of achieving financial gain or physical pleasure. After bluntly telling Mike to 'fuck off' when he tries to hit on her, she is intrigued by his boast that he is 'hung like a horse' and invites him to stay after checking his claim by hand. Bridget also uses the physical failings and weaknesses of men to her advantage, goading Mike when she uncovers the reason for his humiliating return to Beston's humble surroundings: a hitherto hidden marriage to a transvestite. Fiorentino is a revelation, oozing cold-hearted disdain for the weak, dim-witted males she contemptuously crushes beneath her heels.

Although authentically replicating the stylistic motifs of the genre (disorientating compositions, expressionistic lighting etc.), the film somewhat brazenly and entertainingly exists outside any need for moral rectitude. Thoroughly rotten to the core, Bridget, in a scene reminiscent of the closing moments of *Body Heat* (1981), prospers while her duped male counterparts either die or rot in jail.

Dir: John Dahl; **Prod**: Jonathan Shestack; **Scr**: Steve Barancik; **DOP**: Jeffrey Jur; **Editor**: Eric L. Beason; **Score**: Joseph Vitarelli; **Main Cast**: Linda Fiorentino, Peter Berg, Bill Pullman, J. T. Walsh.

The Living End
US, 1992 – 84 mins
Gregg Araki

Having taught a course titled 'Independent-Guerilla-Underground-American New Wave Neo-realist Cinema' at UC Santa Barbara, Araki put his teaching experience to good use when he went on to direct two micro-budget features. Unconventional in form, experimental in structure (sometimes self-consciously so) and born of a willingness to engage with the artificiality of the medium, both *Three Bewildered People in the Night* (1987) and *Long Weekend (O' Despair)* (1989) were over-burdened by an almost suffocating claustrophobia and cloying ennui.

Bolstered by a moderately increased budget and using equipment loaned by the resolutely independent, increasingly marginalised Jon Jost, Araki seemed to really find his voice – and his audience – with *The Living End*. A punkishly political, agitating and notoriously hard-hitting work, it was another seminal moment in the emerging New Queer Cinema movement of the early 90s. Proudly dubbed 'irresponsible' by the director, the spunky and energetic film wears its cine-literacy proudly, playing hard and fast with the conventions of the couple-on-the-run/road movie genre while frequently referencing Godard's *Pierrot le fou* (1965). Godard's influence is profound, both in terms of the diverse counterculture aesthetics and mimicking of mainstream film-making practices the film employs. and in Araki's 'cute' deconstruction of soundbite culture.

Confrontational, savagely funny (in places the film resembles a screwball comedy) and frequently just savage, *The Living End* tells the story of Luke (Dytri), a gay hustler prone to outbursts of brutal violence, and Jon (Gilmore), a disenchanted Los Angeles movie critic. Both HIV-positive and fiercely attracted to each other, the pair are forced to flee the patently plastic LA environment when Luke carelessly shoots a cop. To the accompaniment of a jagged score from the likes of Braindead Sound Machine, KMFDM and Coil, a fucking and killing rampage through the wastelands of Middle America ensues.

Shot by Araki with a raw tonal intensity, *The Living End* daringly and with heartfelt conviction confronts America's fear of AIDS, existing in stark contrast to Hollywood-sanctioned pictures on the subject, such as Demme's *Philadelphia*, which emerged the following year. The film is also propelled by Araki's rage and indignation, and he ultimately dedicates it to 'the hundreds of thousands who've died and the hundreds of thousands more who will die because of a big white house full of Republican fuckheads'. Roundly antagonistic, Araki even takes a swipe at his US indie peers with a sequence in which Luke murders two gay bashers wearing *Drugstore Cowboy* and *sex, lies and videotape* T-shirts.

Like Todd Haynes and Tom Kalin, Araki also refuses to offer positive, sanitised representations of gay characters. Perhaps as a result *The Living End* (part of a 'teen apocalypse trilogy' completed by *Totally F***ed Up*, 1993, and *The Doom Generation*, 1995) received a largely muted response from gay critics. Feminists also found fault with *The Living End*'s stereotypical depiction of female characters, particularly the film's two inept lesbian serial killers.

Dir: Gregg Araki; **Prod**: Marcus Hu, Jon Gerrans; **Scr**: Gregg Araki; **DOP**: Gregg Araki; **Editor**: Gregg Araki; **Score**: Cole Coonce; **Main Cast**: Craig Gilmore, Mike Dytri, Darcy Marta, Mary Woronov.

Living in Oblivion
US, 1995 – 90 mins
Tom DiCillo

DiCillo was formerly a cinematographer, most notably for Jarmusch, who made the move to directing with the slight if engaging *Johnny Suede* (1991). Much indebted to Jarmusch's work in tone and structure, the film introduced two defining themes in DiCillo's career: masculinity in crisis and the pressures of maintaining artistic principles in a society where philistinism rules. Largely funded through the financial input of many of the cast and crew, most notably Michael Griffiths and Hilary Gilford who put up the $500,000 required to complete the project, *Living in Oblivion* represents DiCillo's most cogent exploration of these themes.

Written when DiCillo was 'the most disillusioned with every aspect of the film-making process; from raising the money to the technical nightmares of shooting' (DiCillo, 1995, p. ix), it's an entertaining look at an idealistic New York director. Nick Reve, played by the talismanic Buscemi (later to reprise his role in DiCillo's *The Real Blonde*, 1997), is struggling to complete his arty, low-budget movie. Despite the best efforts of leading lady Nicole (a film-stealing performance from Keener, one of the most consistently interesting and audacious actors to emerge from the US indie scene), the anxious director is plagued by a cavalcade of malfunctioning machines, the attentions of his overbearing mother and on-set fighting between cameraman Wolf (Mulroney) and petulant, hammy leading man Chad Palomino (LeGros).

Beginning with a black and white dream sequence that was originally a stand-alone short titled *Part One*, *Oblivion* largely proceeds through numerous point-of-view fantasy sequences that instructively reveal the numerous paranoias causing an already fraught shoot to become that bit more difficult. This technique also serves to blur art and life, and fantasy and reality, and creates uncertainty within audience expectations concerning what is 'real' and what is part of the film-within-the-film. A sequence where Keener has to continually re-enact a scene with diminishing returns also marks out both the ardour and the artificiality of the film-making process, stripping it of its mystique and inviting the spectator to consider what actually constitutes performance.

Oblivion has become a classic of its kind, offering a microcosm of the trials and tribulations of independent/low-budget production and its propensity for offering the stuff of both dreams and nightmares. The plot incorporates elements of farce. The fractured and fractious relationships among the cast and crew are, of course, due to the constrictive lack of time and money, but they are exacerbated by a director secretly in love with his leading lady and a philandering, egotistical method-loving actor slumming it in an indie production in order to sharpen his arty credentials (Chad reveals in a fit of pique that he only took the part because he mistakenly believed Nick to be 'tight with Tarantino'). The film is a revealing insight into the currency of 'name' independent directors and a perceptive commentary on how the independent sector is a parasite's paradise offering a short cut to kudos. DiCillo, whose self-penned, Sundance-winning script deftly side-steps any trace of self-indulgence, also shows that he is not averse to making a number of well-aimed jabs at the egos of would-be auteurs, sending up Nick's more ludicrous pretensions to art in a Felliniesque dream sequence involving a precocious dwarf.

Dir: Tom DiCillo; **Prod**: Michael Griffiths, Marcus Viscidi; **Scr**: Tom DiCillo; **DOP**: Frank Prinzi; **Editor**: Camilla Toniolo; **Score**: Jim Farmer; **Main Cast**: Steve Buscemi, Catherine Keener, James LeGros, Dermot Mulroney.

Lonesome Cowboys
US, 1968 – 110 mins
Andy Warhol

One of the major artists of the twentieth century, Warhol had a strong commitment to cinema, devoting equal time to his Factory Studio and to his conceptual art between 1963 and 1968. Warhol had been weaned on classic Hollywood and gay porn films of the 50s, and was later introduced to Jonas Mekas' Film-maker's Co-op. Thereafter, he added to his list of cinematic influences the work of American avant-garde directors Jack Smith, Kenneth Anger, Stan Brakhage and Marie Menken.

Warhol's early films (1963–4) were Bolex-shot, frills-free silent shorts in which the camera – explicitly acknowledged – remained static. Making concession neither to drama, narrative nor indeed the avant-garde, the films were viewed as audacious and provocative. Warhol subsequently worked with scriptwriters Chuck Wein and Ronald Tavel and Factory 'superstars' Edie Sedgwick, Viva and Mario Montez (the approach to performance was idiosyncratic), and his films from 1964 to 1966 began to incorporate both sound and more complex staging, though little in the way of actual plot. Offering a fetishistic depiction of the human body and explicit and destabilised presentations of sex and gender, the films marked Warhol's engagement with fringe cultures of many kinds.

A collaboration with Paul Morrissey, *Lonesome Cowboys* reflects Warhol's attempt to build upon both this and the critical and commercial success of *The Chelsea Girls* (1966), regarded as being as formally important as Godard's work in its use of split-screen technique. Shot on cheap 16mm stock in Arizona, *Lonesome Cowboys* is a synthesis of Western and sexploitation conventions and ultimately resembles an unorthodox pornographic home movie. Featuring a sheriff sporting a black bikini, it's fair to say that the loose incorporation of more traditional realist cinema elements such as characters, plot and costumes is not a tilt at authenticity. The film is frequently hilarious and fleetingly surreal (at one point a cowboy performs ballet exercises), and the props, use of popular songs and the open representation of homosexuality suggest a bold post-modernity. His camera voyeuristically lingering on the muscular torsos of his Western studs (including Hompertz and Joe Dallesandro) as they fuck, frolic, take drugs and generally check each other out, Warhol both popularised cultivated camp (at one point the preening group discuss the correct use of mascara) and provided visual stimuli for the male homosexual gaze.

Moreover, as Peter Gidal comments in *Millennium Film Journal*, in showing the naturalness of sex between men living in close confinement, Warhol posited a far more truthful depiction of the early pioneering days than that revealed in traditional Westerns (Tartaglia, 1979, p. 56). Warhol withdrew from cinema following the attempt on his life by Valerie Solanas, and *Lonesome Cowboys* proved to be his final film as sole director (arms-length Morrissey collaborations aside). But his radicalism and innovatory pioneering spirit endured throughout the late 60s and 70s.

Warhol withdrew his films from circulation in 1972, claiming they were better talked about than seen, but he was later persuaded to donate all existing materials to the Whitney Museum so that they could be preserved and re-exhibited. When they were collectively shown as part of a major retrospective in 1988, the films provided inspiration for a new generation of formally inquisitive and culturally diverse film-makers willing to vocalise their social, racial and sexual experiences and desires.

Dir: Andy Warhol; **Prod**: Andy Warhol; **Scr**: Andy Warhol; **DOP**: Uncredited; **Editor**: Uncredited; **Score**: Uncredited; **Main Cast**: Viva, Taylor Mead, Tom Hompertz, Louis Waldon.

The Loveless
US, 1981 – 84 mins
Kathryn Bigelow, Monty Montgomery

Bigelow emerged from the 70s' New York art scene with the completion of a number of underground experimental shorts. Her idiosyncratic first feature, *The Loveless*, firmly established her reputation as a confident and intelligent visual stylist distilling the themes of violence, voyeurism and sexual politics that were to recur throughout her later work.

The film was conceived and co-directed by Bigelow and future Lynch associate Montgomery and independently produced. *The Loveless* ostensibly examines the impact on a small, isolated township in the American South during the late 1950s of the arrival of a gang of leather-clad bikers, led by the enigmatic Vance (Dafoe). The locals initially fear the worst but it soon becomes apparent that the gang are only interested in preening and exchanging meaningful glances, sipping Coca-Cola and listening to rock and roll on the Wurlitzer jukebox in the neon-lit diner. While repairing his bike, Vance has his attention pricked by the red sports car – driving Debbie (L'Hotsky), who reveals her violent father's responsibility for her mother's death. The pair are coiled in a post-coital embrace at a motel when the liaison is interrupted by the arrival of Debbie's enraged father, who vows to run the bikers out of town. In cahoots with his brother, the father sets upon the gang while they are drinking at a local bar, but his assault is cut short by the intervention of his daughter, who shoots him dead. As Vance helplessly looks on, Debbie returns to her car, places a gun in her mouth and pulls the trigger. The bikers move on to another town.

The Loveless is a dreamy, meticulously detailed and richly evocative celebration of biker culture and 50s' iconography. That said, the unexpected and violent denouement hints at a feminist coda, evidenced by the decisiveness of the female lead and Vance's abject powerlessness and male insecurity. The film's languorousness is accentuated by the relaxed performances, epigrammatic dialogue and extended takes which, in conjunction with arresting colour-coded visuals, contribute to the feeling that Bigelow and Montgomery's primary interest isn't character or story.

Inspiration was taken from three key sources: the premise of *The Wild One* (1953), the fetishism of Kenneth Anger's *Scorpio Rising* (1964), and the alienating environments and emotional vacuity depicted in the paintings of Edward Hopper (Bigelow and Montgomery lovingly linger on painstakingly assembled 50s advertisements, a wardrobe and vending machines). The directors lace the chrome, zips, leather and other erotic and indeed homoerotic material on display with frequent cutaways to tattoos and the mechanics of the aforementioned Wurlitzer. They further lush things up through the sensuous Robert Gordon and John Lurie score.

One of the most visually inspired films of its era, *The Loveless* attained an instant and enduring cult status. The film also acted as the springboard from which Bigelow went on to attain a career in Hollywood (a relatively rare achievement for a female director), directing big-budget action pictures (*Point Break*, 1991) and intelligent genre makeovers (Western/vampire hybrid *Near Dark*, 1987).

Dir: Kathryn Bigelow, Monty Montgomery; **Prod**: Grafton Nunes, A. Kitman Ho; **Scr**: Kathryn Bigelow, Monty Montgomery; **DOP**: Doyle Smith; **Editor**: Nancy Kanter; **Score**: Robert Gordon, John Lurie; **Main Cast**: Willem Dafoe, Robert Gordon, Marin Kanter, Tina L'Hotsky.

Matewan
US, 1987 – 133 mins
John Sayles

Sayles is widely regarded, alongside Cassavetes, as one of the quintessential and most self-sufficient figures in American independent cinema. He is a genuine auteur who, as well as performing numerous technical roles also acts in his own films, a reflection of his college theatre days. Moreover, he is rare even within the indie scene in managing to marry his independence (subsidised through highly paid Hollywood scriptwriting work on projects such as *Apollo 13*, 1995) with both longevity and surprisingly high productivity.

Originally intended to follow the studio-produced *Baby, It's You* (1983), the independently financed *Matewan* collapsed during pre-production when its key investor withdrew commitment. Using his own funds, Sayles instead shot *The Brother from Another Planet* (1984), returning to *Matewan* some three years later. The rising cost of film stock and general inflation during the intervening period increased the original budget from $1.5 million to $3.6 million. Further private investment and a deal structured by Cinecom – the handlers of *Brother* – finally saw the project greenlighted.

The film is based on an amalgamation of material derived from Sayles' own *Union Dues* novel and meticulous research into the coal wars and labour history of the 20s and 30s in America. A good deal of the characters, including Strathairn's Sheriff Sid Hadfield, are based on historical figures, while others are composites of people Sayles read about. *Matewan* is a lyrical period piece set in a small West Virginian mining community in the 20s. Narrated by Danny (songsmith Oldham in an early acting role), a young miner who opens the movie – and as an old man closes it – the film details the struggle between the greedy coal company and the local workers it exploits. Tensions boil when the company begins importing cheap labour in the form of Italian immigrants and blacks from Alabama who become scapegoats for local anger.

Pacifist union organiser Joe Kenehan (Chris Cooper) gradually unifies the striking workers, but a violent showdown builds between the miners and the professional strike-breakers hired by the company when a young miner is murdered.

Matewan is a powerful piece of historical storytelling that merges the personal and the political to examine issues of ethnicity, xenophobia, the birth of the unions and the rights of the working classes. It could not have been more timely, coming shortly after Reagan's union-directed invectives. Sayles neatly orders the historical events by adhering to the conventions and visual iconography of the Western genre. In this he is well served by the veteran Haskell Wexler's naturalistic cinematography and painterly use of artificial light. As well as perhaps sugaring the film's political bent (albeit one cushioned by Sayles' characteristic humility and liberal humanism), the approach also imbues *Matewan* with a resonant mythic clarity that intelligently picks away at America's self-mythology as the land of the free. Music plays an essential role. There is a discussion of the utopian ideal of coexistence, with a beautifully played scene in a camp revealing West Virginian hillbillies, blacks and Italians tentatively bonding over the shared experience of song.

The film perhaps suffers from a caricatured depiction of villainy and corruption, but the performances from both Sayles' regulars and newcomers such as James Earl Jones are of an extraordinarily high standard throughout. Matewan thus stands alongside *Salt of the Earth* (1953) as a pensive, unsentimental and compelling celebration of community and civil action.

Dir: John Sayles; **Prod**: Peggy Rajski, Maggie Renzi; **Scr**: John Sayles; **DOP**: Haskell Wexler; **Editor**: Sonya Polonsky; **Score**: Mason Daring; **Main Cast**: Chris Cooper, Mary McDonnell, Will Oldham, David Strathairn.

Mean Streets
US, 1973 – 110 mins
Martin Scorsese

Post-*Easy Rider* (1969), Scorsese and his New Hollywood contemporaries found themselves in a climate receptive to liberty and daring. Scorsese was advised by mentor John Cassavetes to extricate himself from producer Roger Corman's exploitation movie *Boxcar Bertha* (1972), Cassavetes offering a typically curt, 'You're better than the people who make this kind of movie', Thompson and Christie, 1989, p. 38). Shot on a low budget with many of the *Boxcar* crew, *Mean Streets* bristles with the director's ferocious energy and commitment. On-screen urgency was compounded by a compact shooting schedule involving up to twenty-four set-ups a day and the frequently aggressive chemistry of its actors. Ultimately produced and distributed by Warner Bros. (but owing much to Corman and his associate Paul Rapp), the film represents the cinema of Scorsese in its purest form.

It is set in the violent Little Italy streets of the director's childhood. Returning to the thematic terrain of Catholicism and Italian-American male camaraderie, covered in Scorsese's earlier *Who's That Knocking at My Door* (1968), *Mean Streets* examines the conflicts affecting a closely knit but volatile group of aspirant Italian Americans. Prominent among them is the relatively respectable Charlie (Keitel), whose ascendancy to the running of an ailing restaurant is haunted by his religious sense of the evil around him and his feeling of duty towards his reckless, destructive young friend, Johnny Boy (De Niro in a towering performance of flawed masculinity). Charlie's illicit affair with Teresa (Robinson), Johnny Boy's cousin, ultimately proves the flashpoint that leads to a bloody denouement involving a sharpshooter (Scorsese in a characteristic cameo) hired by the brooding money-lender (Richard Romanus) that Johhny Boy has unwisely antagonised.

Given the restrictive conditions under which the film was made, the expressive and experimental approach to editing, sound and camera work is all the more amazing. Though regarded as a quintessential New York movie, the interiors were largely shot in Los Angeles with only rehearsals and eight days of actual shooting taking place in NYC. Frequently filming in extremely long takes with a mobile camera (as in the prolonged fight scene in a pool hall), Scorsese also uses slow-motion sound and cinematography allied with bold tracking shots – to celebrated and imitated effect. This is most evident in the sequence where Johnny Boy enters a bar to the sounds of 'Jumpin' Jack Flash'. Just

Johnny Boy (Robert De Niro) and Charlie (Harvey Keitel) clash violently in *Mean Streets*

one of many such moments (accredited by the director to the tracking camera style pioneered by Sam Fuller), it moreover illustrates the film's long-lasting influence in the incorporation of popular music as an integral part of its structure.

Scorsese made a powerful connection with his audience, a quality that Michael Powell (a direct influence on the film) cites as being 'the rarest gift given to a movie director. Most directors, however wise, however experienced, however resourceful, however bold, don't have it and never will have it. Marty has always had it' (Ibid. p. xiv). Scorsese's expressiveness also prevailed upon a freshly emerging generation of film-makers, both independent and otherwise, later dubbed the 'sons of Scorsese' (Hillier, p. 92) by critic Amy Taubin. The film is undoubtedly one of American cinema's defining moments. On seeing an initial rough-cut of *Mean Streets* Cassavetes exclaimed, 'Don't cut it whatever you do' (Ibid., p. 48).

Dir: Martin Scorsese; **Prod**: Jonathan Taplin; **Scr**: Martin Scorsese, Mardik Martin; **DOP**: Kent Wakeford; **Editor**: Sidney Levin; **Score**: Various; **Main Cast**: Harvey Keitel, Robert De Niro, David Proval, Amy Robinson.

Metropolitan
US, 1989 – 98 mins
Whit Stillman

Stillman's *Metropolitan*, his writing-directing debut, proved to be one of the key independent films of the decade and a catalyst for the renaissance in intelligent, understated and knowingly literate low-budget comedy dramas. Emerging alongside Soderbergh's *sex, lies and videotape* (1989) and Hartley's *The Unbelievable Truth* (1989), the picture also established Ira Deutchman (who began his career with Faces Films and the release of Cassavetes' *A Woman Under the Influence*, 1974) as an ubiquitous figure in American independent distribution and led to the formation of Fine Line features. The 'classics' division of New Line Cinema and a Mecca for established and emerging talents such as Gus Van Sant and Jim Jarmusch, Fine Line's example in part spurred the formation of similar 'classics' divisions at studio-owned companies.

Against his socialist principles, impoverished Princeton student Tom Townsend (Edward Clements) mixes with a member of the UHB: 'urban haute bourgeoisie' in *Metropolitan*

Made for just $80,000, the film is a smart, articulate, satirical look at the anachronistic children of the 'UHB: the urban haute bourgeoisie', as one character defines them, that's partly informed by Stillman's preppy upbringing as the son of a Republican Democrat on New York's Upper East Side. Into a tightly knit group of privileged Park Avenue bluebloods navigating the endless dinner dress soirées of the debutante season comes Tom Townsend (Clements), an impoverished Princeton student from the Lower West Side whose socialist principles and hired evening attire conflict sharply with the sensibilities and backgrounds of the self-christened 'Sally Fowler Rat Pack'. However, when Audrey (Farina) develops a crush on Tom, he is persuaded to act as an escort and enjoy food, drink and companionship for the remainder of the season.

The film is beautifully performed by its unknown ensemble cast, many of whom became Stillman regulars. Practicalities dictated that *Metropolitan* made a virtue of pithy, perceptive dialogue dripping in social nuances. Recalling Edith Wharton and F. Scott Fitzgerald (by way of Woody Allen), Stillman reveals characters desperately trying to hide their insecurities under social and intellectual facades. Commendably, Stillman takes an egalitarian approach to superiority, gently revealing Tom as a 'public transportation snob who looks down on people who take taxis' and a pseudo-intellectual whose opinions on literature are dictated by other people's critiques.

Metropolitan capitalises on its festive Manhattan backdrops, and economically evokes, through the 1920s' jazz score and the stylised intertitles, the sense that its characters belong to a previous era. These people appear to be merely adhering to customs and traditions outmoded before they were born. Stillman keeps his compositions relatively simple and just so, filming the largely static scenes in uninterrupted medium close-ups. In a telling irony of low-budget production, the characters are often shot leaving the plush Plaza Hotel, but prohibitive filming costs put paid to filming inside it.

The film was described by Rita Kempley in her *Washington Post* review as a 'smart comedy of conversation . . . like *My Dinner with André* but with eight place settings', (Kempley, 1990) *Metropolitan*'s generally warm critical reception was matched by a respectable box-office performance (just under $3 million on a limited release) that once again alerted the industry to the potential profits to be made from low-budget productions. As well as accruing its director an Academy Award nomination for Best Original Screenplay, *Metropolitan* also netted Stillman a prestigious production deal with Castle Rock.

Dir: Whit Stillman; **Prod**: Whit Stillman; **Scr**: Whit Stillman; **DOP**: John Thomas; **Editor**: Chris Tellefsen; **Score**: Mark Suozzo; **Main Cast**: Carolyn Farina, Edward Clements, Christopher Eigerman, Taylor Nichols.

Nashville
US, 1975 – 161 mins
Robert Altman

Altman began his career producing industrial training films in his native Kansas City, and followed this with a successful stint in television (credited as the source of his improvisational methodology) and numerous low-key features. Altman finally rose to prominence during the creatively liberating period ushered in by *Easy Rider* (1969). Beginning with *M*A*S*H* (1970), Altman enjoyed studio support, producing throughout the 70s an unparalleled body of work that combined stylistic and technical daring with an unflinching reflection of the air of disenchantment pervading American society.

A dazzling country music opus set against the political backdrop of an independent presidential candidate's election campaign, *Nashville* follows the intertwining lives, loves and longings of twenty-four disparate protagonists (including performers, agents, groupies, journalists and locals) during an ill-fated, weekend-long music festival in Nashville, Tennessee. Sprawling, ambitious and epic in tone, it is commonly viewed as representing the pinnacle of Altman's career. It certainly acts as a summation of the director's interest in myriad freeform narratives. Frequently co-existing, these divergent strands are tentatively woven together through an impressive marshalling of ensemble scenes and a liberating manipulation of sound and image. The film is further noted for Altman's pioneering incorporation of overlapping dialogue and the use of multiple hidden microphones as opposed to booms.

Nashville also offers, through its mock-documentary format, a compelling union of fiction and reality. Filmed at the Mecca of country music, and made in the shadow of the Vietnam War, *Nashville* typifies Altman's tack of imbuing his subject matter, which is often made under the guise of genre conventions, with a revisionist approach to American history. This refusal to perpetuate mythologies would later see Altman cast out of the system (*Buffalo Bill and the Indians*, 1976, destroyed his

Nashville, a dazzling, multinarrative country music opus set against the political backdrop
of an independent presidential candidate's election campaign

Hollywood standing), but on this occasion it brought him five Academy
Award nominations, including Best Director and Best Picture. The film is
impeccably acted by a large and notable repertory cast (Lily Tomlin,
Geraldine Chaplin and Shelley Duvall appear; Elliot Gould and Julie
Christie offer cameos). The film strikes another perfect note through its
evocative use of country music, with many of the actors writing and
performing their own material; Altman mainstay Keith Carradine won a
Best Song Oscar for 'I'm Easy'.

Popularly viewed as one of the most influential talents to emerge in post-war American cinema (Paul Thomas Anderson is particularly indebted to him), Altman is a true independent whose tremendous longevity spanning over five decades can be attributed to his ability to adapt to the changing economics of the film-making environment. When the studios deserted him, refusing to agree to his stipulation of complete creative control, Altman turned to alternative funding. Ironically, it was *The Player* (1992), a blackly comic exposé of industry morals (or rather lack of them) that saw the director welcomed back to Hollywood.

Dir: Robert Altman; **Prod**: Robert Altman; **Scr**: Joan Tewkesbury; **DOP**: Paul Lohmann; **Editor**: Sidney Levin, Dennis Hall; **Score**: Various; **Main Cast**: Ned Beatty, Ronee Blakley, Henry Gibson, Keith Carradine.

Night of the Living Dead
US, 1968 – 96 mins
George A. Romero

Widely considered to be 'arguably the most influential contribution to the modern horror genre' (Andrew, 1998, p. 23), *Night of the Living Dead* is a landmark of late 60s' cinema. Permeated by a nihilistic sense of abject hopelessness and frantic despair, Romero's film presents a radical and subversive re-reading of horror genre conventions to reflect, like contemporaries such as *The Wild Bunch* (1968) and *Easy Rider* (1969), the pervading mood of pessimism engulfing American society.

The film was independently produced on a meagre budget by a small Pittsburgh company specialising in industrial films and political TV spots. Romero (who personally invested in the project) and his small army of multi-tasking friends and co-workers were forced to be extremely resourceful. Co-writer John Russo and producers Russell Streiner and Karl Hardman were coerced into featuring in the film, alongside a cast of amateur actors and Pittsburgh locals. Filming slowed to a halt on numerous occasions while Romero secured additional financing by showing potential investors completed stock and offering them shares in the picture.

Night is a powerful social allegory dealing with the collapse of society that reflects a growing resentment towards authority, the media and American involvement in Vietnam. It immediately destabilises horror customs when a marauding ghoul kills the male hero in the opening sequence. The man's surviving sister Barbara (O'Dea) flees, finding refuge in an apparently abandoned farmhouse. Shocked into silence, she finds herself among a group of fellow survivors under attack from what a television report reveals to be marauding, cannibalistic flesh-eaters created following a freak molecular mutation. Reluctantly led by the largely inefficient Ben (black actor Jones, though there is no allusion to his colour), the band, which includes members of the same family (later to devour each other) rapidly disintegrates into backbiting and bickering, creating a volatile atmosphere bracketed by the threat of danger from without and within.

Night's relentless, unsparing terror (rendered by eerily effective monochrome cinematography) and gruesome new moral order is carried through to its profoundly despairing conclusion. Having survived the onslaught, Ben, the only character who offers any possible identification for the disorientated spectator, is mistaken for a zombie and shot by a gung-ho policeman.

Rejected by Columbia, allegedly because it wasn't in colour, the film played at out-of-town drive-ins and as part of triple features, accruing a word-of-mouth reputation among horror aficionados. Latterly a fixture on the midnight movie circuit, it attracted the attentions of a number of critics and academics of the time who became convinced of its social relevance and unerring power. *Night*'s was the immediate inspiration for an emerging legion of horror directors keen to merge intellect and gore to allegorical effect. Sam Raimi, Tobe Hooper, David Cronenberg and Wes Craven were perhaps the first to take up *Night*'s gauntlet. The film spawned a number of sequels directed by Romero and make-up artist Tom Savini, and nourished the 70s' cycle of Italian exploitation films such as Lucio Fulci's *Zombie Flesh Eaters* (1979) and those of Dario Argento.

Dir: George A. Romero; **Prod**: Russell Streiner, Karl Hardman; **Scr**: John A. Russo; **DOP**: George A. Romero; **Editor**: George A. Romero; **Score**: Uncredited; **Main Cast**: Judith O'Dea, Duane Jones, Karl Hardman, Keith Wayne.

One False Move
US, 1991 – 105 mins
Carl Franklin

Former actor Franklin turned to directing in frustration at the lack of decent parts available to black actors, and graduated from the Roger Corman school, for whom he directed three uninspiring quickie genre pictures. Having cultivated under Corman's tutelage an appreciation for the structures of genre film-making, Franklin chose to studiously avoid the inner-city milieu and urban tales from the hood currently being mined by many of his African-American contemporaries such as Matty Rich, John Singleton and Albert and Allen Hughes. In its own measured and low-key way, compared to those film-makers' work, *One False Move* is equally revealing of the consequences of violence and the social and economic realities of the African-American experience.

One False Move and the works of hard-boiled pulp novelist Jim Thompson are cut from the same cloth. The film begins with a murderous drugs heist in South Central LA involving a femme fatale with a heart, Fantasia (Williams), her highly strung white boyfriend, Ray (Thornton) and his black partner, Pluto (Beach). Pluto's high IQ is matched only by his thirst for cold-bloodedly stabbing his victims. Pursued by the black and white detective duo Cole and McFeely, the gang is tagged as heading to Star City, Alabama, where Ray has an uncle. Aspirant local police chief Dale 'Hurricane' Dixon (Paxton) is alerted to their imminent arrival as the film expertly cuts between Dixon and the group for maximum suspense . However, when a faxed report arrives revealing Fantasia's involvement in an en-route shooting of a traffic cop, Dixon recognises her as former local flame Lila Walker, with whom, unbeknown to him, he has spawned a mixed-race son. A charged and ultimately violent reunion ensues as Dixon wrestles with his duty and his conscience.

Intelligently adopting classical thriller conventions (with a dash of *High Noon*, 1952), and applying them within a racially charged setting that traces black and white conflict back to its roots in the American South, Franklin avoids the bravura and sometimes sermonising approach of a number of films associated with the 'gangsta' cinema movement. Instead, the theme of race is accorded a subtle and sophisticated treatment that naturally evolves through the characters, environments and the numerous mixed-race relationships and dynamics *One False Move* authentically creates. Written by Billy Bob Thornton and Tom Epperson, the film is similarly perceptive on subjects such as small-town mores, sexual inequality and the interrelationships between race, ambition, money and power.

Newcomer Williams convinces in the complex central role on which the film's revelations and motifs crucially balance, and the performances are generally well judged. So too is the treatment of violence which manages to be explicit, disturbing and thus pertinent by never descending to gratuity. An ultimately humanist and economically executed triumph of insight and import, the film – which suffered rejection by many major film festivals – gave evidence of the ability of African-American directors to escape ghetto stereotyping while also ushering in a new era of neo-noir pictures such as John Dahl's *The Last Seduction* (1992).

Dir: Carl Franklin; **Prod**: Jesse Beaton, Ben Myron; **Scr**: Billy Bob Thornton, Tom Epperson; **DOP**: James L. Carter; **Editor**: Carole Kravetz; **Score**: Peter Haycock, Derek Holt; **Main Cast**: Bill Paxton, Cynda Williams, Billy Bob Thornton, Jim Metzler.

Parting Glances
US, 1985 – 90 mins
Bill Sherwood

According to John Pierson, previous to *Parting Glances*, overtly gay films could largely be reduced to three distinct types: bitchy banter (*The Boys in the Band*, 1970); broad physical farce (*La Cage aux folles*, 1978); and explicit, hardcore 'freak shows' (*Taxi zum Klo*, 1981) (Pierson, 1996, p. 35). Studio attempts to deal with gay sexuality led to predatory caricatures such as *Cruising* (1980) and the insipid *Making Love* (1982). Sayles' impressive lesbian drama *Lianna* (1982) was perhaps alone in presenting an unpatronising and perceptive account of a gay relationship, though it was the product of a straight director.

Independently financed by director Sherwood, a former Juilliard-trained classical musician, *Parting Glances* offers a non-political, but nonetheless from-the-horse's-mouth presentation of gay sexuality. It depicts realistic, fully rounded characters struggling to deal with the universal trials and tribulations that are the by-product of any relationship. Michael (Ganoung) and Robert (Bolger) are two young, well-adjusted, prosperous, New York professionals who consent to put their relationship on hold when Robert decides to spend a year in Africa. Michael remains in New York to comfort Nick (Buscemi), a former lover and mutual close friend dying of AIDS.

Though undeniably stylistically conservative with overly bright production values and, Buscemi aside, performances that echo a day-time soap, *Parting Glances* exhibits a droll humour. There is, too, an endearing affection for and tenderness towards its characters and a refusal to locate its gay characters merely in relation to the heterosexual world around them. A portentous insight into the threat of AIDS and its impact upon the gay community, the film has the distinction of being the first theatrically produced feature to deal with the disease, precipitating a flurry of like-minded pictures such as the TV-produced *An Early Frost* (1985) and the largely anodyne *Longtime Companion* (1990).

The film was treated with kid gloves in the US by its somewhat tentative distributor Cinecom, which played down the explicit gay/AIDS angle and instead firmly positioned the film as another low-budget US indie. *Parting Glances* also brought to the fore the thinly veiled homophobia in the industry. Many companies passed on the film because of its refusal to simply marginalise the sexuality of its characters, and on one infamous occasion a screening theatre projectionist threatened to pull the plug after viewing an early scene featuring two men kissing.

The legacy of the film cannot be undervalued. As well as giving Buscemi his first starring role and acting as the springboard for his enduring association with the US independent scene, *Parting Glances* certainly opened the doors for a new influx of openly gay, in-your-face directors who fought to have their increasingly experimental and uncompromising films positively positioned as such. The ensuing emergence of the New Queer Cinema movement was in no small part due to the activities of Christine Vachon, an assistant editor on *Parting Glances* who went on to form feisty producer alliances with directors such as Gregg Araki, Todd Haynes and Tom Kalin.

Sadly, Sherwood never got to complete another feature, succumbing to AIDS in 1990.

Dir: Bill Sherwood; **Prod**: Oram Mandel, Arthur Silverman; **Scr**: Bill Sherwood; **DOP**: Jacek Laskus; **Editor**: Bill Sherwood; **Score**: Uncredited; **Main Cast**: Richard Ganoung, John Bolger, Steve Buscemi, Adam Nathan.

π *(Pi)*
US, 1997 – 84 mins
Darren Aronofsky

Aronofsky's π marked a literate, challenging and highly original debut. It drew upon inspirations as diverse as Shinya Tsukamoto's body horror classic *Tetsuo: The Iron Man* (1991), the novels of William Gibson and the theories and philosophies of Baudrillard and Hegel.

Maximillian Cohen (Gullette, who, with Aronofsky and producer Eric Watson, came up with the premise for the film) is a reclusive mathematician and electronics whizz kid who believes that mathematics is the language of nature and that everything can be expressed in mathematical terms. From his chaotic Chinatown apartment, Cohen and his self-assembled computer, Euclid, apparently discover a number that signifies the underlying numerical pattern behind the global stock market. Max is befriended by Lenny (Shenkman), a Hasidic Jew who believes that the Kabbalah and the Torah are numerical codes sent from God. Max's findings also arouse the intense attentions of pushy businesswoman Marcy Dawson (Hart). Plagued by migraines and subsisting on a diet of painkillers and exhaustion, Max, despite the warnings of his former teacher Sol (Margolis) to give up his work, teeters on the brink of physical and mental meltdown.

An intense, uncomfortable and often unsettling viewing experience, Aronofsky conveys Max's off-kilter psychosis and apparent descent into a paranoid, psychological hinterland that recalls Lynch's similarly striking *Eraserhead* (1976). The film's surreal, drug-induced hallucinatory sequences (effectively and cheaply shot on high-contrast black and white 16mm stock) also display a Buñuelian eye for the disturbingly absurd. Brian Emrich's impressive, cacophonous sound design further compounds the sense of millennial doom, corporate skulduggery and impending madness, and is augmented by a largely electronic, avant-garde soundtrack featuring Autrechre and Banco de Gaia. Describing the project as a digital take on the story of Faust, Gullette completes the mix, giving a haunted, nervy performance that conveys anxiety and instability with an intensity unmatched on screen since Peter Greene in Lodge Kerrigan's *Clean, Shaven* (1993).

Scholars have questioned the film-makers' understanding of some of the basic tenets of maths and physics that are so essential to its plot and structure. π is certainly guilty of regurgitating certain cinematic stereotypes that constantly equate genius with, in the first instance, eccentricity and, in the second, madness. But, such criticisms aside and at times in spite of the film's wish to stress its impressive IQ, π succeeds as an examination of the destructive nature of obsession and as a surprisingly assured, albeit metaphysical thriller. The film became 1997's must-see independent movie, and provoked a bidding war for distribution rights after a hugely successful Sundance screening that netted the talented Aronofsky the Best Director award. *Requiem for a Dream* (2000) offered confirmation of both Aronofsky's pessimistic worldview and his abilities.

Dir: Darren Aronofsky; **Prod**: Eric Watson; **Scr**: Darren Aronofsky; **DOP**: Matthew Libatique; **Editor**: Oren Sarch; **Score**: Clint Mansell; **Main Cast**: Sean Gullette, Mark Margolis, Ben Shenkman, Pamela Hart.

Pink Flamingos
US, 1972 – 95 mins
John Waters

Born in Baltimore, which, portrayed as a gloriously OTT hotbed of degeneracy has continued as the setting for his films, Waters cites his middle-class, Catholic upbringing and frequent forays into local sex cinemas as formative influences. Waters initially experimented with 8mm shorts in which no subject or act was too profane to represent, and drew together a motley repertory company, including Mink Stole, local legend Edith Massey and larger-than-life transvestite Divine. (Waters continued to work with many of his cohorts long after his assimilation into the Hollywood mainstream as the king of kitsch.)

Pink Flamingos was to act as Waters' breakthrough picture and remains his signature piece, expanding upon the negligible production values, gloriously poor taste and excessive vulgarity of his previous features, *Mondo Trasho* (1969) and *Multiple Maniacs* (1970). The film takes as its premise the attempts of Raymond and Connie Marble (Lochary and Stole), two pornographers, heroin dealers and all-round sexual deviants, to wrest from local rival Divine, a.k.a Babs Johnson, the coveted title of the filthiest person in the world. As the competition hots up, the Marbles throw down the gauntlet by sending Divine a year-old turd before burning down the trailer home she shares with the egg-guzzling Mama Edie (Edith Massey) and her chicken-fixated son Crackers (Danny Mills). Swearing revenge, Divine captures the Marbles and tars and feathers them before slaying them in front of reporters, declaring, 'I am God . . . killing and blood make me cum'. The film famously concludes with Divine reaffirming her right to the title by devouring freshly laid dog excrement, an act that one hopes required but a single take.

(Opposite page) 'I am God . . . killing and blood make me cum'. Divine, a.k.a. Babs Johnson as the self-proclaimed 'filthiest person in the world' in *Pink Flamingos*

Waters has on occasion insisted that for him the act of someone throwing up during one of his movies would be the equivalent of a standing ovation; *Pink Flamingos* delivered a hearty and sustained round of applause. Not for sensitive souls, though! In addition to the memorable final shot, there are also numerous other notable and vaguely disgusting moments, including copulation with a chicken (Waters quipped that it was subsequently cooked and eaten), a plethora of scatological references, a close-up shot of a youth flexing his anus and references to rape, torture and incest. Those not seduced by Waters' gleeful revelling in abominable behaviour and general irreverence have pointed to fascistic overtones in the film and deemed its unique brand of humour corrupting and irresponsible.

Pink Flamingos is defined by a primitive visual style, performances that are intentionally camp and uneven, and an at-best rudimentary grasp of film skills. The frills-free camera work, editing and production values befit the film's guerrilla-style aesthetic and $12,000 budget. Upon release, the film assumed instant cult status, becoming an immediate underground success on the late-night repertory circuit. Gleefully promoted as the most disgusting picture ever made, the film turned New Line from a fledgling outfit into one of the most innovative, daring and successful American independent distributors.

Dir: John Waters; **Prod**: John Waters; **Scr**: John Waters; **DOP**: John Waters; **Editor**: John Waters; **Score**: Uncredited; **Main Cast**: Divine, David Lochary, Mink Stole, Mary Vivian Pearce.

Poison
US, 1990 – 85 mins
Todd Haynes

Former art, semiology and psychology student Haynes was courted by Disney and United Artists after having shown considerable promise with the subversive and formally daring *Superstar: The Karen Carpenter Story* (1987), a witty and perceptive meditation on how popular culture affects society on multiple levels. Resisting their overtures, Haynes opted to establish an independent partnership with *über* producer Christine Vachon. The result was *Poison*, Haynes' $200,000 debut feature. Conceived as a tribute to the work of Jean Genet and expressing an explicit gay sensibility, the provocative and intelligent film won Sundance's 1991 Grand Jury Prize and placed Haynes at the vanguard of the emerging New Queer Cinema movement.

The film was prompted, in part, by the American Right's dismissal of the AIDS crisis and a rejection of a 'positive' image of gay cinema in favour of a more complex analysis of what society regards as transgressive or deviant. *Poison* calculatedly adopts a disparate range of styles and genres. Tripartite in structure, each separate narrative segment interweaves with little apparent overlap, allowing the spectator a refreshing opportunity to reflect on the issues with which Haynes engages, namely sexuality, oppression, alienation, non-conformity and persecution.

Poison begins with *Hero*, a mockumentary that adopts the form of a suburban TV news location report into the disappearance of Richie Beacon, a seven-year-old boy, who apparently flew away after murdering his father. The statements of Richie's peers reveal the retaliatory nature of the crime, committed in response to the beatings his father administered to his mother on discovering that his wife was sleeping with their Hispanic gardener (echoes of Haynes' *Far from Heaven*, 2002, abound). Concerned with violence and small-town hysteria, *Hero* remains the most elusive segment. The black and white *Horror* is a historically acute pastiche of 50s' B-movie sci-fis, in which a scientist researching the mysteries of the sex drive accidentally imbibes his own serum. Suffering hideous physical mutations that make him repellent to society, Dr Graves becomes the subject of a police witch-hunt after he kills a woman in a bar that he has infected with his condition. The most accessible section, *Horror* serves as a parable about AIDS and about mainstream cinema's and popular culture's tendency to stigmatise illness as an object of horror and equate sex, particularly of the non-heterosexual variety, with disease and decay.

The only sequence that relates directly to Genet's work (it's based on the autobiographical *Thief's Journal*), *Homo* is part claustrophobic, grim prison drama and part lyrical homage to a more innocent era of sexuality that traces the shifting sexual relationship between two inmates who knew each other as youths in reform school.

Dr Graves (Larry Maxwell) with his sex drive serum in the *Horror* segment of *Poison*. An evocation of the 1950s' horror movie, *Horror* mediates on the stigmatisation of illness and the equation of sex with disease within the mainstream media

Concluding with a brutal rape, *Homo* examines contrasting notions of 'masculine' and 'feminine' behaviour in the restricted prison environment.

Poison was condemned as pornography by the Reverend Donald Wildmon's American Family Association. Wildmon also conducted a campaign against the National Endowment for the Arts, which had contributed completion funding. Ironically, Wildmon's objections merely increased the film's media profile and added to its impressive commercial performance in the States, where the film (initially released on a single print but later increased to seven) took just under $790,000. It remains challenging and compelling viewing.

Dir: Todd Haynes; **Prod**: Christine Vachon; **Scr**: Todd Haynes; **DOP**: Maryse Alberti; **Editor**: James Lyons, Todd Haynes; **Score**: James Bennett; **Main Cast**: Edith Meeks, Scott Renderer, James Lyons, John R. Lombardi.

Portrait of Jason
US, 1967 – 100 mins
Shirley Clarke

Portrait of Jason is the engrossing final part of a 60s' trilogy of films in which former experimental film-maker Clarke challenged practices of the American cinema vérité movement. In works such as 1961's *The Connection* (Clarke's first collaboration with her black lover Carl Lee) and 1963's *The Cool World*, Clarke purposefully blurred the line between documentary and fiction, and offered compelling portraits of under-represented and marginalised African-American figures. This approach called into question the position of natural authority and objective reality asserted by vérité documentarists such as D. A. Pennebaker and Richard Leacock.

Entirely self-funded and filmed in Clarke's room at the Chelsea Hotel, *Portrait* stands as Clarke's most sustained critique of vérité techniques, and shares Warhol's distrust of artifice and his preference for frills-free filming techniques. The 100-minute film evolved from a continuous twelve-hour, single-take interview with Jason Holliday (real name Aaron Paine), a black, thirty-three-year-old homosexual prostitute and would-be raconteur. Filmed on a single camera in real time as a response to Pennebaker and co'.s offering of climactic, edited highlights, Jason's initially highly entertaining and colourful monologue recounting his childhood, service as a houseboy and 'white boy fever' is punctuated only by brief, out-of-focus, extreme close-ups followed by fades to black. These moments signal Clarke's changing of the camera magazine.

Jason smokes and sips scotch, his reminiscences initially encouraged and guided by the off-screen voices of Clarke and Carl Lee (Clarke makes explicit her role as director by issuing technical instructions and directions regarding Jason's positioning). They prompt, 'Hey Jason, do one of your nightclub routines'. However, as Jason's histrionics for the benefit of the camera increase, Clarke and Lee become aggressive and antagonistic, questioning the authenticity and veracity of his comments with mocking slurs such as 'be honest, motherfucker'. At this point, Jason is reduced to tears. Displaying a continued preoccupation with ghetto subcultures (the film profoundly influenced Marlon T. Riggs in its willingness to engage with issues of black maleness and sexuality), *Portrait* serves as a provocative investigation and riff on the manipulative nature of performance and the supposedly impartial mediation of 'truth' in documentary film-making.

Despite the validity and intelligence of Clarke's intentions there are however, undoubtedly moments in which *Portrait* feels uncomfortably exploitative. Holliday is no doubt seduced by the opportunity to regale an audience with his outrageous, 'autobiographical' tales, and the suspicion remains that his trust is somewhat betrayed by Clarke, who ultimately uses Holliday's personal confessions merely to prove an admittedly cogent point about the nature of filmed reality. Given Jason's

Jason Holliday (real name Aaron Paine) reaches breaking point. *Portrait of Jason*

showmanship there's no denying that there is a degree of mutual media manipulation, but Jason's closing comment that he found the experience 'beautiful' would seem to suggest a lack of complicity and an endorsement of the fact that Clarke, as director and editor, ultimately wields the greater power.

Dir: Shirley Clarke; **Prod**: Shirley Clarke; **Scr**: N/A; **DOP**: Jeri Sapanen; **Editor**: Shirley Clarke; **Score**: N/A; **Main Cast**: Jason Holliday (Aaron Paine).

Reservoir Dogs
US, 1991 – 99 mins
Quentin Tarantino

Acquired by Miramax following a frenzied Sundance screening at which even US indie sage John Pierson admits to having been 'blown away' (Pierson, 1996, p. 213), *Reservoir Dogs* had an impact on the industry that was almost as radical as *sex, lies and videotape* (1989). The film's success placed its celluloid junkie director, a former clerk at LA's Video Archives store, at the forefront of a new wave of aspirant young film-makers.

Imbued with a vast array of stylistic and structural references to the works of other film-makers, *Reservoir Dogs* is a tale of honour among a bunch of nameless, low-life crooks assembled by an old-time hood. The spirit of *Mean Streets* (1973) looms large as does *The Killing* (1956), *City on Fire* (1987) and *The Wild Bunch* (1969). The exaggerated, amoral violence and nihilistic denouement also recalls Takeshi Kitano. This tendency to homage or freely borrow from the work of others inspired conflicting critical reactions. Some saw Tarantino as a cine-literate and inspired genre stylist or *metteur en scène* in the style of Godard; others, such as Geoff Andrew have discerned a disregard for originality and tendency to 'sample' the work of others that for older viewers 'may smack of plagiarism' (Andrew, 1998, p. 317).

But skilfully crafted, originality does lie in Tarantino's daring and elaborate approach to narrative and structure. *Reservoir Dogs* unfolds as a series of elaborate tales within tales, allowing for minutely detailed and seemingly inconsequential but ultimately intrinsic plot and character digressions. Audaciously, the heist is never revealed; Tarantino's real interest lies in events leading up to its thwarted execution and bloody aftermath. Thus, from the opening diner sequence the film abruptly cuts to the sounds of a fatally wounded Mr Orange (Roth) being driven by Mr White (Keitel, who alongside Monte Hellman co-produces) to the abandoned warehouse where the criminals reconvene. As Orange slowly bleeds to death, Tarantino inserts episodes from the past to reveal the machinations of the recruitment process and intersecting lives of the criminals. Of equal note and influence (perhaps the most recognisable motif of his career) is Tarantino's gift for snappy, conversational dialogue, which riffs on popular culture: *Reservoir Dogs* begins with the sharp-suited criminals expansively discussing the connotations of the lyrics to Madonna's 'Like a Virgin'.

Bolstered by a recognisable cast, including Buscemi and Keitel, and a modest budget funded by a home video company, the film generated controversy for its blunt violence. To the ironic radio airing of 'Stuck in the Middle with You', Michael Madsen's psychopathic Mr Blonde goes to work on a policeman's ear with a razor. During this, the film's most infamous moment, Tarantino pans the camera to avert our gaze from the act itself. Indeed, though Tarantino could be said to use violence as a means of providing spectacle, it is more often purely a generic convention and a further component in his gleeful approach to the art of storytelling.

Though only a modest commercial success in part due to its restrictive rating, *Reservoir Dogs'* appearance on home video ensured that it became a cultural phenomenon. A loyal legion of dedicated Tarantino admirers sprang up and, seduced by the stylised violence and hip post-modern dialogue, crowned him the future of American cinema. Similarly awed and inspired by the film's potentially lucrative appeal, the industry frantically looked for duplicates, precipitating an unwholesomely prolonged period that produced a slew of brash, knock-off imitations made by second-rate copyists.

Dir: Quentin Tarantino; **Prod**: Lawrence Bender; **Scr**: Quentin Tarantino; **DOP**: Andrzej Sekula; **Editor**: Sally Menke; **Score**: Karyn Rachtman; **Main Cast**: Harvey Keitel, Tim Roth, Michael Madsen, Steve Buscemi.

Return of the Secaucus Seven
US, 1979 – 110 mins
John Sayles

Having penned a number of short stories and two ambitious novels while working as an actor in summer stock, Sayles carved a name for himself as an intelligent, literate writer of superior, humanist exploitation films produced by Corman's New World Pictures. Diligently accruing the proceeds earned on *Piranha* (1978), *The Lady in Red* (1979), and future contracted titles *Alligator* (1980) and *The Howling* (1980), Sayles, in the manner of Cassavetes before him, ploughed the money into his own self financed (to the tune of $60,000), -written and -directed $125,000 debut feature, *Return of the Secaucus Seven*.

Shot on free locations with actors drawn from the writer-director's Eastern Slope Playhouse (they provided their own wardrobe and make-up), the 16mm film, partly inspired by Alain Tanner's *Jonah, Who Will Be 25 in the Year 2000* (1975), is an affectionately observed ensemble drama that deals with the annual New Hampshire reunion of several college friends. The group were formerly bound by the shared moral and political activism of 60s' campus life (Sayles subtly reveals the origin of their radical titular collective: a night spent in jail en route to a Washington demonstration), and since graduation they have all chosen different paths. Despite the passage of time and the changing nature of their relationships, they remain linked by shared experience and common humanity.

The film displays a rare willingness to focus on the concerns of the thirty-something generation, whose values were all but dismissed by Reagan-era America, and an acuity that arises from Sayles' intelligent dialogue. This stock-in-trade of the resourceful low-budget writer-director, and the film's acute sense of character, in part mask Sayles' technical limitations (overcome in later films) and economic constraints. Sayles kept camera movement to a relative minimum, and cited *Nashville* (1975) as the inspiration for the frequent cutting between characters as fresh allegiances and interrelationships evolve.

Made pre-Sundance, the film was screened at various American festivals before being transferred to 35mm and commercially released in a grass-roots fashion on the East and West coasts. A critical and commercial success (making a profit of $120,000 with estimated gross film rentals of $800,000), the film brought Sayles the Los Angeles Film Critics Best Screenplay award and a 'genius' grant from the MacArthur Foundation. With its liberal sensibilities, psychologically rounded characters and an interest in communities under threat, *Secaucus Seven* set the template from which Sayles has continued to work. His works are self-financed through his intermittent journeyman script work on Hollywood pictures. The film was also important in establishing an ongoing repertory group of collaborators, including his partner and producer Maggie Renzi, composer Mason Daring and actors David Strathairn and Gordon Clapp.

Over and above the role the film played in shaping Sayles' career, *Secaucus Seven* is a milestone picture in the history of American independent cinema. It became one of the first films to actively promote the virtues of its minuscule budget in relation to its domestic gross and provided a timely reminder of a cinema that was in all ways at odds with mainstream Hollywood.

Dir: John Sayles; **Prod**: Jeffrey Nelson, William Aydelott; **Scr**: John Sayles; **DOP**: Austin De Besche; **Editor**: John Sayles; **Score**: Guy Van Duser, Bill Staines, Timothy Jackson, Mason Daring; **Main Cast**: Bruce Macdonald, Adam Lefevre, Gordon Clapp, Maggie Renzi.

(Opposite page) Made for just $125,000 and successfully released in a grass-roots fashion on the East and West coasts, John Sayles' *Return of the Secaucus Seven* represents a milestone moment in American independent cinema

Roger & Me
US, 1989 – 90 mins
Michael Moore

In the same year that Soderbergh's *sex, lies and videotape* (1989) was changing perceptions of low-budget features, former investigative journalist turned film-maker Moore was about to have a similar effect on the documentary. Shot on 16mm (but blown up to 35mm) for an approximate budget of $160,000, *Roger & Me* not only ignited a heated debate concerning documentary aesthetics but also transformed the ways documentaries were distributed, marketed and consumed.

Filmed under the title of *A Humorous Look at how General Motors Destroyed Flint, Michigan*, the film is an often hilarious and scathing examination of industrial ruthlessness which traces the decline of Moore's hometown of Flint, Michigan, after General Motors' systematic and poorly implemented closure of its production plants. Sanctioned by General Motors' chairman Roger Smith, this action resulted in social and economic deprivation, most directly through the loss of thousands of local jobs. *Roger & Me* was filmed over a three-year period. Archive footage and interviews with local celebrities, dignitaries and former General Motors' employees are inventively interspersed with Moore's dogged attempts to track down and confront Smith with the consequences of his actions.

Viewed as a precursor of the 'subject pursued' style of documentary refined by figures such as Nick Broomfield (similarly chastised for being too prominent a figure in his work), *Roger & Me* is ostensibly simplistic. It is even at times primitive in style (basically Moore tracked by a very small camera crew). The alchemy and subsequent controversy arose from Wendy Stanzler and Jennifer Beman's stylish editing which, in providing the film with a distinctive narrative thrust, plays fast and free with chronology in favour of humour, metaphor and exaggeration. The film premiered to ecstatic notices at the Telluride Film Festival and subsequently enjoyed significant critical and public support. However,

Moore's approach also led to accusations that he'd sacrificed the principles of journalistic accuracy and betrayed the documentary format. Moore, as John Pierson describes in *Spike Mike Slackers and Dykes'* excellent chapter on the film, was understandably defensive, making no apologies for breaking the cardinal rule of documentary by being entertaining and accessible (Pierson, 1996, pp. 137–76). Moore described the work as belonging to a new sub-genre: the 'docucomedy'.

Roger & Me's irreverent attitude to chronology and its emphasis on entertainment may have sabotaged what appeared to be a sure-fire Academy Award nomination in the Best Documentary category, but this did the film no harm in terms of securing a lucrative distribution deal. Warner Bros. eventually won the race for distribution rights, after agreeing to the asking price of $3 million, and Moore's principled list of contract clauses (including 25,000 free tickets for unemployed auto workers and one empty seat to be left available at every single show in every single theatre for Roger Smith). Aggressively marketed with little mention of the fact that it was a non-fiction work, the film avoided the limited release route (at one point the film was on 307 screens) and was instead promoted to mainstream, multiplex audiences, who in the climate of intense dissatisfaction with Reaganite politics, ensured that with a first-run theatrical gross of $7 million it became one of the most successful non-concert documentaries in history.

Dir: Michael Moore; **Prod**: Michael Moore; **Scr**: Michael Moore; **DOP**: Christopher Beaver, John Prusak, Kevin Rafferty, Bruce Schermer; **Editor**: Wendy Stanzler, Jennifer Beman; **Score**: Uncredited; **Main Cast**: Michael Moore, Roger Smith.

Salt of the Earth
US, 1953 – 94 mins
Herbert J. Biberman

Salt of the Earth is a subversive, courageous and profoundly radical work. Its independence lies not only in the adverse circumstances surrounding its production and the autonomous spirit in which it was made but also in its rigorous ideological and political opposition to McCarthyism.

Director Biberman, producer Paul Jarrico, screenwriter Michael Wilson, composer Sol Kaplan and actor Will Geer were among the 'Hollywood Ten' blacklisted because of their refusal to co-operate with the House Un-American Activities Committee. Biberman declined to answer Congressional questions on First Amendment grounds, a stance that resulted in a stay in federal prison. *Salt of the Earth* therefore represents nothing less than acute defiance. Independently financed by the Mine, Mill, and Smelter Workers of America (one of eleven unions expelled by the Congress of Industrial Organizations in 1949 because of Communist sympathies), the production suffered not only continual harassment from the FBI but the repatriation of veteran leading Mexican actress Rosaura Revueltas before filming could be completed. Opposition to the picture continued post-production and it was largely the intervention of Electrical Workers Union film-maker Haskell Wexler that enabled the finished film to be processed. Wexler would go on to become one of America's most renowned cinematographers, working on John Sayles' *Matewan* (1983), a picture owing a huge debt to *Salt of the Earth* in both subject matter and sensibility.

Set in the New Mexican community of Zinc Town and based on actual historical events, *Salt of the Earth* deals with the uprising of Mexican mineworkers in protest against the unbearable conditions in which they are forced to live. In stark contrast is the reasonable quality of life enjoyed by their Anglo co-employees. Featuring among its cast many non-professional actors and real mineworkers, and efficiently shot in black and white to capture the grime of its environment, the film focuses on a downtrodden Mexican worker, Ramon Quintero (Chacon) and his long-suffering pregnant wife (Revueltas). Targeting racism, workers' rights and the rapidly developing divide emerging in the wake of America's post-war economic boom, the film's modern, forward-thinking sensibility is also reflected in its proto-feminist undertones. The women are initially forced to defer to a traditional macho male ethos, but as the strike and the violent actions of company-employed officials intensify (Geer, incidentally, plays a venal local sheriff) they begin to take a more active role in events, standing side by side with their husbands both on the picket line and in jail.

The decision of the Projectionists' Union to refuse to screen it ensured that *Salt of the Earth* was effectively banned in America. Consigned to independently owned drive-ins and a smattering of sympathetic theatres, the film received only nominal distribution and exhibition in its homeland (wider circulation was secured in Latin America) and so passed largely unseen. However, the film was greeted with acclaim in Communist circles (it was apparently approved of at the highest levels in Moscow) and in more liberal publications, and retrospectively its reputation and impact have continued to grow.

Dir: Herbert J. Biberman; **Prod**: Paul Jarrico; **Scr**: Michael Wilson; **DOP**: Stanley Meredith, Leonard Stark; **Editor**: Ed Spiegel, Joan Laird; **Score**: Sol Kaplan; **Main Cast**: Rosaura Revueltas, Juan Chacon, Will Geer, Mervin Williams.

Schizopolis
US, 1996 – 96 mins
Steven Soderbergh

Having scaled the critical and commercial heights with *sex, lies and videotape* (1989), Soderbergh's career seemed to flounder after three poorly received, esoteric and intelligent studio projects, *Kafka* (1991), *King of the Hill* (1993) and *The Underneath* (1995). The latter film left the director so dissatisfied with the practices of mainstream production that for his next project he next turned his back on commercial film-making in order to give free rein to his increasingly repressed anarchic personality and puckish approach to directing; *Schizopolis* (1996) is the dazzling result.

Shot guerrilla-style on old Arri camera equipment over a ten-month period in Florida, *Schizopolis* was made with $250,000 Soderbergh had coaxed out of Universal, having assured them he was making something they would never want to see. With a small crew, many of whom doubled as technicians and actors (the director himself undertook script and photography duties and also played the two lead roles), Soderbergh set about producing a film that grew out of his interest in parallel time structures, New Age religion and the American obsession with dentistry.

A succinct synopsis is impossible, suffice to say that *Schizopolis* tells the tale of Fletcher Munson (Soderbergh), a man beset by work anxieties who may or may not be having an affair with his own wife, played, with post-modernist verve, by Betsy Brantley, Soderbergh's real-life spouse from whom he separated prior to filming. It is certainly film as therapy. As well as displaying an interest in selfhood and identity, the film is also concerned with the complexity of language, as evidenced by the progressively intelligible gibberish in which the characters converse.

Working assiduously to defy convention and easy categorisation, the film is peppered with numerous narrative deviations and comical visual asides, such as a naked lunatic intermittently pursued by hospital orderlies. *Schizopolis* adopts a wilfully irreverent, free-form style and approach to narrative cause and effect with the speeded-up action sequences and faux straight-to-camera character interviews recalling the work of Soderbergh's hero, Richard Lester. Influences as disparate as Luis Buñuel and Jacques Tati can also be discerned.

The general reaction to the film ranged from incomprehension to barely suppressed hostility. In Cannes, where Harvey Weinstein wanted to buy it sight unseen for a million dollars, Soderbergh told him he'd be wise to see it first. He did and withdrew his offer; the mass walk-outs in Cannes were an eerie portent. Even among the independent sector, positive reaction was minimal. 'The irony of the situation really amused me – here I'd made about as independent minded a film as one could make, and the independents are all afraid of it' (Soderbergh, 1999, p. 46).

An entirely uninhibited, determinedly complex and delightfully comic work that acts as an intelligent commentary on the medium of film itself, *Schizopolis* was a bold and rewarding move that restored Soderbergh's appetite and confidence. His most rarely seen work, it has in tone, structure and approach served as a touchstone for his subsequent output and is credited by the director as allowing him to find the right balance between experimentation and convention in subsequent studio outings.

Dir: Steven Soderbergh; **Prod**: John Hardy; **Scr**: Steven Soderbergh; **DOP**: Steven Soderbergh; **Editor**: Sarah Flack; **Score**: Cliff Martinez; **Main Cast**: Steven Soderbergh, Betsy Brantley, David Jensen, Mike Malone.

sex, lies and videotape
US, 1989 – 100 mins
Steven Soderbergh

sex, lies and videotape ranks among the most auspicious feature debuts
in contemporary cinema. Few debuts since Hopper's *Easy Rider* (1969)
have had so lasting an effect on the American production landscape in
generating a clamour for low-budget projects. It was also by many
yardsticks the most important and influential American independent
picture in recent memory, though the majority of the film's $1.2 million
budget was provided by the video division of Columbia.

Soderbergh was a cineaste from an early age with a taste for the
formal and structural characteristics of European cinema. He drew upon
the fall-out from a recent failed relationship and the premise of his earlier
short, *Winston*, for his risqué-titled but subtle, thought-provoking and
insightful ensemble drama. Head on, it tackles sexuality and its off-
shoots: inhibition, insatiability and impotence. Moreover, the film calls
into question the way sexuality is portrayed and sold in the media while
also acting as a profound meditation on voyeuristic viewing experiences.

Graham Dalton (Spader), an impotent drifter who makes videotapes
of women recounting their sexual experiences, returns to Baton Rouge to
visit John Mullaney (Gallagher), a successful lawyer whose marriage to
the sexless Ann (MacDowell) is lent added spice by his affair with her
voracious sister, Cynthia (Giacomo). Filmed quickly and relatively cheaply
in Louisiana with relative unknowns and a crew largely made up of
Soderbergh's cohorts from his student days, the film combines an
ostensibly simplistic formal aesthetic (relatively static medium long shots),
a talk-is-cheap philosophy (the writer-director's assured and pithy
dialogue is used to intelligent effect), and an experimental aspect, shown
by the incorporation of the low-density video footage on which Graham
conducts his interviews. It is through this medium that Soderbergh,
belying the film's humble origins and his own relative lack of experience
as a film-maker, is able to explore the concept of dual time frames, the

way in which we seek to catalogue experiences through video documentation, and the spectator's desire for visual gratification.

Debuting at the Sundance Film Festival, the film was immediately hailed as the most original American feature in recent memory. Soderbergh was tagged by the press as the successor to figures such as Cassavetes and Sayles as the doyen of indie directors. And it exploded onto the international scene following its 1989 Cannes Palme d'Or success. An unsuspecting Soderbergh, the youngest-ever winner of the award, was catapulted even further into the limelight; 'It's all down hill from here', he was heard to bemusedly remark. As well as helping to establish the US independent distributor powerhouse Miramax, the film also put Sundance on the map, turning it into a major event and an attractive and lucrative shop window for new talent, producers and distributors. John Pierson describes the film as having 'radically and demonstrably changed the business' (Pierson, 1996, p. 2).

The critical fanfare and industry repercussions the film generated were more than matched by its commercial success. In making back its

Life through a lens: Andie MacDowell as Ann in *sex, lies and videotape*

cost many times over (to date it has grossed over $100 million worldwide), *sex* became a key work in the rejuvenation and development of US independent cinema and, according to Pierson, the fluke financial benchmark of potential for an independent film. Precipitating Soderbergh's remarkable film-making career and exhibiting similar thematic concerns so eloquently mined by Canadian film-maker Atom Egoyan, particularly in early work such as *Family Viewing* (1987), it is an enduring triumph of intelligent, low-budget film-making.

Dir: Steven Soderbergh; **Prod**: Robert Newmyer, John Hardy; **Scr**: Steven Soderbergh; **DOP**: Walt Lloyd; **Editor**: Steven Soderbergh; **Score**: Cliff Martinez; **Main Cast**: James Spader, Andie MacDowell, Peter Gallagher, Laura San Giacomo.

Shadows
US, 1959 – 87 mins
John Cassavetes

Viewed as the *Citizen Kane* (1941) of American independent cinema, *Shadows* opened the door for a new kind of uncompromising and self-sufficient film-making: 'There were no more excuses. If he could do it, so could we', commented Scorsese (Thompson and Christie, 1989, p. 15). Intermittently made between 1957 and 1959, the film evolved from an improvisation dealing with miscegenation in one of Cassavetes' acting workshops.

Intrigued by the notion of 'off-Broadway movies' (Carney, 2001a, p. 56), Cassavetes gave an interview to the *New York Times* announcing his plans to turn the piece into a $7,500 amateur production. 'We had no intention of offering it for commercial distribution. It was an experiment all the way' (Ibid., p. 57). After persuading cameraman Erich Kollmar to join up, Cassavetes appeared on Jean Shepherd's 'Night People' radio show, imploring listeners to send donations for a film about the ordinary people seldom seen in Hollywood movies. The irrepressible Cassavetes also talked Deluxe Film Labs into donating stock and processing facilities and borrowed 16mm equipment from fellow film-maker Shirley Clarke. Intended to capture the spontaneity of the actors and lend empowering mobility to the film-maker (much of the film was shot without permission on New York's sidewalks), the lightweight Arriflex camera provided by Kollmar would lend *Shadows* its influential hand-held, free-focus visual aesthetic. It was named after an actor's etching, and shot in black and white with a skeleton six-person crew.

Shadows offers a frank observation of the tensions and lives of three siblings in an African-American family in which two of the siblings, Ben and Lelia, are light-skinned and able to 'pass' for white. Cassavetes demanded that the actors retain their real names to reflect the actual conflicts within the group, but saw the film as being concerned with human problems as opposed simply to racial ones. The film features an

The *Citizen Kane* of American independent cinema? John Cassavetes' influential *Shadows*

elliptical narrative, ten-minute takes and jagged editing. Cassavetes attributed *Shadows*' conception and style to the Italian neo-realists while also professing admiration for Welles' pioneering spirit. Landmark picture though it is, Cassavetes expert Ray Carney describes the common tendency to view the film as the first American independent as displaying an 'ignorance of the history of the American independent film' (Ibid., p. 61) and a disregard for the early 50s' work of Morris Engel, Lionel Rogosin and Shirley Clarke.

Having shot and printed 60,000 feet of material, the editing process confirmed Cassavetes' inexperience and technical limitations. The sound was so poorly recorded that much of it was unusable. Nobody had kept a record of what was said, so Cassavetes was forced to employ lip readers so that dialogue could be dubbed. Featuring a be-bop score by Charles Mingus and Shafi Hadi, *Shadows* was finally screened in

November 1958 at New York's Paris Theatre, almost two years and $25,000 after filming originally began. The screening was not a success, acting, according to Cassavetes, as a 'shattering admission of our own ineptness' (Ibid., p. 81). Having destroyed much of the unused footage, Cassavetes was forced to collaborate with screenwriter Robert Alan Aurthur on over an hour of new scenes that were intercut with the original print during the summer of 1959. The final budget rose to $40,000, much of it financed by Cassavetes' studio acting roles. With less than twenty-five minutes of the original version remaining, the version of *Shadows* now known today was blown up to 35mm and screened in a Cinema of Improvisation programme. Shortly before his death, Cassavetes confessed to Carney that little of the finished film was in fact improvised.

Shadows influenced many aspects of independent film-making, redefining film distribution in particular. It was a critical and commercial sensation in Britain and Europe, but the American release was blighted by constant references to its low-budget origins and technical deficiencies by reviewers still largely in thrall to Hollywood production values. Chastened by the experience (and his ill-fated studio sojourns), Cassavetes formed Faces Films to enable him to self-distribute his work and retain ownership of it.

Dir: John Cassavetes; **Prod**: Maurice McEndree; **Scr**: John Cassavetes; **DOP**: Erich Kollmar; **Editor**: Len Appelson, Maurice McEndree; **Score**: Charles Mingus, Shafi Hadi; **Main Cast**: Lelia Goldoni, Ben Carruthers, Hugh Hurd, Anthony Ray.

Sherman's March
US, 1985 – 160 mins
Ross McElwee

A former Richard Leacock student, McElwee emerged from what William Rothman in *Documentary Film Classics* terms the second generation of American cinéma vérité directors (Rothman, 1997). The work of this group, according to Rothman, was distinguished by the acknowledgment on camera of their presence and personal participation in the stories they told. *Sherman's March* (for Rothman, the 'grand epic', Ibid., p. xii) also introduces an ironic perspective that makes explicit the extent to which the documentarist has knowingly become the subject of his own story. Michael Moore, Nick Broomfield and Nanni Moretti are key practitioners of this approach; the proliferation of made-for-television video diaries is its ugly conclusion.

Described by John Pierson as 'an enormously charming and moving personal essay', (Pierson, 1996, p. 107) *Sherman's March* originated when McElwee received a grant to make a documentary tracing American Civil War General William Tecumseh Sherman's devastating march through the American South and the consequent (and as yet unhealed) wounds of the civilian population. The pervading anxieties of the global politics of the 1980s and the impending threat of nuclear war made suitable parallels for Sherman's destructive trail. Abandoned by his girlfriend on the eve of filming, McElwee returned dejectedly to his family home in Charlotte, North Carolina, with the intention of aborting the project. Encouraged, however, by his sister's promptings that he use his camera as a conversation piece to meet women, McElwee returned to the project, adopting the subtitle, *A Meditation on the Possibility of Romantic Love in the South During an Era of Nuclear Weapons Proliferation*. He then appropriated Sherman's conquering march for his own journey in search of an understanding of Southern womanhood and a flickeringly vengeful quest for romantic fulfilment.

Though historical ironies are revealed about the feared general (a series of disastrous business ventures left him with an obsessive sense of failure), after the narrated introduction Sherman only fleetingly appears as a metaphor for McElwee's own expedition and romantic misadventures. On his travels McElwee turns his camera on several invariably resilient women, including Mary, a former girlfriend; Pat, an aspiring actress whose dreams centre on meeting Burt Reynolds (a model of the larger-than-life masculinity McElwee feels himself to lack); Claudia, a survivalist; Jackie, a nuclear campaigner; and Charleen, who advises him, 'This isn't art Ross. This is life.' Each responds differently to the attentions of the camera, with McElwee well aware of its intrusive nature. Towards the conclusion, McElwee – who we later learn finds love with a teacher in Boston – steps out from behind the camera to be filmed by a third party. The moment, which occurs while addressing a statue at the site of Sherman's final victory, is illustrative of what Ellen Draper, writing in *Film Quarterly*, describes as a 'complex discussion of its own nature as a movie' (Draper, 1987).

Narrated in McElwee's frequently hilarious and self-mocking voiceover (the *Washington Post*'s Paul Attanasio likened him to Woody Allen), the film's intelligence and interest in structure and representation are tempered by its comic tone. At the beginning of the film, McElwee appears dressed as the pillaging Sherman, but is reduced to addressing his camera in a barely audible whisper so as to not wake his sleeping parents. The film was widely admired for McElwee's maverick and entertaining approach, but there were dissenting voices, notably the *Monthly Film Bulletin*'s Louise Sweet, who criticised the director for treating the Southern preoccupation with war as a backdrop to an 'irritating' personal quest (Sweet, 1988).

Dir: Ross McElwee; **Prod**: Ross McElwee; **Scr**: Ross McElwee; **DOP**: Ross McElwee; **Editor**: Ross McElwee; **Score**: Uncredited; **Main Cast**: Ross McElwee.

She's Gotta Have It
US, 1986 – 85 mins
Spike Lee

Prior to *She's Gotta Have It*, Lee had only two film projects to his name: a student short, *Joe's Bed-Stuy Barbershop: We Cut Heads* (1983) (the first film to be selected for the New Directors/New Films series at the Museum of Modern Art), and an aborted 1984 feature *The Messenger*. But he forever altered the landscape for African-American film-makers with this idiosyncratic, independent debut feature. The cast and crew were composed of many of Lee's collaborators from his student days, and the evocative, effervescent jazz score came from father Bill. The film was completed in the face of economic adversity, which was exacerbated when the American Film Institute withdrew the funding it had earmarked for Lee's earlier project. Made up largely through deferments, the total budget was just under $115,000, a mere $15,000 of which was Lee's writing, producing, directing and acting fee.

She has as its heroine Nola Darling (Johns). An independent, sexually liberated black woman simultaneously involved with three disparate though equally needy male lovers, Nola finally resolves to choose between the caring and sincere Jamie (Hicks), the preening, self-obsessed model Greer (Terrell) and the vivacious though immature courier Mars (Lee).

Lee's film wears its stylistic debt to the French new wave with aplomb. Arrestingly shot in high-contrast black and white by Ernest Dickerson (save for a colour interlude the director intended as a homage to Vincente Minnelli and *The Wizard of Oz*, 1939), Lee deploys jump cuts, documentary-style direct-to-camera address and digressive vignettes, and makes innovative use of sound effects and montage sequences to profound, irreverent and humorous effect. Perhaps most memorable is a riotously funny sequence involving twelve black men recounting for the camera their favoured and often lascivious pick-up lines: 'Girl, I got plenty of what you need, ten throbbing inches of USDA, government inspected, prime-cut, grade-A tube steak'.

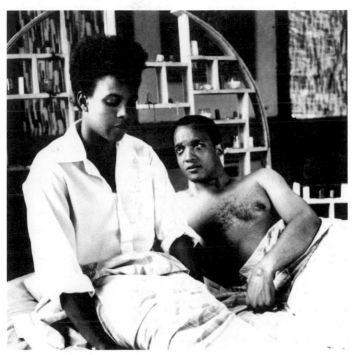

Pillow talk: Nola Darling (Tracy Camila Johns) and Jamie (Tommy Redmond Hicks) in Spike Lee's *She's Gotta Have It*

Selected as part of Director's Fortnight at Cannes, where it carried off the Prix la Jeunesse, *She* was still initially greeted with scepticism and incomprehension by much of the largely white critical cognoscenti. Also, and despite focusing on a strong-willed black female character and revealing men to be absurd and slightly pathetic, the film drew criticism from female commentators, including Amy Taubin, for what were perceived to be its misogynist overtones. Especially contentious was the scene in which Nola is virtually raped by Jamie, an act of punishment for her promiscuity.

However, after a cannily marketed New York opening the film rapidly became a cultural and commercial phenomenon, finding favour with both art-house aficionados and, more pertinently, African-American audiences unaccustomed to seeing their lives and sensibilities faithfully depicted. Since the demise of blaxploitation there were few black directors working in the American film industry. Lee almost single-handedly opened the door for a new generation of African-American film-makers, such as John Singleton, Leslie Harris and Matty Rich, who followed in his trailblazing wake. For this and for its own particular merits, *She* remains one of the most momentous contemporary American independent pictures. To this day, independent sage John Pierson (who acted as a rep on the film) still cites Lee as his hero.

Dir: Spike Lee; **Prod**: Shelton J. Lee; **Scr**: Spike Lee; **DOP**: Ernest Dickerson; **Editor**: Spike Lee; **Score**: Bill Lee; **Main Cast**: Tracy Camila Johns, Tommy Redmond Hicks, John Canada Terrell, Spike Lee.

Shock Corridor
US, 1963 – 101 mins
Samuel Fuller

Fuller's punchy, straight-to-the-gut narratives and sheer visual ferocity passed unappreciated by the American critics of his day. The director was a former crime journalist and war veteran who worked tirelessly in relative obscurity on quickly shot, low-budget pictures invariably released as B movies. Focusing on unsympathetic, deeply flawed protagonists comprised of soldiers, cops and bigots, Fuller's work was inaccurately charged with expressing fascistic leanings. He worked outside the studio system as writer, producer and director, and his independence enabled him to deliver subversive and unflinchingly honest critiques of American society in which 'film is a a battleground of alienated human energies' (Thomson, 2002, p. 318).

Shock Corridor, deemed trashy, vicious and irresponsible by the American press, is characteristic Fuller fare. Beginning with a quote from Euripides ('Whom God wishes to destroy, he first turns mad'), it examines the attempt by ambitious crime reporter Johnny Barrett (Breck) to win the Pulitzer Prize by solving the murder of a patient at a mental institution. He decides to pose as an inmate at the institution. In order to be committed, Barrett persuades his stripper girlfriend Cathy (Towers) to pretend that she is his sister and has been subjected to his incestuous advances. While undergoing sexual therapy, Barrett interviews the three witnesses to the murder: Stuart (Best), a disgraced American soldier who has returned from the Korean War believing himself to be a Confederate general; Boden (Evans), an atom bomb developer who has regressed to the state of a six-year-old; and Trent (Hari Rhodes), a black student who was among the first to enter an all-white Southern university, but who now believes himself to be a white supremacist. His grip on reality wavering, Barrett himself begins a slow descent into madness.

Originally intended as an exposé of the harrowing conditions in American mental facilities, the film delivers a riveting précis of the fundamental issues troubling a 1960s' America awash with paranoia and ideologically enforced anti-communist sentiments. Detractors bemoaned a lack of subtlety in Fuller's sociological observations, but there's no doubting the passion and force with which *Shock Corridor* articulates both the racial divide in American society (continued in Fuller's *White Dog*, 1982) and unease concerning nuclear weapons. Formally, the film heralds an advance on the vibrant use of camera that had already become a signature of Fuller's work (and which was to so influence Scorsese), with the constant tracking shots accentuating the escalating hysteria. Fuller's stylistic achievements are all the more impressive given the parameters within which he worked. Save for two colour sequences, the film is effectively shot in stark black and white by Stanley Cortez (*The Magnificent Ambersons*, 1942) and boasts noir-inspired chiaroscuro lighting pregnant with menace and foreboding.

Fuller became revered as an auteur throughout Europe (in 1977 Wenders cast him in *The American Friend*) and particularly in France. His domestic standing rose following the publication in 1968 of Andrew Sarris' *The American Cinema*, in which the critic described the director as an authentic American primitive and an estimable artistic force. More recently Fuller has been accorded statesmanlike status by the American independent sector, a position cemented by a full retrospective of his work at the 1988 Sundance Film Festival.

Dir: Samuel Fuller; **Prod**: Samuel Fuller; **Scr**: Samuel Fuller; **DOP**: Stanley Cortez; **Editor**: Jerome Thoms; **Score**: Paul Dunlap; **Main Cast**: Peter Breck, Constance Towers, Gene Evans, James Best.

Simple Men
UK/US, 1992 – 105 mins
Hal Hartley

The last of Hartley's Long Island pictures (though it was actually largely filmed in Texas), *Simple Men* gave evidence of the director's desire to explore new thematic, stylistic and geographical terrain. However, being a Hartley film, it still retained many of the characteristics that had rendered *The Unbelievable Truth* (1989) and *Trust* (1990) so endearing and original: the aphoristic, epigrammatic dialogue ('there's only trouble and desire' became the promotional hook); the deadpan performances from repertory actors; crisp, highly stylised compositions courtesy of the ubiquitous Michael Spiller; and a determinedly pared down, minimalist and elliptical approach to narrative and editing. The film had a $2 million budget, a sizeable improvement on Hartley's previous productions.

Thematically, *Simple Men* continues the director's interest in class and culture conflicts and the quest for self-fulfilment. The stupidity of men, the superior intellect of women, and the ways in which men objectify and 'seek to reconcile their various needs in them' (Fuller, 1992, p. xi) are central to the film. Also central are familial dysfunction and the rancour and rumour associated with a small-town mentality. *Simple Men* follows Bill McCabe (Burke), a small-time career criminal, and his brother Dennis (Sage), an overly serious student, as they embark on a trip to track down their father. A former baseball shortstop turned radical political activist, William McCabe (John Mackay) is preparing to make good his escape from the law. Aiding him are Kate (Sillas) and Elina (Löwensohn), two women with whom the brothers forge fraught relations.

Though defined by characteristic tableau-like compositions, *Simple Men* makes good use of its extra funds and, compared to Hartley's previous films, is distinguished by increased camera movement (there's a prolonged tracking shot involving a motorbike pursuit) and a doubling of the number of principal characters, allowing for interesting digressions.

As befits a director establishing an authorial style, the film feels more assured than Hartley's previous efforts, with the blending of the personal and the political especially deftly handled.

The sense that each Hartley film should be considered part of a work in progress is readily apparent. Cited by the director in an interview with Graham Fuller (Ibid.) as a reference to Lindsay Anderson's *O Lucky Man!* (1973), two characters from *The Unbelievable Truth* reprise their roles. There are also continued allusions to the recurring Ned Rifle, most notably as the title under which Hartley composes. Hartley shows an interest in referencing popular culture, here having his characters discuss Madonna's right to exploit her sexuality. A direct tribute occurs in a musical interlude inspired by *Bande à Part* (1964), directed by Godard, to whom he is frequently compared. This beguiling moment, in which the principal characters dance to a Sonic Youth track, demonstrates both the director's playful irreverence and the importance he places on the relationship between sound and image.

Simple Men served notice of Hartley's increasing international stature when it was selected as part of the Official Competition at the 1992 Cannes Film Festival.

Dir: Hal Hartley; **Prod**: Ted Hope, Hal Hartley; **Scr**: Hal Hartley; **DOP**: Michael Spiller; **Editor**: Steve Hamilton; **Score**: Ned Rifle; **Main Cast**: Robert Burke, William Sage, Karen Sillas, Elina Löwensohn.

Slacker
US, 1991 – 97 mins
Richard Linklater

Seldom seen, Linklater's debut feature, *It's Impossible to Learn to Plow by Reading Books* (1988), helped establish the youth-specific motifs that would recur throughout the largely self-taught director's career: fractured attempts at communication; disenchantment; an agonising over choices; and travel. His breakthrough picture *Slacker* consolidated these themes and precipitated a coherent run of films, including *Dazed and Confused* (1993) and *Before Sunrise* (1995), that briefly placed the director at the forefront of the American independent scene.

Slacker's unconventional, freewheeling and essentially plotless narrative offers a *True Stories* (1986)/documentary-style snapshot of a town's various obsessive and eccentric slacker inhabitants. It is set over a twenty-four-hour period in Linklater's hometown of Austin, Texas. Surprisingly, the film is in fact entirely scripted. Included in the often bewilderingly expansive mix of characters (the poster for the film simply listed the cast as 'a lot of people') are hipsters, bar-room philosophers, conspiracy theorists, anarchists and general oddballs, one of whom is selling what she claims to be Madonna's cervical smear. The film begins with a frantic traveller (Linklater himself) theorising on parallel realities, and then unfolds as a series of ostensibly random and largely comic vignettes. The intersection between episodes is provided by the fleeting moment of contact between one subject and the next. In one instance this occurs mid-scene when the restless, attentive camera simply picks out a passing figure of greater interest than the one currently shadowed.

Almost entirely self-financed (completion money was provided by a $35,000 German television sale), the film was produced by Linklater's own Detour Productions (named after the 1945 Edward G. Ulmer classic). The simply but effectively 16mm-shot film suffered initial rejection by almost every major and, indeed, minor festival. Undeterred, Linklater was confident that the film could succeed in his hometown, having nurtured a burgeoning film community through the formation of the Austin Film Society (a self-confessed cineaste, Linklater cited the art-house sensibilities of Antonioni, Ophuls, Buñuel and Fassbinder as influences). Acting as his own distributor, he opened it at an on-campus cinema, where it was a phenomenal success, enjoying consecutive sell-out weeks. Orion Classics acquired the film for national release one year after its Austin platform, sensing the film's *Zeitgeist* factor in its ability to directly connect with the rapidly emerging Generation X types being heavily hyped by the media. As a result, *Slacker* not only enjoyed a commercial and critical resurgence but also coined a new lifestyle approach, in the process ensuring the title term an indelible place in the modern lexicon.

  Slacker exerted a profound influence on a new generation of emerging directors (Linklater was himself barely into his twenties), including Kevin Smith who, dragged from his traditional multiplex haven to a downtown art cinema, suffered something of an epiphany. It made a highly visible and esoteric mark on the post-*sex, lies and videotape* (1989) independent landscape. As detailed by John Pierson, another of the film's legacies was the blow it struck at a grass-roots level in its daring launch strategy (Pierson, 1996, p. 185).

Dir: Richard Linklater; **Prod**: Richard Linklater; **Scr**: Richard Linklater; **DOP**: Lee Daniel; **Editor**: Scott Rhodes; **Score**: Uncredited; **Main Cast**: Richard Linklater, Rudy Basquez, Jean Caffeine, Jan Hockey.

Smithereens
US, 1982 – 93 mins
Susan Seidelman

The debut feature from New York Film School graduate Seidelman, *Smithereens* was an independent triumph in the face of adversity. Largely self-funded through the forming of limited partnerships, the film was shot for $80,000 in three stints over a year-long period in less than salubrious Lower East Side locations. Mas'ud Zavarzadeh in *Film Quarterly* described the film as a 'postmodern classic' (Zavarzadeh, 1984, p. 54).

Smithereens follows Wren (Berman), a punkish, working-class girl from the wrong side of the Hudson River, who descends upon Lower Manhattan in search of an express ticket to rock and roll fame. By day, she ekes out a menial living; by night, she trawls the clubs and bars of the New York punk scene, stubbornly promoting her flimsy talents. Wren is partly embroiled in a potentially fulfilling relationship with Paul (Rinn), an artist from Montana, but her ruthlessly ambitious streak, and her eviction from her apartment for non-payment of rent, leads to a chance encounter with Eric (Hell), the self-obsessed lead singer of much-fancied band the Smithereens. Could a ride on Eric's coat-tails turn Wren's dreams to reality?

With only limited previous acting experience, Berman is astonishing in an unattractive central role. Wren is fed by an almost tyrannical ego and narcissism: she is seen early on in the film pasting pictures of herself inscribed with the enigmatic question, 'Who is this girl?' Paul describes her as being morally deficient, in that people only matter to her in so far as they can be of use to her prospective career. Wren's abject lack of talent is emphasised by the fact that she works in a copy shop, 'a job characterised by re-production instead of production' (Ibid.). Having set out ostensibly to portray the New York punk rock scene and its subculture, Seidelman accurately exposes a movement in its dying embers, when it was barely sustained by waning media attention and irreparably tarnished by a perversion of values and artistic and ethical decay.

Seidelman has said in a *New York Times* interview that she 'wanted to people the film with characters who were products of the mass culture of the 1970's and 80's kids who grew up on rock and roll' (Armstrong, 1984, p. 4). She resonantly cast charismatic Richard Hell as a last-minute replacement for another unnamed actor. The author of the 1976 album *Blank Generation* and an acclaimed punk performer, Hell was one of the most visible figures of the era. Playfully aware of the hierarchies of cool involved in any creative movement, Seidelman also cast New York underground associates such as Amos Poe and Cookie Mueller in cameo roles.

Seidelman herself edited the film, which has a soundtrack that includes tracks by seminal New York acts The Feelies and ESG. Chirine El Khadem's realistic cinematography and its functional aesthetic authentically capture the squalor underpinning the facade of bohemian living. The film was acquired for domestic distribution by New Line, following an impressive showing at Telluride and its surprising selection for the main competition at Cannes. Marketed as a film with a lot of attitude, *Smithereens* played to packed houses on New York's alternative cinema circuit. Describing her goal to the *New York Times* as achieving a balance between Hollywood and non-Hollywood film-making, Seidelman perfected the formula for the following year's *Desperately Seeking Susan*.

Dir: Susan Seidelman; **Prod**: Susan Seidelman; **Scr**: Ron Nyswaner, Peter Askin; **DOP**: Chirine El Khadem; **Editor**: Susan Seidelman; **Score**: Glenn Mercer, Bill Million; **Main Cast**: Susan Berman, Brad Rinn, Richard Hell, Nada Despotovich.

Spanking the Monkey
US, 1994 – 100 mins
David O. Russell

Writer-director and executive producer Russell's independently produced
$200,000 feature debut is a poignant and accomplished Oedipal drama.
It was another mid-90s picture to generate controversy and a must-see
hysteria following its impressive showing at Sundance, where it carried
off the Best Picture award. Key among the film's numerous virtues is the
composed treatment of the taboo subjects of incest and suicide.

When medical student Raymond Aibelli (Davies) returns to upstate
New York after completing his freshman year, he expects to stay just a
few days before taking up a prestigious internship in Washington. He is
shocked to be informed by his father (Hendrickson), a dour, tyrannical
travelling videotape salesman, that he must in fact spend the summer
with his attractive, depressed mother (Watson), who has recently
fractured her leg in a bungled suicide attempt. Presented with an
exhaustive list of instructions to maintain the family infrastructure,
Raymond begins to suffer numerous frustrations. Moreover, his mother's
constant demand for back rubs and thigh massages begins to engender
a slide towards a transgressive intimacy.

For all its masturbation references *Spanking the Monkey* adroitly
reveals itself as a distinguished, subversive strike at the heart of the
aspirations and lifestyles of the dysfunctional American middle-class
family. Russell's deft screenplay skilfully navigates the constantly shifting
plays for power and authority that serve as the dynamic for the film,
which also speaks of the unspeakably restrictive claustrophobia of
suburbia and the difficult passage from adolescence to adulthood.

The sex between mother and son is handled with a refreshing
ambiguity and a frisson of eroticism that manages to impart an
audacious yet sensitive and non-judgmental tone. In this regard, the
compelling performances of Watson and Davies assist immeasurably.
Russell employs a bold, confident style and has an impressive eye for

detail, managing to suggest the ridiculous facade of the Aibelli's supposedly stable, structured existence (Tom Aibelli is later revealed as a serial philanderer and a failing businessman, evoking *Death of a Salesman*). Russell further denotes the pent-up frustrations in loose montage sequences that show Raymond forlornly performing a variety of mundane, designated tasks, such as mowing the lawn and brushing the deteriorating gums of family dog Lucky.

It's also through such attention to details that Russell communicates the sense of disgust and loathing that the characters feel for their thwarted existences – hence, the quibbling over semantics through which Raymond's mother reveals her resentment at being forced to give up her own career, and the look of horror on Raymond's face when manipulative local girl Toni (Gallo) removes her cumbersome brace in advance of a sexual embrace. The film's potent, provocative and measured undercurrent of melancholy is further embellished by the use of Morphine's plaintive 'In Spite of Me' on the soundtrack.

Dir: David O. Russell; **Prod**: Dean Silvers; **Scr**: David O. Russell; **DOP**: Michael Mayers; **Editor**: Pamela Martin; **Score**: David Carbonara; **Main Cast**: Jeremy Davies, Alberta Watson, Benjamin Hendrickson, Carla Gallo.

Static
US, 1985 – 93 mins
Mark Romanek

Romanek's feature debut, *Static* is a relatively obscure and all too little known picture of genuine originality. The film boasts a formal and thematic inventiveness and an unforced and enigmatic sensibility, but Romanek wholly disowned it while promoting *One Hour Photo* (2002), his belated follow-up feature.

Written by Romanek and leading man Gordon (a talented director in his own right with *A Midnight Clear*, 1991, among his credits), *Static* begins as an almost whimsical, if Lynchian tale of small-town weirdness before departing for altogether darker terrain. By day, nerdish, insular Ernie Blick (Gordon) toils away at a provincial crucifix factory, ferreting away the deformed rejects from the assembly line for his own private collection. By night, he decamps to his oppressive motel room where he is perfecting an invention that he believes gives people a glimpse of heaven through a specially adapted channel on their television sets. Unable to assert the legitimacy of his invention – all others see is uninterrupted static – Blick hijacks a bus in an attempt to gain a media platform and local air-time as the forum from which he will finally satisfy those who doubt the magnitude of his labours.

A convincing parable about conformity, community and small-town mentality, the film looks at decaying lines of communication in contemporary society. It acts too as a perceptive comment on the role of the media, and specifically television, in the forming of popular opinions and ideas. Moreover, *Static* offers an in-depth look at the various ways in which people choose to interpret faith and religion. In this regard, though perhaps lacking its acerbic fervour, *Static* bears close comparison to Huston's *Wise Blood* (1979); both pictures share a keen interest in the concept of martyrdom. More recently, Aronofsky's π (*Pi*) (1997) provides a point of reference, concerning as it does the claustrophobic and disturbing sense of living with the knowledge that something exists outside the realms of popular comprehension.

The lead is endearingly performed by the bug-eyed Gordon, who makes a convincing and sympathetic oddball. Plummer offers able support. Cinematographer Jeff Jur's intricately constructed compositions, aided by the other-worldly Utah and Arizona locations, display a canny eye for the off-kilter and visually surreal. Brian Eno's suitably austere, contemplative score is yet another formal flourish. Perhaps most impressive, however, is *Static*'s concentrated ambiguity concerning Blick's invention. Common sense would seem to suggest that his claims are poppycock, but Romanek's unforced optimism and refusal to offer ridicule or castigation wills the viewer to suspend disbelief and concede the possibility that Blick really was able to offer a glimpse of celestial paradise on earth after all.

Despite an eye-catching marketing campaign featuring two children sporting outlandish monster masks and a Grand Jury Prize nomination at the 1986 Sundance Film Festival, the film did little to capture critical or commercial attention. It remains rarely screened in the UK. Though hardly epoch-defining and ultimately of little industrial consequence in terms of the development of American independent cinema, *Static* is a genuinely esoteric and idiosyncratic addition to American indie ranks.

Dir: Mark Romanek; **Prod**: Amy Ness; **Scr**: Keith Gordon, Mark Romanek; **DOP**: Jeff Jur; **Editor**: Emily Paine; **Score**: Brian Eno, Various; **Main Cast**: Keith Gordon, Amanda Plummer, Bob Gunton, Lily Knight.

Stranger Than Paradise
US/W. Germany, 1984 – 89 mins
Jim Jarmusch

One of American independent cinema's defining films, *Stranger Than Paradise* was directly responsible for pushing many new films and directors into production and for inaugurating what John Pierson perceives as a halcyon period (1984–94) in intelligent, esoteric but accessible low-budget movies (Pierson, 1996). Moreover, the film (Jarmusch's second after 1982's disappointing *Permanent Vacation*) coined a laconic, minimalist visual style that was in part informed by the works of Bresson, Ozu and Rivette. It also borrowed confidently from avant-garde and punk rock aesthetics. Kevin Smith recognised the 'look' to which Jarmusch aspired, and in the credits for *Clerks* (1993) thanked Jarmusch for 'leading the way'.

The film originated as a thirty-minute short shot over a weekend on leftover stock donated by Wenders following the completion of *The State of Things* (1982). Jarmusch screened the short on portable projectors at clubs throughout New York in order to attract further finance. Later shown at the Hof Festival in Germany, the short captured the attention of director Paul Bartel and chocolate entrepreneur Otto Grokenberger, with the latter stepping forward to provide the completion funding that allowed Jarmusch to extricate himself from his soured relationship with Gray City Films, Wenders' distribution company.

Exploring the effects of an unwanted visit from a Hungarian cousin (Balint) on detached, taciturn New Yorker Willie (Lurie) and his gambling buddy Eddy (Edson), the film offers a perceptive look at exile, existential solitude and the possibilities of communication beyond cultural differences. Jarmusch also studies the effects of geography on human emotions, tracking the trio as they travel from New York, to snowy Cleveland and then on to an out-of-season Florida.

(Next page) Welcome to Florida. From left to right, Eddie (Richard Edson), Eva (Eszter Balint) and Willie (John Lurie) playing it cool in *Stranger Than Paradise*

Suture
US, 1993 – 96 mins
Scott McGehee, David Siegel

Though they have met just once at the funeral of their murdered father, wealthy, unprincipled sophisticate Vincent Towers (Michael Harris) invites his identical half-brother Clay (Haysbert), a lowly construction worker, to spend some time with him in Phoenix, Arizona. The visit is ostensibly a bonding exercise, but Clay is dismayed to learn upon arrival that an unannounced business trip necessitates Vincent's immediate attention. After dropping his preoccupied brother at the airport, Clay is involved in a terrible car explosion that leaves his face burned beyond recognition and his memory erased. With the aid of Freudian psychoanalyst Dr Shinoda (Shimono) and leading plastic surgeon Renée Descartes (Mel Harris), Clay is slowly pieced back together. The only problem is, he's reconstructed as Vincent, the prime suspect in his father's death.

Executive produced by Soderbergh, *Suture* is a sophisticated, post-modernist and intertextual first feature that borrows freely from the B-movie thriller, the American avant-garde, and the thematic and stylistic staples of film noir. There is highly stylised chiaroscuro lighting, a complex flashback structure and a focus upon a moral landscape predicated by corruption and greed. The directors acknowledge *Spellbound* (1945) as a key structural influence. *Suture* nonetheless brings its own intoxicating and inventively cerebral embellishments to the Hitchcockian mix.

Suture is an intelligent analysis of identity, class, the duality of mind and body (the film alludes to Lacanian psychoanalysis which, in part, also lends the film its title), and the physical and mental means by which we define ourselves. It features at its core two compelling, non-naturalistic performances by Harris and Haysbert. Harris is slight and white, Haysbert is muscular and black – facts that go unmentioned within the film. For the spectator, the men's racial differences highlight the illusory nature of identification. 'Our physical resemblance is striking' remarks Vincent at one point in a moment that is indicative of the film's deadpan dialogue and entertainingly existentialist sensibilities. The naming of a character after the philosopher Descartes and the engaging use of Johnny Cash's 'Ring of Fire' as a charred Clay is rushed to emergency offer further evidence of the film-makers' mischievous but effective daring.

Shot in austere black and white by Greg Gardiner (who won the Cinematography Award at 1994's Sundance) and boasting Kelly McGehee's stunning production design (the use of modish 60s' office interiors evokes Godard's *Alphaville*, 1965), *Suture* is also visually arresting in its spatial dexterity and compositional assurance. The final face-off between Vincent and Clay, shot from high above in an ornate bathroom, is especially memorable. Also memorable are the film's disjunctive editing and the overlapping use of sound to intrude from one scene to another, techniques that reference the pioneering work of the late 60s' theorist Jean-Pierre Oudart, who drew parallels between the psychic processes that establish subjectivity and the structuring language of cinema.

Clay (Dennis Haysbert) and Vincent (Michael Harris) in *Suture*, a film in which nothing is simply black and white

Suture can be enjoyed on multiple levels. A gripping thriller where nothing is black and white (both literally and metaphorically), it's an ambitious example of the possibilities of the medium and a notable entry to the pantheon of inspired American independent movies.

Dir: Scott McGehee, David Siegel; **Prod**: Scott McGehee, David Siegel; **Scr**: Scott McGehee, David Siegel; **DOP**: Greg Gardiner; **Editor**: Lauren Zuckerman; **Score**: Cary Berger; **Main Cast**: Dennis Haysbert, Mel Harris, Sab Shimono, Michael Harris.

Sweet Sweetback's Baadasssss Song
US, 1971 – 97 mins
Melvin Van Peebles

A watershed film in the history of black American cinema, *Sweet Sweetback's Baadasssss Song* was an act of great defiance that had major ideological repercussions in its polemical treatment of white oppression and its challenge to the discriminatory regime of Hollywood and American society in general. Independent by any definition – production, politics, aesthetics and economics – its signficance and influence cannot be overstated.

Van Peebles was unsurprisingly unable to obtain studio funding for the project. A former novelist blessed with entrepreneurial flair, Van Peebles acted as his own producer to raise a shoestring budget largely composed of contributions from wealthy black businessmen and entertainment figures, including Bill Cosby. As well as undertaking writing and directing duties, Van Peebles would also go on to star, edit and alongside Earth, Wind and Fire, compose the R & B score.

The film is dedicated to 'all the Brothers and Sisters who had enough of the Man' and billed simply as 'starring The Black Community'. The simple plot concerns an apolitical black stud, Sweetback (Van Peebles), who becomes a reluctant hero after impulsively beating two white cops guilty of brutalising Mu Mu (Hubert Scales), a young black revolutionary. Sweetback is forced to go on the run, his escape to Mexico being punctuated with various altercations with the law and encounters with numerous women, who are suitably chastened by his sexual prowess.

The film is set amid the Los Angeles ghettos frequently glossed over on screen. While *Sweetback*'s narrative may at times border on the repetitive and its central character, whose actions lack any real political motivation, reinforces stereotypes of black male potency, the film is still an uncompromising and provocative vision that begins with the epigraph, 'these lines are not an homage to brutality that the artist has invented, but a hymn from the mouth of reality'. Perhaps the film's single most transgressive gesture is that Sweetback's anti-authoritarian stance is met not with death (as would traditionally be the case) but with liberty and a final warning shot emblazoned on the screen: 'Watch Out! A baadasssss nigger is coming back to collect some dues.' The film's activism is mirrored by Van Peebles' striking formal approach. Making a mockery of his budget and his limited film-making experience, he vigorously employs multiple experimental new-wave techniques such as split screen, freeze frames, overlapping images and the exposure of the film negative.

Sweetback's impact was immediate and enduring, despite it being rated X by the Motion Picture Association of America. Van Peebles personally ordered the addition to the posters of the statement, 'rated X by an all-white jury') and largely condemned to limited circulation by an industry fearful of its content and repercussions. Deemed mandatory viewing by the Black Panthers, the film is credited with fathering the blaxploitation movement of the early 70s and offered a positive advance in terms of the cinematic visibility of African Americans. Moreover, it opened the door for subsequent black film-makers, including Haile Gerima, Billy Woodberry, Charles Burnett and, latterly, Spike Lee. It also opened up the potential for such figures to ply their trade both within and independent from the Hollywood system.

Dir: Melvin Van Peebles; **Prod**: Melvin Van Peebles; **Scr**: Melvin Van Peebles; **DOP**: Robert Maxwell; **Editor**: Melvin Van Peebles; **Score**: Melvin Van Peebles; **Main Cast**: Melvin Van Peebles, Rhetta Hughes, John Amos, Simon Chuckster.

Swingers
US, 1996 – 96 mins
Doug Liman

Swingers was one of the ubiquitous films of its year (in part due to the goofy but irrepressible charm of its characters and its eminently quotable pop-culture referencing dialogue), and briefly established director-cinematographer Liman as one of the brightest directorial talents to emerge in the post-Tarantino era. From an autobiographical script by leading man Favreau (who also co-produced), the Miramax-backed film marries Favreau's perceptive, anthropological observations of male group behaviour and masculinity in crisis to Liman's hip, retro stylised cinematic sensibility. The result is a work that comfortably exists at the commercial/independent intersection.

Liman used a skeleton crew and filmed on a small, portable Aaton camera, lending the film, and particularly its interior moments, a casual naturalism. This feeling is further engendered by the casting of Liman's real-life actor friends and former coffee bar nighthawks. The film takes a keenly observed look at the largely fruitless efforts of Favreau (Mike), Vaughn (Trent), Livingston (Rob) and Van Horn (Sue) to make it big in Hollywood and add some romance to their lacklustre lives. An aspirant comedian suffering a crisis of confidence following the break-up of a long-term relationship, Mike is the most disconsolate of the bunch. A trip to glitzy Las Vegas (cue sharp suits and a medley of Rat Pack-era show tunes in keeping with the film's retro sensibilities and Liman's interest in 60s' culture and design) does little to assuage his pain, and so he dejectedly returns to his sparse apartment. The men are unable to get past first base with the opposite sex, and the closest any of them come to an acting gig is an offer to play Goofy, to which another observes, 'Hey, at least it's Disney'. Convinced by the more cocksure Trent that there are 'honey babies' available for their picking, the unemployed bunch trawl the hippest Hollywood Hills clubs in search of romantic fulfilment and an end to Mike's torpor.

Though hardly pinned on the most original of ideas, *Swingers* achieves an impressive and affecting perspicacity by virtue of well-judged performances (Favreau's hangdog yearning just shading the acting honours over Vaughn's unreconstructed playboy) and the leading man's deft and often painfully funny script. The determinedly uncomfortable sequence where Mike tries to leave a message on the answerphone of a potential date, only to be repeatedly cut off mid-flow, achieves a new high in on-screen embarrassment and frustration. Trent's use of the word 'money' as an adjective (to mean looking good, an apt choice given Hollywood's ability to reduce everything to currency exchange) instantly found its way into the lexicon. Liman also displays a playful reflexivity and awareness of contemporary film culture, cheerfully and cheekily referencing the films of Tarantino and Scorsese in a number of impressively orchestrated, diversionary sequences.

Made for just $200,000 (rendering the visual panache of the Las Vegas sequence all the more impressive), *Swingers* was originally released in the States on just eight screens. However, as positive word of mouth spread, the film was expanded to multiple theatres and quickly racked up a healthy $4.5 million domestic box-office gross.

Dir: Doug Liman; **Prod**: Victor Simpkins; **Scr**: Jon Favreau; **DOP**: Doug Liman; **Editor**: Steve Mirrione; **Score**: Justin Rheinhardt; **Main Cast**: Jon Favreau, Vince Vaughn, Ron Livingston, Patrick Van Horn.

Swoon
US, 1991 – 94 mins
Tom Kalin

Kalin is a former producer for AIDSFILMS, an AIDS prevention and educational organisation, and the director of the provocative and experimental short *They Are Lost to Vision Altogether*, a look at the media's treatment of AIDS information within America. He made a compelling feature debut with the self-written and edited *Swoon*. Produced by Christine Vachon (with initial funding from Apparatus, the company established by Vachon and Todd Haynes) after Kalin had raised $100,000 himself by writing to granting organisations, the film became one of the key pictures of the New Queer Cinema movement, alongside works such as Haynes' *Poison* (1990) and Gregg Araki's *The Living End* (1992).

Swoon offers a bold and modernist account of the 1924 Leopold and Loeb murder case in which eighteen-year-old Nathan Freudenthal Leopold Jr and Richard Loeb, two aesthetes from wealthy Chicago Jewish families, kidnapped and murdered fourteen-year-old Bobby Franks purely for the intellectual stimulation of the crime. The pair were bound by Nietzschean concepts of superiority and by a sadomasochistic sexual relationship (Leopold was a homosexual, Loeb a sociopath who allowed himself to be used sexually in return for Leopold's involvement in his criminal activities). They were sufficiently arrogant as to be clumsy in their execution of the crime and thus were quickly brought to justice.

The case had been previously filmed on two occasions, firstly by Hitchcock as the famously one-take *Rope* (1948), which did explore the pair's fascism and grounding in Nietzschean philosophy, and then by Richard Fleischer as *Compulsion* (1959), a more conventional thriller based on Meyer Levin's novel. Kalin's revisiting of the material was inspired by his desire to 'state publicly, once and for all, in an unabashed and direct fashion the facts of the case' (Okewole, 2001, p. 88), particularly Leopold and Loeb's homosexual relationship. Perhaps unsurprisingly this facet was consciously avoided by the earlier productions, which were made in a more morally proscriptive climate. Determinedly eschewing a positive depiction of homosexuality (which later led to criticism from some sections of the gay media), *Swoon* begins with an examination of the sadomasochistic nature of the pair's sexual relationship and the transgressive games they played. Kalin means to show just how important a factor the pair's sexuality was in regard to their subsequent actions. For Kalin, the crime did not happen because of the sexuality of the perpetrators, but it was undeniably linked to it.

The film is exhaustively researched and factually accurate, to the extent that almost all the confession speeches and courtroom material of the latter half were literally transcribed from court records. Kalin examines defence attorney Clarence Darrow's argument that the pair's homosexuality was a sign of pathological deviance and that they could not be held fully accountable for their crimes. A fascinating depiction of racism, repression and rabid homophobia emerges. Using what Kalin has described as a 'revisionist aesthetic' influenced by the photographs of Bruce Weber, *Swoon*'s impressive and non-naturalistic collage of fictional footage and courtroom re-enactments is beautifully captured in monochrome by Sundance Cinematography Award winner Ellen Kuras. The film also boasts a decadent, well-tailored retro style that communicates the period's atmosphere and extravagance and Leopold and Loeb's just-so glamour.

Dir: Tom Kalin; **Prod**: Tom Kalin, Christine Vachon; **Scr**: Tom Kalin, Hilton Als; **DOP**: Ellen Kuras; **Editor**: Tom Kalin; **Score**: James Bennett; **Main Cast**: Daniel Schlachet, Craig Chester, Ron Vawter, Michael Kirby.

The Thin Blue Line
US, 1988 – 101 mins
Errol Morris

The Thin Blue Line evolved from *Dr Death*, another much-mooted and fastidiously researched Morris project which took as its subject Dr James Grigson, a Dallas psychiatrist who often appeared as a witness for the prosecution in death penalty cases. It was while interviewing death row inmates for that project that Morris first encountered and interviewed Randall Adams, a young drifter imprisoned in 1977 for the fatal shooting of Dallas police officer Robert Wood, a case in which the authorities had been under pressure to deliver an assailant. The chief witness against Adams was David Harris, also on death row for an unrelated murder. Adams had continually professed his innocence, and slowly Morris began to believe him, realising that tracking the situation on film was an opportunity to clear Adams' name and spare him from execution.

The film takes its title from the judge recalling the prosecutor's summary concerning 'the thin blue line' that maintains the social fabric, and is described by the director as 'the first murder mystery that actually solves a murder'. It is an impressive and provocative piece of photojournalism that serves as a sobering meditation on the failings of the American justice system, and also offers an at times blackly comic, decidedly Lynchian peep into the troubled American psyche. Fascinated more by incongruities than the facts themselves, Morris painstakingly interviews all the principal figures in the case, slowly piecing together an alternative and more probable picture of the fateful events from multiple perspectives. Though conventionally framed, Morris's interview technique is captivating and unique. Honing in on idiosyncratic word choices and patterns of speech, he draws the most intimate, revealing and previously

(Opposite page) Documentary evidence: Errol Morris's *The Thin Blue Line* was pivotal in the re-trial of convicted cop killer Randall Adams and indirectly led to the quashing of his conviction

suppressed details from his subjects, including, ultimately, Harris's audio confession to the crime.

Morris eschews the low-key aesthetic conventionally associated with the documentary (an approach that offended purists, hence the film was a no-show in the Academy Award nominations), characteristically adopting a more visually arresting and inventive approach to structure, design and execution. The distinction between documentary and fiction is blurred (acquired by Miramax, the film was aggressively marketed as a 'non-fiction feature') as immaculately conceived reconstructions (including a dramatic slow motion re-enactment of Woods' bullet-ridden body slumping to the floor), actual footage and close-ups of objects and hitherto overlooked details blend to cogent and seductive effect. When excerpts from *Swinging Cheerleaders*, the late-show B-movie that was used as an alibi, are incorporated, shots of a ticking clock are intercut to reveal glaring discrepancies in chronology (Morris unearths the fact that there was no late show on the night of the murder). Sensitively scored by Philip Glass, *The Thin Blue Line* also boasts felicitous sound design, including strikingly repeated amplified gun shots, that contributes to the overall rhythmic thrust. Little wonder that J. Hoberman described the film as 'impressive, haunting and brilliantly stylised' (Hoberman, 1988, p. 60).

The film was entered as evidence when Adams was granted a re-trial, which became a media furore that contributed to the film's notable home video popularity. The instant impact of the film was magnified when it aired on American Playhouse – one of the project's financiers – to coincide with Adams' release from prison.

Dir: Errol Morris; **Prod**: Mark Lipson; **Scr**: N/A; **DOP**: Stefan Czapsky, Robert Chappell; **Editor**: Paul Barnes, Elizabeth King; **Score**: Philip Glass; **Main Cast**: Randall Adams, David Harris, Edith James, Dennis White.

Tongues Untied
US, 1989 – 55 mins
Marlon T. Riggs

Along with Isaac Julien's *Looking for Langston* (1988), *Tongues Untied* was one of the first black independent productions to openly address the thorny issue of black homosexuality. Intelligently and passionately exploring the intersections of racism and homophobia, the film gives a committed and defiant voice to the previously silenced black gay male community.

Tongues Untied is hugely politically charged, being set in the shadow of AIDS. The film is largely autobiographical, beginning with a childhood spent among the rednecks of Georgia where the director remembers being referred to as a 'motherfuckin' coon'. It depicts numerous encounters of racism and homophobia as Riggs subsequently comes out into a largely white gay environment, shedding 'shades of nigger boy for pigments of faggot and queer'. The initial wonder of San Francisco's Castro area soon dissipates when Riggs realises his invisibility remains because 'I was a nigger boy still'. Giving evidence of a shared black gay male experience and mutual recognition, while further tapping into the African-American tradition of witness and testimony, Riggs eloquently structures the film around the poetry of a chorus of black gay voices, including Essex Hemphill, Reginald Jackson and Steve Langley. The music of the *a cappella* outfit the Lavender Light Quartet also prominently features, as does, on the film's soundtrack, artists such as Sylvester, Roberta Flack and Nina Simone.

The film impressively draws upon Riggs' experience of working within disparate media, resembling an at times complex and skilfully edited kaleidoscopic collage. Among the inserts intercut with the poetry and personal reminiscences are an Eddie Murphy routine in which homosexuals are roundly condemned, a street mime performed by a troupe of young black kids, and a profoundly lyrical, slow-motion sequence of a black man smoking a cigarette wearing a look of pained contemplation. Accompanying the latter sequence is Billie Holiday's *Loverman*, here transformed into a paean for black gay longing.

Despite attracting criticism from black gay women and feminist critics for its seemingly segregative closing coda of 'black men loving black men is the revolutionary act' (Amy Taubin labelled it 'heedlessly misogynistic': Taubin, 2001a, p. 91) *Tongues Untied* nonetheless articulated a new collective sexual and racial identity and placed Riggs at the vanguard of the renaissance of black culture in the 80s and early 90s. Made on a tight budget with a grant from the National Endowment for the Arts, the film, also produced, edited and shot by Riggs, achieved a recognition far beyond black or gay audiences when its airing on US television was used by far-right sympathisers to attack George Bush for what they regarded as his misuse of tax-payers' money to fund a rainbow coalition. Riggs fired back, defending the right of all to representation, while highlighting the anti-gay bigotry with which the political establishment now laced its racial slurs.

Dir: Marlon T. Riggs; **Prod**: Marlon T. Riggs; **Scr**: Reginald Jackson, Steve Langley, Alan Miller, Donald Woods, Joseph Bream, Craig Harris, Marlon T. Riggs, Essex Hemphill; **DOP**: Marlon T. Riggs; **Editor**: Marlon T. Riggs; **Score**: Alex Langford, Steve Langley, Marlon T. Riggs; **Main Cast**: Kerrigan Black, Blackberri, Bernard Brannier, Gerald Davies.

Trees Lounge
US, 1996 – 95 mins
Steve Buscemi

Buscemi's nervous, haunted presence graced seemingly every self-respecting 90s' US independent picture, making his 'king of the indies' title (Kemp, 2001) seem entirely appropriate. His understanding of and association with the indie milieu was extended by having played low budget directors in Rockwell's *In the Soup* (1992) – which also gave him the opportunity to helm the short film contained therein – and DiCillo's *Living in Oblivion* (1995). Buscemi's familiarity with the territory therefore ensured that it came as little surprise when he made his impressive writing-directing debut with the partly autobiographical *Trees Lounge*.

Shot in Valley Stream, the blue-collar suburban belt of Long Island where Buscemi grew up, it's a well-observed and ultimately quietly poignant character study of Tommy Basilio (Buscemi), an unemployed

Barflies Tommy Basilio (Steve Buscemi) and Bill (Bronson Dudley) in the director-star's autobiographical *Trees Lounge*

mechanic whose life has fallen apart since his girlfriend Teresa (Bracco) left him for his former boss, Rob (LaPaglia). Tommy wastes his days hanging around the garage and his nights drinking himself into oblivion at the Trees Lounge bar, conveniently situated right below his apartment. Finally finding work driving an ice-cream truck, his downward spiral nonetheless continues when he beds his seventeen-year-old niece, Debbie (Sevigny).

Described by Buscemi as a projection of 'what would have happened if I'd stayed in Valley Stream' (Ibid., p. 16), *Trees Lounge* is a perceptive and authentic account of barroom blue-collar life and the perils of constant libation. Vividly realised by Buscemi's credible, world-weary dialogue and its coterie of well-drawn leather-skinned bar lizards drunkenly pontificating on life, the Trees Lounge bar is a wonderfully murky, beer-sodden creation of the kind Charles Bukowski may have frequented. Tommy's attempts to rally his co-drinkers into a hospital visit to see Bill, the Lounge's longest-serving patron, immediately collapse under the collective weight of apathy; a moment that perhaps encapsulates the central concern of the film.

The film is beautifully performed by its ensemble cast, not least Buscemi's former stand-up comedy partner Mark Boone Junior, and the director himself, who brings a wounded sympathy to two-time loser Tommy. *Trees Lounge* is appropriately shot in a relaxed, understated and unhurried deadpan style that suggests that Buscemi's time with Jarmusch and the Coen brothers was formally instructive. The defining influence and sensibility is, however, that of Cassavetes, whose spirit is evoked through the film's unforced naturalism and its favouring of colourful, digressive and often painfully funny character-driven vignettes in place of a rigid structural cohesion. Moreover, a well-judged cameo from Cassavetes' stalwart Seymour Cassel apart, *Trees Lounge* also maintains a lineage with Cassavetes in its willingness to engage with the underbelly of American life. Like many indie directors of his generation, Buscemi is forthright in his admiration for Cassavetes and of his alternation of an independent film-making career with lucrative acting parts in Hollywood movies. This is a tactic increasingly employed by Buscemi himself, with his subsequent feature, *Animal Factory* (2001), being partly built upon fees accrued for work in fare such as *Con Air* (1997) and *Armageddon* (1998).

Told by a Valley Stream barfly during shooting that *Trees Lounge* was a terrible idea because it was not remotely commercial, Buscemi took the comment as a compliment, replying 'that's the point' (Ibid., p. 16). Nominated for two Independent Spirit Awards (Best First Feature and Best First Screenplay), the film was actually no slouch at the US box office either. Initially opening on just two screens, the film took $39,830 on its opening weekend, and later expanded to fifty-one screens and a final box-office gross of $749,741.

Dir: Steve Buscemi; **Prod**: Brad Wyman, Chris Hanley; **Scr**: Steve Buscemi; **DOP**: Lisa Rinzler; **Editor**: Kate Williams, Jane Pia Abramovitz; **Score**: Evan Lurie; **Main Cast**: Steve Buscemi, Chloë Sevigny, Anthony LaPaglia, Elizabeth Bracco.

Triple Bogey on a Par Five Hole
US, 1991 – 88 mins
Amos Poe

Working cheaply and prolifically on black and white 16mm film stock, art-film cineaste Poe became a central figure for a whole new generation of underground film-makers (Jarmusch chief among them) that emerged from the New York scene circa the late 70s and mid-80s. Poe's *The Blank Generation* (1976) proved to be the seminal documentary on the punk movement and made explicit his own punk-inspired sensibilities.Later works such as *Subway Riders* (1981), starring John Lurie revealed a formal debt to the minimalism of Warhol and to Godard's unconventional approach to film grammar. *Triple Bogey on a Par Five Hole* marked Poe's first feature since *Alphabet City* (1984), and augured a return to independent film-making following a lengthy and largely uneventful scriptwriting sojourn in Hollywood.

Triple Bogey is a knowingly post-modern riff on *Citizen Kane*'s (1941) investigative structure and concern with the reconstruction of identity and self. It features fellow independent director Eric Mitchell (*Underground U.S.A.*, 1980) as screenwriter Remy Gravelle. Hired to research the story of the Levys, a glamorous pair of crooks who up until their untimely end made a perfectly good living robbing wealthy golfers, Gravelle decides to spend time in the company of the Levys' progeny, Amanda (Hall), Bree (Goethals) and Satch (McBride), as they endlessly circle Manhattan on their luxury yacht, the *Triple Bogey*. Beset by squabbling and neuroses, none of the precocious children is able to shed much light on the lives of their parents (whom Satch refers to as 'pathetic losers'), and the obsessively compiled Super 8mm home movies (apparently footage of Poe's own family and the only colour material to appear in the film) also prove unenlightening. Remy turns first to the family lawyer Steffano Baccardi (Robbie Coltrane) and then to his niece Nina (Alba Clemente) for much-needed answers.

An often wry and amusing satire on the mores of both Hollywood and the biography format, it is also part philosophical detective story that pays homage to Welles' *The Lady from Shanghai* (1947). (The film's depiction of the eccentricities and caprices of the idle rich would also seem to have influenced Wes Anderson's *The Royal Tenenbaums*, 2001.) Poe adopts a chimeric, stimulating approach to narrative and composition that includes the technique of having Remy, charismatically rendered by Mitchell, remain largely unseen until the picture's conclusion. A marginal figure in the frame, Remy's presence is denoted through the sound of his voice (the film in part uses a voiceover structure) and visual and aural signposts from other characters.

Intelligently juxtaposing expansive Manhattan vistas (stunningly shot by Joe DeSalvo, whose previous credits include *Johnny Suede*, 1991, Tom DiCillo's directorial debut) with below-deck claustrophobia and verbal sparring, *Triple Bogey* is suitably marked by the director's willingness to explore the intellectual possibilities of the medium. Tempered by Poe's decidedly playful and irreverent tone, the result is an entertaining and often seductive cocktail.

Dir: Amos Poe; **Prod**: Amos Poe; **Scr**: Amos Poe; **DOP**: Joe DeSalvo; **Editor**: Dana Congdon; **Score**: Anna Domino, Michel Delory, Mader, Chic Streetman; **Main Cast**: Eric Mitchell, Daisy Hall, Angela Goethals, Jesse McBride.

Trouble in Mind
US, 1985 – 112 mins
Alan Rudolph

Rudolph began his career with minor low-budget horror flicks
Premonition (1972) and *Nightmare Circus* (1973) before establishing an
association with Altman that would prove instructive in terms of his own
working practices and sensibilities. After serving as Altman's assistant
director and co-authoring *Buffalo Bill and the Indians* (1976), Rudolph
directed the highly personal and idiosyncratic *Welcome to L.A.* (1977). A
kaleidoscopic, largely free-form satire about the lives of various LA
denizens, the film displays an elegant visual style, slightly off-kilter
characters and locations and sense of doomed romanticism (all evident in
Trouble in Mind) that were to become Rudolphian hallmarks. However,
the commercial failure of *Welcome to L.A.* necessitated Rudolph's signing
up for a number of impersonal and largely inferior studio projects that
did little but allow the director the opportunity to try out different genres
and squirrel away finance for the pictures he wished to make; it's a
pattern Rudolph has, frustratingly, been forced to follow ever since.

The film was made hot on the heels of 1984's *Choose Me*, Rudolph's
most commercially successful though wholly independent feature.
Trouble in Mind takes place in the mythical, dangerous and retro-futurist
Rain City. Fresh out of jail for the slaying of a mobster, former cop Hawk
(Kristofferson) returns to a familiar haunt, a neon-lit café run by old
flame Wanda (Bujold). He soon finds himself falling under the spell of a
young mother, Georgia (Singer), whose reckless, feckless husband Coop
(Carradine) is slowly sinking into a life of crime and extravagance. To
protect her after a scheme involving Coop and his partner Solo (Joe
Morton) goes disastrously wrong, Hawk must confront his old adversary
Hilly Blue (Divine, impressive in a rare straight role), a wealthy and
extremely powerful crime lord.

Featuring many of Rudolph's regular performers, most notably Bujold
and Altman alumnus Carradine (who in a display of the film's inherent

Coop (Keith Carradine), seen here with Hawk (Kris Kristofferson), has another bad hair day in *Trouble in Mind*

humour and sense of the absurd sports increasingly outlandish hairstyles and clothing as his criminal activities increase), *Trouble in Mind* is a characteristically eccentric, ambiguous and decidedly offbeat delight. Rudolph's talent for invoking atmosphere is well complemented by a suitably moody, melancholy and eclectic collaborative score from regular composer Mark Isham, here ably assisted by chanteuse Marianne Faithfull. The film borrows freely from melodrama, the Western, film noir (Rudolph's regular source of inspiration) and even sci-fi/fantasy (Rain City, actually Seattle, Washington, seems to be set some time in the future during what looks like a state of martial law). The various influences merge and react to dazzling and often dreamlike effect. Similarly disparate, the film's imaginative and at times distinctly surreal production design and *mise en scène* (particularly evident in Hilly Blue's opulent home) positively revels in stylistic excess.

Perhaps, though, the minimalist, achingly lonely paintings of Edward Hopper ultimately win out as the most pronounced influence on the film

– which is fitting given that *Trouble in Mind* is an elegiac meditation on regret, love and longing. It is certainly among the most visually striking of Rudolph's intermittently independent works, with Toyomichi Kurita's cinematography winning an Independent Spirit Award. The film offers confirmation that Rudolph's esoteric talents are not best suited to the commercial demands of mainstream production.

Dir: Alan Rudolph; **Prod**: Carolyn Pfeifer, David Blocker; **Scr**: Alan Rudolph; **DOP**: Toyomichi Kurita; **Editor**: Tom Walls, Sally Coryn Allen; **Score**: Mark Isham; **Main Cast**: Kris Kristofferson, Keith Carradine, Lori Singer, Genevieve Bujold.

Two-Lane Blacktop
US, 1971 – 101 mins
Monte Hellman

Like Paul Bartel, Hellman is a product of the Roger Corman stable. Early Hellman pictures configure to the low-budget genre knock-offs with which Corman made his name. Hellman's starkly original Westerns *Ride in the Whirlwind* and *The Shooting* (both 1966, but not released until two years later), however, though made at Corman's behest and shot back-to-back in the Utah desert for a combined $150,000, display a less commercial and more cryptic, European sensibility than the earlier films. *Two Lane Blacktop* offered an advance on Hellman's wilfully esoteric approach and withdrawn visual style, and considered man's abject futility and mythical search for identity in an existentialist landscape of the kind more commonly found in the films of Antonioni and the literature of Sartre and Camus.

Greenlit by Universal boss Lew Wasserman along with Hopper's *The Last Movie* (1971) and Peter Fonda's *The Hired Hand* (1971), the $850,000 project was seen as an opportunity to capitalise on the chord that *Easy Rider* (1969) had struck with America's youth market. The omens were initially good; *Esquire* was so impressed by the Wurlitzer/Corry screenplay that it made the film its April 1971 cover, printed the script in its entirety and proclaimed the film, which they had yet to see, the movie of the year. However, after viewing a film that was even more determinedly oblique and intransigent than the director's Westerns, *Esquire* awarded themselves a prize for over-hyping. The film was accorded a few positive endorsements by critics who admired director-editor Hellman's ability to capture the contemporary mood of alienation without resorting to the visual clichés of drugs, sex and violence, but it was largely marginalised by reviewers and the public, who were left cold by what J. Hoberman termed 'absurdly inert' characters (Hoberman, 2000).

Opaque, with little investment in character or plot consequentiality, the film centres on two young car enthusiasts, The Driver (singer Taylor) and The Mechanic (Beach Boy Wilson), who trek across the American Southwest in their finely tuned '55 Chevy, occasionally competing in drag races to maintain the car's upkeep. Barely speaking, except when a discussion of the car necessitates it, the duo experience friction after allowing a girl (Bird) to enter their circle. At a gas station the trio encounter GTO (Oates), a middle-aged braggart who travels the highways in his Pontiac picking up hitch-hikers and listening to loud music; in one of the more lucid moments he divulges that his job and family have 'fallen apart'. A challenge is suggested, a race to Washington D.C., in which the victor will claim the loser's car. A mesmeric duel unfolds over the two-lane blacktops of Oklahoma, but gradually the race fizzles out as the nomadic participants lose interest.

Two-Lane Blacktop's self-destructive final image is of the film jamming in the projector and igniting, a 'closure' that highlights Hellman's disregard for convention, while acting as a metaphor for his subsequent career: unable to assimilate into the system, Hellman returned to the fringes with the relentlessly bleak *Cockfighter* (1974). Excising all possible tension, Hellman revels in the abstract, creating a stunningly and languorously shot parable about desolation and inertia. The film has itself subsequently attained a mythic status (Malick and Wenders took note) and is now commonly regarded as the quintessential road movie.

Dir: Monte Hellman; **Prod**: Michael Laughlin; **Scr**: Rudolph Wurlitzer, Will Corry; **DOP**: Jack Deerson; **Editor**: Monte Hellman; **Score**: Billy James; **Main Cast**: James Taylor, Warren Oates, Laurie Bird, Dennis Wilson.

The Unbelievable Truth
US, 1989 – 90 mins
Hal Hartley

Hartley's feature debut, following three well-received shorts, was made while working for a TV company specialising in public service announcements. It is an early expression of the thematic and formal concerns that have remained throughout the director's subsequent career. It also reveals the then thirty-year-old to be a tyrant of economy (both textural and in terms of working within the tight confines of a seemingly prohibitively low budget) and a master chronicler of the minutiae of suburban life

Made for just $75,000 and financed by Jerome Brownstein, Hartley's sympathetic boss, it boasts no stars, though all the actors involved went on to form part of Hartley's regular repertory company. The film has a highly idiosyncratic and elliptical structure coupled with a non-naturalistic ambience and an at times endearingly goofy affection for European art movies – particularly those of Godard. In a video interview, the director cites Howard Hawks and Preston Sturges as other influences (Anipare and Wood, 1997). Moreover, in what was to become a defining motif in later works such as *Trust* (1990) and *Simple Men* (1992), the film displays a winning reliance upon the writer-director's immaculately constructed, highly comic and tersely delivered dialogue. Hartley has been compared to the playwright Harold Pinter for his epigrammatic aphorisms and interest in patterns of speech and repetition. Here, Hartley reaffirms the independent film-maker's mantra: talk is cheap.

In terms of narrative, it's a characteristic study of the journey towards selfhood and knowledge. Here the journey is made by Audry (Shelly), a politically committed, bookish intellectual whose dreams of attending college are dented by her fear of impending apocalypse and the lucrative modelling career that seems to be unfolding. Also making the pilgrimage is Josh (Burke), a sombre slaughterman returning from prison to his home town of Lindenhurst, where he takes a job as a mechanic in a

Trouble and desire: Audry (Adrienne Shelly) and Josh (Robert Burke) discuss the mechanics of love in *The Unbelievable Truth*

garage run by Audry's father. A shared appreciation of George Washington ensures that romance ensues between the enigmatic pair, but in a small town ruled by idle tittle-tattle and prejudice, misconception haunts their every action and conspires to keep them apart.

Quizzical in spirit and in terms of the playful approach to *mise en scène* and structure (jump-cuts, overlapping dialogue and gently comic intertitles such as 'Meanwhile', 'A month, maybe two months later' recur) *The Unbelievable Truth* also reveals Hartley's often undervalued eye for crisp compositions. The film may have been made on the cheap, but cinematographer Michael Spiller makes sure that it doesn't look it. Another defining feature is the absence of establishing shots, a format Hartley has declared his disinterest in, with many scenes often beginning as if interrupted mid-flow. Light-hearted it may appear (a fondness for outlandish, almost cartoonish physical humour such as staccato slaps and punches is revealed), but the concerns are unmistakably serious: the corrupting nature of money, the division between ambition and achievement and between truth and hearsay, the fraught nature of relationships, and the decay of the American family.

A Grand Jury Prize nominee at 1990's Sundance, *The Unbelievable Truth* was a seminal work in terms of American independent cinema in the immediate aftermath of *sex, lies and videotape* (1989). Though freely borrowing from melodrama and the Western (a genre Hartley studied), it largely eschews and positively defies convention, existing in a world all of its and Hartley's very own.

Dir: Hal Hartley; **Prod**: Bruce Weiss, Hal Hartley; **Scr**: Hal Hartley; **DOP**: Michael Spiller; **Editor**: Hal Hartley; **Score**: Jim Coleman, Phillip Reed, Wild Blue Yonder, The Brothers Kendall; **Main Cast**: Adrienne Shelly, Robert Burke, Christopher Cooke, Julia McNeal.

Variety
Germany/UK/US, 1983 – 100 mins
Bette Gordon

Originating from a short story by Gordon, an experimental film-maker and leading light in New York's post-punk scene, *Variety* attracted heightened interest due to its Kathy Acker credit. Acker was invited to add a number of key discussions about men and the pivotal sex monologues delivered by the film's female protagonist, Christine, played by Sandy McLeod. McLeod later became a script supervisor on John Sayles' films, including *City of Hope* (1991). The film was independently produced by Variety Pictures, Channel Four and Germany's Zweites Deutsches Fernsehen, with further financial assistance from the New York State Council on the Arts.

Variety begins with struggling writer Christine accepting a lowly job selling tickets at the Variety, a New York sex cinema. Alienated from her boyfriend Mark (Patton), a journalist investigating a story about union links with the Mob, Christine becomes increasingly drawn to the images on screen and to entertaining strangers with graphic, monotone descriptions of hardcore sex. Christine also begins to obsess over Louis (Richard Davidson), a powerful and affluent regular at the Variety whose shady activities suggest Mafia links. Segueing into thriller territory (with allusions also to film noir), the film concludes unresolved with Christine waiting on a darkened street corner, seemingly on the cusp of being drawn into Louis' nefarious world.

Made at the height of feminist debates on pornography, *Variety* is regarded as a feminist work, a perception Gordon refutes: 'My life, my sexual identity is as a feminist, but my films don't fit easily into that category' (quoted in Jenkins, 1984, p. 138). Moreover, though various pornographic discourses appear (soundtracks, images from men's magazines and Christine's aforementioned monologues), *Variety* is not specifically about women and pornography at all. It is more an examination of how Christine deals with sexuality, which she does in a way that women are seldom shown doing. Gordon deliberately sets out to raise eyebrows by 'saying things about my own sexuality that won't be popular, in talking about things that contradict the positive view of women that you are supposed to show' (Ibid.), and compares her approach to Fassbinder's attempts to force the audience to question prescribed notions of race, class and sexuality.

Asserting that Christine re-makes herself and takes charge of her own actions, Gordon is also at pains to make clear the patriarchal culture that surrounds her central character. This is most evident in a montage sequence in which Christine recalls various men shaking hands, the circle of handshakes symbolising patriarchy and the unwritten bond between men that women have to break into. This was replicated by the director's own experiences making the film, when she frequented porn emporiums to find that men would move away from her, 'unable to deal with a real woman, only a woman on the page' (Ibid.).

As befits a film set in a sex cinema, *Variety* intelligently reflects an interest in the act of looking. Christine's initial objectification in the opening swimming pool section is commented upon through use of dissecting close-ups. *Variety* is a technically accomplished work featuring the cinematography of Tom DiCillo and John Foster; the equally classy jazz and blues score is courtesy of John Lurie. Closer inspection of the credits yields similar riches and further establishes the film's independent pedigree: Christine Vachon is a production assistant, and among the cast are Steve Buscemi's writing partner Mark Boone Junior, photographer Nan Goldin and John Waters' regular and ubiquitous figure on the New York underground scene, Cookie Mueller.

Dir: Bette Gordon; **Prod**: Renee Shafansky; **Scr**: Kathy Acker; **DOP**: Tom DiCillo, John Foster; **Editor**: Ila von Hasperg; **Score**: John Lurie; **Main Cast**. Sandy McLeod, Luis Guzmán, Will Patton, Nan Goldin.

Walking and Talking
UK/US, 1996 – 85 mins
Nicole Holofcener

Walking and Talking is one of the most notable female debuts of the 90s. It owes much to writer-director Holofcener's shorts *Angry* (1992) and *Your Name in Cellulite* (1995), which have similar preoccupations with physical imperfection and relationship anxieties. A segue into a lucrative career in television helming *Sex and the City* followed Holofcener's first feature. The lengthy gap that elapsed before the completion of her next film, *Lovely and Amazing* (2002), raises questions as to why the follow-up should have taken so long.

Frequently described, for better or worse, as a US independent chick movie, *Walking and Talking* is a touching, wry and often painful comedy about the pressures put on a long-term female friendship by romantic rivalry and impending change. The film begins with a prologue showing two pre-teen girls intently studying a sex manual, and fast forwards to the girls' adulthood, revealing two professional, thirty-something New Yorkers: Laura (a pre-fame Heche) and Amelia (Keener exuding vulnerability). When Laura accepts the marriage proposal of her live-in boyfriend, Frank (director-in-waiting Field), unlucky-in-love Amelia, whose previous relationship floundered when her partner Andrew (Liev Schreiber) became obsessed with porn, begins to fear that she will be left on the shelf. Could a video store assistant (scene-stealing Corrigan) obsessed with cheapo horror flicks offer a final chance of salvation?

The film is written with consummate attention to the nuances of contemporary dialogue and with an intimate understanding of the hidden meanings of uncomfortable silences, qualities that are enhanced by editor Alisa Lepselter's inventive cutting from master shots to intense, intimate close-ups). *Walking and Talking*'s perceptive examination of neuroses and desires, and its cultured New York milieu, left critics unable to resist Woody Allen comparisons. Moreover, a frequent though never overstated sprinkling of post-modern references to the lower echelons of popular culture and knowledge of the murkier aspects of the male psyche also prompted parallels with indie stalwarts Kevin Smith and Richard Linklater. Formally, it is the work of Hal Hartley that looms largest, little surprise given that the cinematographer on the film is Hartley regular Michael Spiller, who makes a customarily arresting use of framing and composition and conceals the film's relatively low-budget origins with crisp visuals and pinpoint colours.

However, to contextualise the film purely in relation to the work of others does a disservice to Holofcener and fails to acknowledge the wit and vitality on display – emphasised by Billy Bragg's perceptive, observant score – and Holofcener's creation of sympathetic, though staunchly unsentimental, male and female characters (brilliantly realised by the cast), whose failings and foibles are presented with refreshing candour. Endlessly quotable, such as when a tearful Laura, after her bridal makeover, says that she looks like a drag queen, *Walking and Talking* also contains a number of extremely funny if often excruciating set-pieces, including a terribly unromantic offer of marriage made by Frank while urinating and the worst cinematic first date since Travis took Betsy to a porno theatre in *Taxi Driver* (1976).

Dir: Nicole Holofcener; **Prod**: Ted Hope, James Schamus; **Scr**: Nicole Holofcener; **DOP**: Michael Spiller; **Editor**: Alisa Lepselter; **Score**: Billy Bragg; **Main Cast**: Catherine Keener, Anne Heche, Todd Field, Kevin Corrigan.

Wanda
US, 1970 – 100 mins
Barbara Loden

A remarkable directorial outing from Loden, the actor wife of director
Elia Kazan, *Wanda* is a relatively little-known classic of American
independent/underground cinema. The film's reputation rests largely on
its impressive past showings at international film festivals such as London
and Venice, where it won the Prix FIPRESCI (the European Film Academy
Critics' Award) as best first feature.

The film, written by Loden, also stars her in a poignant if miniaturist
and utterly convincing performance as the meandering, emotionally
confused and half-destitute Wanda of the title. The film opens with her
rising from her grubby bed to impassively attend the divorce proceedings
that will see her ejected from the lives of her family. Having all too easily
relinquished her sense of security and permanence, she subsequently
drifts through drab, semi-industrial American townships and from one
dead end and unfulfilling sexual relationship to the next. Wanda
eventually takes up with a hapless, volatile crook (the superb Higgins)
who coerces her into acting as his getaway driver in a poorly conceived
bank robbery. Characteristically, but perhaps fortuitously, Wanda botches
her involvement by getting lost in a traffic jam on the way to the bank.
Back on the road again, Wanda winds up in yet another run-down
backwater bar where, disconnected from her fellow revellers, she
embarks on yet another meaningless affair with a stranger.

Wanda was shot in real, largely unremarkable and down-at-heel
locations with available (i.e. limited) resources on poor-quality 16mm
stock that was subsequently blown up to 35mm. It is unassuming,
understated and at times unapologetically rough and ready in style, and
draws on influences as diverse as Italian neo-realism (Fellini's *Nights of
Cabiria*, 1956, is frequently cited as an inspiration), the documentaries of
Shirley Clarke, and the cinema vérité approach adopted by John
Cassavetes. Loden also used untrained actors to authentically capture the

semi-articulate nature of everyday speech. The film portrays America as a sad and shabby environment of aimless losers. Perhaps as importantly, *Wanda* also achieves a kind of transgressive objectivity through its ambiguous recording of Wanda's total and at times infuriating passivity, with Loden signalling her central character's abject powerlessness and the ultimate oppression of women like her without immediate recourse to heavy-handed politicising.

Others took a different view. Writing in *Jump-Cut*, Chris Kleinhans criticised the film for never revealing Wanda's consciousness of her oppression, describing the viewing experience as ultimately depressing and unnecessarily nihilistic (Kleinhans, 14). Similarly, the film was also targeted for unsympathetically portraying Wanda as little more than a confused and vapid mess, whose subservient nature makes her a conduit for male desire. *Wanda*, however, has grown in reputation in the years since its release and remains an uncompromising, fascinating and socially salient work. Tragically it was to be Loden's sole directorial effort; she died from cancer in 1980.

Dir: Barbara Loden; **Prod**: Harry Shuster; **Scr**: Barbara Loden; **DOP**: Nicholas Proferes; **Editor**: Nicholas Proferes; **Score**: Uncredited; **Main Cast**: Barbara Loden, Michael Higgins, Charles Dosinan, Frank Jourdano.

Welcome to the Dollhouse
US, 1995 – 88 mins
Todd Solondz

Such was the impact of *Welcome to the Dollhouse* on the independent
landscape that it was mistakenly believed to be New Jersey-born
Solondz's debut feature. In fact, he'd made his first feature six years
earlier, the studio-produced *Fear, Anxiety and Depression* (1989). That
film was re-cut against Solondz's wishes. The incident caused him to turn
his back on the business to teach English as a second language to
Russian immigrants, an experience that informed his third film, the
remarkable and hugely controversial *Happiness* (1998).

Self-penned and self-produced, *Dollhouse* marked a triumphant
return to film-making for Solondz, a move achieved entirely on his own
terms and capped by the Grand Jury Prize at Sundance. The film stakes
out the terrain he has continued to make his own: the depiction of
suburbia as a peripheral, excruciating hell in which gawky, adolescent
teenagers interminably suffer the physical and verbal taunts of their
equally maladjusted parents and peers.

At times unbearably cruel with extremely violent, callous overtones,
the film is also an uncannily authentic and perceptive account of
outsiderism and the desire to belong as depicted through the eyes of
dorky Dawn Wiener (the astonishing Matarazzo), an eleven-year-old New
Jersey seventh grader reviled and hated by her classmates. Dawn's home
life is little better; her mother makes it patently clear that her affections
lie with her pampered, prissy ballerina-wannabe sister Missy, while her
computer nerd brother refuses to let her anywhere near the high-school
heart-throb with whom he has formed an uneasy musical alliance. In
fact, the only friendship Dawn enjoys is with her equally ostracised, runty
neighbour Ralphy, with whom she forms a 'Special Persons' club. An
altercation with local thug Brandon (Sexton Jr) brings fresh complications
when he threatens to rape her after school – but at least that would
involve physical contact, put an end to the 'lesbo' rumours and perhaps

precipitate the much-sought onset of puberty.

Solondz directs with the judicious precision and formal economy that goes hand-in-hand with working in the independent sector. The approach of Solondz and his production designer Susan Block (the *mise en scène* alone signals a clarion call for help) also perfectly captures the details of thoroughly unremarkable, suburban life. Sharply satirical and written with a darkly comic attention to detail, the film invites an autobiographical reading: the anguish of the agonisingly painful, lonely youth of its 'geeky', bespectacled author.

As with his subsequent work, Solondz refuses to pull his punches, tackling issues such as abuse, petty crime, sexual confusion and pre-teen sex with candour, directness and a staunchly unsentimental tone far removed from mainstream treatments of juvenile disaffection. At times, the film seems to wilfully exacerbate the barbaric inhumanity on show (a charge levelled at Solondz with increasing regularity) but the ultimately insightful *Dollhouse* also offers moments of extreme tenderness that reveal the hidden depths of this very darkest of black comedies.

Dir: Todd Solondz; **Prod**: Ted Skillman, Todd Solondz; **Scr**: Todd Solondz; **DOP**: Randy Drummond; **Editor**: Alan Oxman; **Score**: Jil Wisoff; **Main Cast**: Heather Matarazzo, Victoria Davis, Christina Vidal, Brendan Sexton Jr.

You Can Count on Me
US, 2000 – 111 mins
Kenneth Lonergan

Enjoying the double-whammy of Best Picture and Best Screenplay awards at the 2000 Sundance Film Festival, *You Can Count on Me* marked playwright-turned-screenwriter Lonergan's (*Analyze This*, 1999) confident, perceptive and engaging directorial debut.

Set in Scottsville, upstate New York, the film maps the fallout of a bereavement, shown in a pre-credit sequence in which two children, a brother and sister, lose their parents in an accident. The children grow up to be Sammy (Linney) and Terry (Ruffalo), two people who are poles apart. Sammy is a respected, God-fearing single mother of a young son. Her neatly allotted life runs like clockwork until a priggish new boss (Broderick) arrives at her bank and makes her life hell. Close behind is the returning brother Terry, who after spending time in prison has drifted from one dead-end situation to the next in the hope of finding himself. Terry has returned to borrow money, but he's persuaded to stay on in the environment he finds suffocating after nurturing an initially fractious rapport with Sammy's son, Rudy (Culkin). Unfortunately, Terry's presence serves as a destructive catalyst.

Stephen Kazmierski's autumnal photography manages to capture both the visual beauty and the boredom of the region, condensing the minutiae of small-town life to a suffocating conformity and obsession with neatness and order. Linney (who earned a Best Actress Academy Award nomination for her impressive performance), and Ruffalo are utterly convincing as the contrasting but equally scarred siblings. Broderick (a friend of the director from high school) and Culkin offer effective support. Continuing the tradition of independent directors acting in their own films, Lonergan appears as the faintly embarrassed local priest who seems ill equipped to provide ecclesiastical assistance.

Lonergan directs with assurance, economy and a flab-free precision, which is fortified by Anne McCabe's judicious editing. Perhaps the main virtue of *You Can Count on Me* is Lonergan's astute, intelligent and gently humorous script that treats its characters with respect while tenderly revealing the fragile fabric of their individual credos and moralities: Terry rails against the conformity of Scottsville and a settled family life, but finally appears reluctant to leave; Sammy preaches the virtues of Christianity and the constraints of small-town existence, but wilfully jeopardises her place in the community by screwing her boss. Moreover, the film bristles with an understated melancholy and ennui and a highly developed sense of ambiguity that raises it above the standard story of familial tension in a small town.

Similarly, Lonergan assiduously avoids mawkishness and a pat conclusion. 'Everything is going to be all right *Comparatively*,' proffers Terry, as he prepares to board the bus that will once again take him out of Sammy's and Rudy's lives.

Dir: Kenneth Lonergan; **Prod**: John N. Hart, Jeffrey Sharp, Barbara De Fina, Larry Meistrich; **Scr**: Kenneth Lonergan; **DOP**: Stephen Kazmlerski; **Editor**: Anne McCabe; **Score**: Lesley Barber; **Main Cast**: Laura Linney, Mark Ruffalo, Matthew Broderick, Rory Culkin.

Useful websites

A good many of the films included in this volume will be familiar to the majority of readers. Evergreen and lesser-known titles alike have undoubtedly been viewed, discussed and argued over.

Many of these films are available on video and DVD, the latter format also usually offering insightful access to behind the scenes materials, commentaries and director interviews. Listed below are a number of British and US websites that I recommend to those who wish to purchase videos and DVDs. For those with multi-region DVD players, the US sites have a distinct edge in regard to general availability. It is also worth looking out for specialist home entertainment distributors such as Anchor Bay (<www.anchorbay.co.uk> and <www.anchorbayentertainment.com>) and Pioneer (<www.pioneer-ent.com>).

<www.blackstar.co.uk>
<www.amazon.co.uk>
<www.amazon.com>
<www.moviem.co.uk>
<www.dc-dvd.net>

Of the above sites, Moviem (Movie Mail) is particularly recommended as it specialises in world and cult cinema titles. Blackstar is also worth a visit as it offers a useful and often fruitful Video Hunt Service for rare and out-of-print titles. Pick of the bunch, however, is probably the US-based dc-dvd, which usually comes up trumps.

Of course, one of the aims of this book is to lead you down less well-travelled paths, encouraging you to seek out less frequently celebrated works. And therein lies the rub. Not only are many of these titles no longer available for hire on 35mm or 16mm and therefore unlikely to be showing at a screen near you any time soon, but also they are still to appear on home video. Therefore, while secretly toasting my own obsessive recording of almost every feature film to have appeared on British television from about 1986 onwards, I regrettably list the films that you may have the most trouble tracking down: *Angel City*; *Another Girl, Another Planet*; *Born in Flames*; *Candy Mountain*; *Chan Is Missing*; *Clean, Shaven*; *Impostors*; *Killer of Sheep*; *The Kill-Off*; *Metropolitan*; *Portrait of Jason*; *Return of the Secaucus Seven*; *Sherman's March*; *Static*; *Tongues Untied*; *Triple Bogey on a Par Five Hole*; and *Variety*.

In this regard, the British Film Institute (<www.bfi.org.uk>) and the American Film Institute (<www.afi.com>) are worth contacting. Both bodies provide excellent viewing resources due to committed archiving and preservation policies. Other organisations dedicated to specific groups, concerns or film-making practices can also be approached. One such example is Cinenova, the ultimate resource for women's film and the rights-holders for a number of key titles (*Born in Flames* included) by, for or about women. They can be reached at: <www.cinenova.org.uk>.

Finally, it is also worth noting that a fairly high number of independent directors maintain their own websites and in some instances directly sell or provide screening and/or other availability advice. I have often, as in the case of D. A. Pennebaker (<www.pennebakerhegedusfilms.com>) and Hal Hartley (<www.possiblefilms.com>), found such repositories extremely helpful. An Internet search should be sufficient to direct you to your chosen destination. Good luck.

Bibliography

Alexander, Karen, Review of *Daughters of the Dust*, in Hillier, 2001.

Allon, Yoram, Del Cullen and Hannah Patterson (eds), *The Wallflower Critical Guide to Contemporary North American Directors* (London: Wallflower, 2000).

Anderson, Melissa, 'The Vagaries of Verities: On Shirley Clarke's *Portrait of Jason*', *Film Comment*, vol. 35, no. 6, Nov/Dec 1999.

Andrew, Geoff, *Stranger Than Paradise: Maverick Film-makers in Recent American Cinema* (London: Prion Books, 1998).

Andrew, Geoff, *Directors A–Z: A Concise Guide to the Art of 250 Great Film-makers* (London: Prion Books, 1999).

Anipare, Eileen and Jason Wood, *Trouble and Desire: An Interview with Hal Hartley* (video), 1997.

Armstrong, Dan, 'Wiseman's *Model* and the Documentary Project: Toward a Radical Film Practice', *Film Quarterly*, vol. 37, no. 2, Winter 1984, quoted in uncredited interview with Susan Seidelman, *New York Times*, 26 Dec 1982.

Barrowclough, Susan, Review of *Born in Flames*, *Monthly Film Bulletin*, vol. 51, no. 601, Feb 1984.

Biskind, Peter, *Easy Riders, Raging Bulls* (New York: Simon & Schuster, 1998).

Burn, Gordon, 'Rising Below Vulgarity', *Sight and Sound*, vol. 6, no. 12, Dec 1996.

Carney, Ray (ed.), *Cassavetes on Cassavetes* (London: Faber & Faber, 2001a).

Carney, Ray, *Shadows* (London: BFI Publishing, 2001b).

Cheshire, Ellen and John Ashbrook, *Joel and Ethan Coen* (Harpenden: Pocket Essentials, 2000).

Combs, Richard, Review of *Killer of Sheep*, *Monthly Film Bulletin*, vol. 49, no. 581, June 1977.

Cook, Pam (ed.), *The Cinema Book* (London: BFI Publishing, 1987).

DiCillo, Tom, Living in Oblivion *and Eating Crow: A Film-maker's Diary* (London: Faber & Faber, 1995).

Don't Look Back, Review (author uncredited), *Monthly Film Bulletin*, vol. 36, no. 428, Sept 1969.

Draper, Ellen, Review of *Sherman's March*, *Film Quarterly*, vol. 40, no. 3, Spring 1987.

Ebert, Roger, Review of *Boyz N the Hood*, *Chicago Sun-Times*, 12 July 1991.

Ebert, Roger, Review of *Hoop Dreams*, *Chicago Sun-Times*, 21 Oct 1994.

Felperin, Leslie, Review of *High Art*, *Sight and Sound*, vol. 9, no. 4, April 1999.

Field, Simon, Review of *Impostors*, *Monthly Film Bulletin*, vol. 49, no. 577, Feb 1982.

Fuchs, Christian, *Bad Blood: An Illustrated Guide to Psycho Cinema* (London: Creation Books, 1996).

Fuller, Graham, 'Finding the Essential', Hal Hartley interview in Hal Hartley, Simple Men *and* Trust (London: Faber & Faber, 1992).

Giles, Jane, 'Auteur of the OTT', *Guardian*, 16 Jan 1995.

Goodeve, Thyrza, Review of *Tongues Untied*, *Cinéaste*, vol. 18, no. 1, 1990.

Guerrero, Ed, 'Be Black and Buy', in Hillier, 2001.

Hillier, Jim (ed.), *American Independent Cinema: A Sight and Sound Reader* (London: BFI Publishing, 2001).

Hoberman, J., 'The Wrong Man', *Village Voice*, 30 Aug 1988.

Hoberman, J., Review of *Two-Lane Blacktop* (re-release), *Village Voice*, 27 Sept–3 Oct 2000.

Hoberman, J., 'Blood, Sweat and Tears', *Village Voice*, 5–11 July 2000.

Hoberman, J., Review of *Donnie Darko*, *Village Voice*, 24–30 Oct 2001 <www.villagevoice.com/issues/0143/hoberman.php>.

hooks, bell, 'Dreams of Conquest', *Sight and Sound*, vol. 5, no. 4, April 1995.

Jenkins, Steve, Review of *Variety*, *Monthly Film Bulletin*, vol. 54, no. 604, May 1984.

Journal of the University Film and Video Association, XXXV, 2, Spring 1983 (author uncredited).

Kemp, Philip, Review of *Clean, Shaven, Sight and Sound*, vol. 5, no. 2, Feb 1995.

Kemp, Philip, 'Mr Pink, Mr Indie, Mr Shh', *Sight and Sound*, vol. 11, no. 8, Aug 2001.

Kempley, Rita, Review of *Metropolitan*, *Washington Post*, 14 Sept 1990.

Keogh, Peter, 'Home and Away' (Jim Jarmusch interview), in Hillier, 2001.

Keyssar, Helene, *Robert Altman's America* (Oxford: Oxford University Press, 1991).

King, Stephen, *Twilight Magazine*, Nov 1982.

Kleinhans, Chuck, 'Seeing through *Cinéma Vérité*', *Jump-Cut*, no. 1–11, 1971

Leigh, Danny, 'Boy Wonder' (Kimberly Peirce interview), in Hillier, 2001.

Leigh, Danny, 'The Beat Up Kid', in Hillier, 2001.

Maslin, Janet, Review of *Gummo*, *New York Times*, 17 Oct 1997.

Newman, Kim (ed.), *The BFI Companion to Horror* (London: Cassell, 1996).

Okewole, Seun, 'Tom Kalin', in Hillier, 2001.

Patterson, Richard 'How to Make a Successful Feature for $22,315.92', *American Cinematographer*, vol. 64, no. 2, Feb 1983.

Pierson, John, *Spike Mike Slackers & Dykes: A Guided Tour Across a Decade of Independent American Cinema* (London: Faber & Faber, 1996).

Pym, John, Review of *Angel City*, *Monthly Film Bulletin*, vol. 45, no. 528, Jan 1978.

Rayns, Tony, 'Chinese Boxes', (interview with Wayne Wang), *Monthly Film Bulletin*, vol. 52, no. 621, Oct 1985.

Renan, Sheldon, *An Introduction to the American Underground Film* (New York: E. P. Dutton, 1967).

Rich, B Ruby, 'What's New Pussycat?', *Village Voice*, 17 Jan 1995.

Rich, B. Ruby, 'Comings and Goings', in Hillier, 2001.

Rich, B. Ruby, 'Queer and Present Danger', in Hillier, 2001.

Rodley, Chris and Paul Joyce, *Made in the USA* (video), Lucida Productions (for Channel Four), 1994.

Rosen, Dan, with Peter Hamilton, *Off Hollywood: The Making and Marketing of Independent Films* (New York: Grove Press, 1990).

Rothman, William, *Documentary Film Classics* (Cambridge: Cambridge University Press, 1997).

Sarris, Andrew, *The American Cinema* (New York: Da Capo Press, 1968).

Sarris, Andrew, Review of *Don't Look Back*, *Village Voice*, 21 Sept 1967, quoted in Elizabeth Thompson and David Gutman (eds), *The Dylan Companion* (New York: Delta Books, 1991),

Sayles, John, *Thinking in Pictures, The Making of the Movie Matewan* (Boston, MA: Houghton Mifflin, 1987).

Smith, Gavin (ed.), *Sayles on Sayles* (London: Faber & Faber, 1998).

Smith, Gavin, 'Dealing with the Now', in Hillier, 2001.

Smith, Gavin, 'Night Fever', in Hillier, 2001.

Soderbergh, Steven, *Getting Away with it, Or: The Further Adventures of the Luckiest Bastard You Ever Saw* (London: Faber & Faber, 1999).

Sweet, Louise, Review of *Sherman's March*, *Monthly Film Bulletin*, vol. 55, no. 654, July 1988.

Tartaglia, Jerry, 'The Gay Sensibility in American Avant-Garde Film', *Millennium Film Journal*, no. 4/5, Summer/Autumn 1979.

Taubin, Amy, 'Beyond the Sons of Scorsese', in Hillier, 2001.

Taubin, Amy, 'Girl n the Hood', in Hillier, 2001.

Thomas, Kevin, Review of *Heavy*, *Los Angeles Times*, 28 June 1996.

Thompson, Cliff, 'The Devil Beat His Wife: Small Moments and Big Statements in the Films of Charles Burnett', *Cinéaste*, vol. 13, no. 1, 1983.

Thompson, David and Ian Christie (eds), *Scorsese on Scorsese* (London: Faber & Faber, 1989).

Thomson, David, *Rosebud: The Story of Orson Welles* (London: Little Brown, 1996).

Thomson, David, *The New Biographical Dictionary of Film* (London: Little Brown, 2002 [4th edn]).

Zavarzadeh, Mas'ud, Review of *Smithereens*, *Film Quarterly*, vol. 37, no. 2, Winter 1984.

Index

Page numbers in *italics* denote illustrations; those in **bold** indicate detailed analysis

List of Illustrations

Whilst considerable effort has been made to correctly identify the copyright holders, this has not been possible in all cases. We apologise for any apparent negligence and any omissions or corrections brought to our attention will be remedied in any future editions.

Another Girl, Another Planet, Nabu Productions; *The Blair Witch Project*, Artisan Entertainment/Haxan Films; *Blood Simple*, © River Road Productions; *Born in Flames*, Lizzie Borden; *Clerks*, View Askew; *Crumb*, Superior Pictures; *Drugstore Cowboy*, Avenue Entertainment; *Easy Rider*, Pando Company/Raybert Productions; *Eraserhead*, © David Lynch; *Gas Food Lodging*, Cineville; *George Washington*, © Youandwhatarmy Filmed Challenges; *Gummo*, Independent Pictures/New Line Productions, Inc.; *Just Another Girl on the I.R.T.*, Truth 24 F.P.S./Miramax Films; *Killer of Sheep*, Charles Burnett Productions; *Mean Streets*, Taplin-Perry-Scorsese Productions/Warner Bros.; *Metropolitan*, Westerly Films; *Nashville*, © American Broadcasting Company/© Paramount Pictures Corporation; *Pink Flamingos*, Dreamland Productions; *Poison*, © Poison L.P.;*Portrait of Jason*, Shirley Clarke/Film-Makers' Distribution Center; *Return of the Secaucus Seven*, Salsipuedes Productions; *sex, lies and videotape*, Outlaw Productions; *Shadows*, © John Cassavetes; *She's Gotta Have It*, 40 Acres and a Mule Filmworks; *Stranger Than Paradise*, © Cinesthesia Productions; *Suture*, Kino-Korsakoff; *The Thin Blue Line*, Third Floor Productions; *Trees Lounge*, Addis/Wechsler and Associates/Seneca Falls Productions/LIVE Entertainment/LIVE Film and Mediaworks; *Trouble in Mind*, Raincity Incorporated/Island Alive/Embassy Home Entertainment; *The Unbelievable Truth*, Action Features.